Business Intelligence and Espionage

BUSINESS INTELLIGENCE AND ESPIONAGE

RICHARD M. GREENE, JR., Editor

1966

DOW JONES-IRWIN, INC.
Homewood, Illinois

Library of Congress Catalog Card No. 66–25591

Printed in the United States of America

INTRODUCTION

Business executives must make the decisions that lead the firm or organization toward its desired goals. Business intelligence helps to make those decisions rational ones and optimizes the likelihood of their resulting in steady progress toward the firm's goals.

The process of making business decisions is illustrated on the following page. As may be seen, a decision depends upon having rules (what we will do under certain circumstances), having data (data tells us that those circumstances now exist), and a time requirement specifying when the decision must be made.

Decision data have been defined to be of two types—that which is about the inside operations of the firm, called "Management Information," and that which concerns the environment of the firm or about things occurring outside of the firm, "Business Intelligence."

Business Intelligence tells us of our competition—his plans, his sales techniques, his pricing. It tells us, too, of our customers—what they want, who they are, and how much they can spend. It tells us about our suppliers—what they charge, to whom they sell, what their quality reputation is, and if they are facing labor trouble. It tells us of our customers' credit ratings and of new developments of interest to our production staff. In general, it is a vital part of our work from the start of our firm to its demise. It helps us find, sell, and hold our customers.

Such an important function cannot be left to trial and

error. Yet, this is exactly what many firms do. Bankruptcy marks the way of those who overlook it when their competition does not.

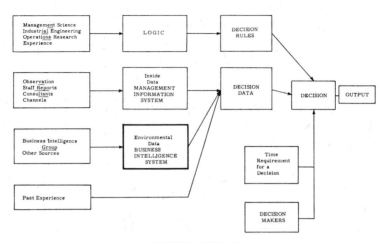

ILLUSTRATION I

The Requirements for Decisions and the Role of Business Intelligence.

Every serious student of business and every executive should be aware of the field of Business Intelligence. Ethical and moral fears may have held back the development of this area as an occupation. Other business specialties such as PERT, Line of Balance, Gantt Charting, Milestone systems, Value Analysis and Zero Defect programs all have had their time, one by one, in the mid-1960's. A survey of most of the major U.S. universities showed in 1964, however, that no course on Business Intelligence per se was available although some aspects of this work were taught in other courses such as "Business Forecasting," "Economic Cycles and Trends," and "Competitive Marketing."

A 1959 Harvard University student survey and our own work at R. M. Greene & Associates showed that most large companies use some form of Business Intelligence and Espionage and, that nationally, some 113 million dollars annually go toward such items as estimating the competition's strength and predicting RFP publication, etc.

Counterintelligence is also of importance. If one defines the steps in Business Intelligence as; *a*) identification of data of interest, *b*) collection, *c*) storage and retrieval, *d*) evaluation, *e*) collation of relevant data, *f*) interpretation, and finally, *g*) dissemination to appropriate executives, then counterintelligence seeks to thwart these. It tries to becloud what data will be of use, to stymie collection, to prevent storage and confuse retrieval, to baffle evaluators, to make collation impossible, to mislead interpretation, and to block dissemination. Methodology for counterintelligence ranges from planting false data to creating elaborate security systems with guards and electronic countermeasures and detectors.

Market research, business forecasting, competitive analysis, economic prediction, and influence analysis are all subsets of a total Business Intelligence program. Corporate planning, both short-range or tactical and long-range or strategic, depends upon good Business Intelligence. Although an old art, its recent development into a science, its emergence as a possible career field, and its use of modern techniques and equipment such as operations analysis and computers, are all strikingly new.

Now and then, from 1930 to 1964, there have been meetings and conferences on Business Intelligence, many of them privately directed through business associations or organizations. Typical of these was an American Management Association meeting, held in 1958, which dealt mostly with forecasting. Other than a study by Harvard students in 1962, the only major activity in this area recently was a series of conferences in Los Angeles sponsored by R. M. Greene and Associates. Broad participation from a variety of industries was gained and demand for the "Proceedings" of this series led to the preparation of this book.

The purpose of this book is to introduce the subject of Business Intelligence to those who are unfamiliar with it, to provide useful material for those already in the field, to provide a text for courses on this topic and to establish even more clearly the concepts, methods, values, ethics and future of this field.

I would like to express appreciation to the chapter authors who, without financial remuneration, have labored to present their points of view, and to Betty Ann Peterson who prepared the first draft from the conference tapes, and to Frank Douglas for editorial rewriting. Also, our thanks to Rozalia deKanter who laboriously edited each page for typographic and language errors.

RICHARD M. GREENE, JR., Editor

Los Angeles, 1966

TABLE OF CONTENTS

PART I: ORGANIZATION AND ADMINISTRATION

PART II: TECHNIQUES

PAGE

BIBLIOGRAPHY

APPENDIXES

NOTE

The authors of chapters have contributed from their personal experiences. No inference should be drawn that the firms for which they now work either agree with, or practice, the concepts discussed.

The Editor

Organization and
Administration

Chapter One

MANAGEMENT, BUSINESS INTELLIGENCE AND ESPIONAGE

RICHARD M. GREENE, JR.*

INTRODUCTION

THIS IS A BOOK on an unusual subject. It talks openly about a topic which normally is not even discussed. Many business executives doubt that the field exists. The editors of *Business Management* took the trouble to check approximately 20 persons in the security field to see if commonly used techniques described in a submitted article were in use. The reply was "yes." They then published the material (October, 1965) in two parts ("A professional spy tells 'How I Steal Company Secrets,'" and "How Your Company Can Thwart a Spy").

---

*Richard M. Greene, Jr., President of R. M. Greene & Associates, is a well-known management consultant located in Glendora, California. He works with the top leadership of firms to improve their total management systems. He teaches for the extension division of the University of California, Los Angeles, Irvine, Santa Barbara and Riverside, and holds degrees in psychology as well as advanced graduate studies in business. His clients include some of the nation's top aerospace firms, the Air Force and well-known electronics corporations.

Those of us who consult with management are often aware of the amount of business intelligence and espionage work being carried out. Although often seen in marketing work, it also occurs in long-range planning, site location studies, and new product development. Heavily prevalent in the drug, fashion, chemical, automobile, and toy industries, BI is found in almost all industries and companies of various sizes. It is a big business; it is a growing business.

Let us look into the field, not only for academic interest, but so that we may protect ourselves should the occasion arise.

THE FIELD OF BUSINESS INTELLIGENCE

Managers must have data to make decisions. They also must have decision rules, a time cue and, if they are to succeed, good judgment. The data comes from both the inside of the organization and the outside. Inside data is collected and made useful by what may be called management information systems. Such data would include sales volume, personnel actions, expenditures, plant and facilities status, etc.

Data arising outside of the organization deals with the present or future environment in which the business is to be conducted. Examples of this type of data which determine management decisions are: competitor site location, competitor pricing, market demand, population shifts, labor availability, and government regulations. This data is collected and made useful by what we chose to call business intelligence systems.

Some of the environmental data is easy to get, because it is "available." This includes newspaper articles, competitor stockholder reports, and government regulations. Some of it is not easy to get because for various reasons someone does not want you to know it. This desired data may have to be acquired by "unusual means." This term often implies a form of business espionage.

The information itself we may call source material, data, or basic or primary data. When processed it becomes intelligence. *Business intelligence, therefore, is processed information of interest to management about the present or future environment in which the business is operating.*

Actions taken by an organization to prevent unauthorized disclosure or release of information, such as the use of file cabinets with locks, "keep our business to ourselves" campaigns or the use of security guards is classified as "counterintelligence" or "security."

WHO USES BUSINESS INTELLIGENCE

All organizations and businesses have some degree of business intelligence operation. Many do not formalize it or give it a name but others assign whole departments to this work.

Take, for example, a sole-owner such as a corner newsstand operator. He is aware of such items as: plans to change routes of public transportation near his stand; anyone who intends to open a nearby newsstand; and the establishment of new newspapers in the city. In addition, if he desires to keep secret how well (or badly) he is doing, he may apply counterintelligence measures. He may hide his receipt box, code his accounting entries, and in conversation purposely mislead others on the state of his business.

Counterintelligence

Counterintelligence or counterespionage, as previously mentioned, is the organized attempt upon the part of a firm to prevent its secrets from disclosure. Although occasionally represented by a staff specialist in a large firm, it is often the subject of a contract for services between a firm and an outside consultant who specializes in the field. Most major firms in the defense industry, following the dictates and spirit of the *Guide to Industrial Security,* have people working in their employee relations units who develop "keep it quiet" programs of various types. A good example of such material from the Litton Industries Data Systems Division publication *News & Opinion* (Monday, June 13, 1966) is that below:

A Special Message To DSDers

YOUR HELP VITAL IN GUARDING DIVISION'S SECRETS

Did you know that Data Systems division has something of value in addition to its products—four "P's": Plans, Performance, Prices and Problems. In the past quarter of a century one of the many enigmas facing industry has been the loss of business advantage.

Assume that Jones and Smith are competitors. They operate independent service stations across the street from each other. In this case, would Jones deem it important to know that within the next three months Smith will completely modernize and renovate his station? If you agree that this would be nice information to have you will agree that the first "P"—Plans— could reveal significant data to a competitor.

Performance

While mulling over this advance information, Jones' thoughts invariably turn to the second "P"—Performance. He would like to know Smith's gallonage which has either permitted or instigated the expenditure of this capital. How does Smith's performance compare with Jones'?

The next thing that Jones would like to know is what Smith is going to do about the third "P"—Prices. If Smith's modernization program includes the addition of tanks and pumps, will Smith cut his prices and depend on the added volume, or will he simply rely on a more attractive station to keep the additional equipment busy at the same price?

Problems

The last of the four "P's" is a little more obscure—Problems—but just as important as the other three. Now, if Jones knew of the first three, would it have any impact on his own counteraction to know that Smith had to borrow all of the money for his program on a short-term loan at an extremely high interest rate?

Surely all businessmen will agree that knowledge of Smith's problem might cause Jones to react in such a manner that a "buyer's market" would soon be prevalent on their corner.

Everyone can relate the importance of plans, performance, prices and problems to their own business. In essence, most companies want to know about the four "P's" of their competitors to better assist their own penetration of the available market and to evaluate whether or not they are directing their own efforts in the most rewarding paths.

Disclosure Hurts

How do we lose competitive information? We can immediately categorize the manner of possible loss under willful disclosure or negligent disclosure.

Willful disclosure is, of course, the most serious because it may become systematized and progress in scope until it covers all four of the "P's" in every section, branch, department or facility that the dishonest employee can victimize. This type disclosure is by far the most difficult to guard against because an employee who willfully discloses proprietary information is lacking in that quality known as "fidelity to trust."

Negligence Varies

Negligent disclosure is the most prevalent type of disclosure, and almost always involves a present employee. It should be of little solace to note that negligent disclosure is usually limited in scope to only a portion of the four "P's" since that portion could be the very information that has the greatest impact on profits.

It is even less reassuring to observe that the employee guilty of such negligence "meant well" but only "talked too much."

Almost any employee who has knowledge of the four "P's" can negligently disclose them. The type of negligence can vary from carelessness in handling or storing important papers to a salesman boasting of his company's four "P's" to the wrong person or in the wrong place, but the end result is always reflected in the same way—less business. A scientist might be quite careful in preparing a paper or a speech to protect patentable or trade secret data, but not at all careful in keeping the four "P's" out. A purchasing agent zealously doing his job of getting the best quantity price possible, can give a vendor or supplier a staggering number of the four "P's" and either be unaware of it or think it was necessary to do so.

Not Always Negligence

One might conclude that the loss of the four "P's" always involves an employee who is either negligent or out-and-out dishonest. This is not always the case. There is an instance where a very carefully arranged tour disclosed sensitive performance data to an entire industry. A reporter on the tour mentally kept track of the number of test machines he saw in various product departments and spaced two casual questions over ten minutes. "What is the approximate volume of units per hour for that type testing machine?" "How many shifts are you working?" His calculations and subsequent article in a national publication made the company officials feel he had read their production reports.

Prevention

The first step in preventing our competitors from obtaining competitive intelligence is to develop an awareness of the possibility of compromise of the four "P's." Information relating to compromise should immediately be brought to the attention of the DSD Security Manager's office.

We have tried to alert you to the dangers and earnestly solicit your help as trustworthy employees in retaining DSD's four "P's" for DSD's own use.

(Reprinted by permission.)

When data required cannot be collected by more ordinary means such as studies of news releases, stockholder reports, letters of inquiry, discussions with friends and customers of the subject organization, and similar means, it may be necessary to move to industrial espionage to gather the data. This is usually done by one or more of the following techniques:

A. Overhearing
 Planting tape recorders
 Planting microphones
 Introducing an outsider to the subject plant who listens for data (a VIP, a salesman, a visitor, job applicant.)
 Tapping telephones
 Mingling with key employees at a club, lunch or professional meeting.
 Calling into the subject organization under a guise of being an employee or a reporter.

B. Following
 Following special persons, such as proposal engineers, marketing men or advanced R & D personnel, to find their contacts, who they visit, how often.

C. Pilfering
 Taking, without authority, plans, reports, documents, cultures, breadboards, from a subject firm.

D. Photographing
 Obtaining photos of mock-ups, designs, control panels, management displays, parking lots, and so on.

E. Infiltration
 Planting an informer as an employee of a subject firm, or using consultants, reporters or others whose access is easier.

F. Informers, subject firm
 Drawing desired data from an employee of the subject firm by appeal to financial need, fear of disclosure

for some real or imagined wrongdoing, or by appeal to
negative attitudes due to a real or imagined slight.

G. Search of Output/Input
    Examination of trash of subject firm, electric usage,
    use of unusual or esoteric materials, metals, fuels,
    remote pickup of computer processing, obtaining de-
    tailed phone company call listings.

There are numerous stories of how a large organization can
be bilked or caused to deliver data by straightforward, although improper means. In one recent case a competitor
dressed a laborer as a member of a trash removal firm. This
person, armed with an unsigned, but official looking memo
on the subject firm's letterhead, proceeded to do the rounds
of the engineering design departments with a large locked
barrel on a cart. The memo message and cart sign said, "We
are checking if latest design memos are properly marked for
security. Deposit here and they will be returned tomorrow."
Of the some 250 employees who deposited vital documents,
not one asked for identification.

In another recent case a representative of a competing firm
had his name placed on the internal distribution list of administrative memos by means of a "blind" firm listing. The
value was that among the administrative memos is a periodic
listing of all technical memos and their classification, title and
author. This permitted the outside firm to keep up on the
latest R&D work of the subject firm for almost two years
before a review of who was on the distribution list caused his
name to be removed, and then it was only removed for
"budget limitation reasons." If the "plant" had been spotted,
the subject firm would have had a wonderful opportunity for
some counterintelligence. They could have made up special
lists including all sorts of hypothetical projects, fantastic
developments and strange items which would have kept the
spying firm busy to the hilt in figuring out what was going

on, and in addition to spending lots of money trying to emulate these weird developments, they would have been punished also by the fact that their normal R&D efforts were disrupted. Imagine the consternation that would have been caused by a listing such as this:

Technical Bulletin #310   Director: Dr. Sisch.
Company Confidential

Title: "Continued Development of Discovery
of use of Ordinary Water as Weapon
to Hypnotize Entire Cities"

The main methods used in counterintelligence are:

Education—educating employees (1) to avoid disclosure, and (2) to report attempts by others to obtain data.

Investigation—careful inquiry using multiple methods to determine existence of leaks, motivations, methods used, amount of data compromised and optimum tactics to recover or close.

Physical barriers—fences, gates, locked doors, safes, files and similar means, also, use of electronic devices to block possible radio transmissions such as the antibug.

Planting—periodic: planting of known false data to see if it turns up in a suspected end-point.
—special: planting of data when a leak is known, to throw off the suspect, to confuse or cause him loss of funds or prestige.

Responsibility—careful tracking of personal responsibility for vital data with adequate security checks on the background of those involved.

Search—periodic or special searches for hidden microphones, search of the person of visitors and workers to prevent removal of blueprints, samples, and similar material.

Security status sampling—using planned random and other
sampling techniques, especially discovery sampling, to
assess the quality of the firms normal security program.
Immediate feedback helps maintain quality.

Staff coordination—through membership on the top corporate staff, and by sitting-in on key planning meetings,
marketing meetings and having access to other top activities, a counter-intelligence group can (1) be aware of
what is worth guarding, (2) allocate priorities of security,
(3) advise others on methods, locations, techniques or
hazards in their planned activities which may reveal some
key data.

With regard to this last point, in order to impress upon a
corporate staff how much data they were revealing through
their employment ads, a team was assigned for one month to
follow the personnel ads placed by the firm. They then made
a report to the firm of their estimation of what was going
on. To the great surprise of the firm's leadership, not only
were they quite accurate in almost all areas, but they spotted
three problems in production and quality control that the top
brass did not even know existed!

Large companies usually have a formalized structure, both
for gathering intelligence and for security or counterintelligence. In the former class fall market researchers, economic
forecasters, and market analysts. In the latter are guards and
possibly specialists in counterintelligence. General Dynamic's
(Pomona) chief of security is FBI trained. Timothy J. Walsh,
Sperry Gyroscope's security manager was with the Office of
Strategic Intelligence (OSI) during World War II and later
with the Office of Naval Intelligence. The Central Intelligence Agency (CIA) and Federal Bureau of Investigation
(FBI) have been training grounds for almost one hundred
industrial security leaders. Many are members of the American Society for Industrial Security. Others work free lance
or as consultants on counterespionage as do: Saul D. Astor

of Management Safeguards, Inc., in New York; Crawford Research, Inc., of Washington D.C.; R. M. Greene & Associates of Glendora, Cal.; Crest Detective Agency of Santa Monica; and Harvey G. Wolfe. Wolfe is characterized by a *Los Angeles Times* article (February 11, 1962) as "49-year-old wartime agent of the Army's Counter Intelligence Corps (who) has been quietly developing his own organization in Los Angeles for the past 15 years, specializing in counterespionage for industrial and business firms who have been 'penetrated' by the competitor." One prominent firm in this field, Norman Jaspan Associates, claims 500 employees and although listed as a management engineering company, specializes as a counterespionage agency. Fidelifacts, another firm in the field, describes itself as "a cooperative of 400 ex-F.B.I. and Secret Service agents throughout the United States."

HOW IMPORTANT IS BUSINESS ESPIONAGE?

The action of taking information from another by force or subterfuge implies that no easier way exists to get the data, and that the data is absolutely vital. In most cases these two conditions are not met. Either the majority of firms are willing to do without the data which may require improper or illegal methods to obtain or, if they must have the data, they prefer to substitute similar data or parallel data. There is, however, evidence that a good number of firms use business espionage.

The New York Times, for example, on a typical Sunday carries on the last page of its sports section at least one, if not several, ads for equipment primarily designed for spying. One such ad is reproduced in Figure 1–1.

Admiral Ellis Zacharias, Deputy Chief of Naval Intelligence during World War II has indicated that the U.S. Navy obtained about 95 percent of its peacetime intelligence through public sources, 4 percent from semipublic sources and only 1 percent from secret agents. (See Capt. E. M.

FIGURE 1–1

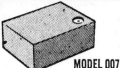

Zacharias (USN), *Secret Missions, The Story of an Intelligence Officer* [New York: G. P. Putnam's Sons, 1946], pp. 117–18).

However, business espionage is far from being unpublicized and its disproportionate publicity is what makes it appear more widespread than is the case. Such matters do make interesting reading. To get the flavor of such publicity, let us examine some newspaper articles avoiding names, but otherwise as they appeared on this topic.

From the periodical *Electronic News* for Monday, October 10, 1964:

W ... SUED BY M. CO. AGAIN OVER SECRETS

Los Angeles—The M. Electronic Co. has filed another suit in Federal Court here against W... Research Corp. here, and others over secret developments of M.'s Adv. Division for a laboratory recorder-reproducer.

The new action is also against J. M., who was an Adv. Lab. field sales manager . . . and now top W... Co. officials and former Lab. Div. employees.

They are charged with violating their fiduciary and contractual obligations to the Lab. Div. Mr. A. and Mr. B. are charged with offering to design for the Government a complete laboratory reproducer using secrets developed at the Lab. Div. Camarillo, California plant.

The suit seeks $50,000 damages and an injunction against Mr. B. disclosing confidential details of their new developments, customer lists and customer requirements for the developments.

From the *Los Angeles Times* of May, 1960:

AUTO INDUSTRY RUNS BIG ESPIONAGE RING
by Jack Vandenberg

Detroit—April 30 (UP)—The auto industry operates one of the world's largest espionage setups outside of government circles. Right now almost any auto company could tell you what its competitors have on the drawing boards for 1962.

. . . Actually spies for the various companies exchange information among themselves long before their employers are willing to tell the public. . . .

From *Los Angeles's Herald Examiner* of July 24, 1965:

MILLION-DOLLAR SPY QUIZ; 2 HELD
SECRET PROCESS STOLEN

An alleged cloak-and-dagger melodrama involving what district attorney's investigators believe was the theft of a secret industrial process worth millions is being probed here today. Under arrest are R. and L. booked for grand theft.

The pair were taken into custody as they left the offices of the firm of R. & H.

Investigators said R. and L. had approached officials of R. & H. and offered to make available plans, blueprints and specifications for a highly secret plastics process.

R. & H. asked for $25,000 down payment on the plans and $25,000 later, and both wanted positions as advisors with the firm.

After the arrest of the pair, Attorney O. surrendered all of the missing plans and diagrams to the District Attorney's Office. He said R. & H. had received the plans from a third person and were not aware they were stolen.

In 1964 the following article appeared in *Electronic News:*

COMPANY S. WINS SUIT ON 8 EX-EMPLOYEES

New Haven, Conn.—The S. Corp. has won its suit charging eight former employees with breach of fiduciary duty in making wrongful use of trade secrets when they formed A. B. Company.

Federal Judge Robert P. Anderson ruled S. was entitled to an accounting and award of damages for profits lost through the wrongful activities of the defendants together with court costs. S., in June 1959, sued for $1 million . . .

This interesting situation summary was published in *The New York Times,* August 2, 1964:

LOSS OF "SECRETS" VEXES COMPANIES

STEPS ARE URGED TO REDUCE
INDUSTRIAL ESPIONAGE

by Stacy V. Jones

Washington, Aug. 1—American companies, particularly producers of chemicals and drugs are concerned at the increasing theft of some of their intangible but most valuable assets—trade secrets.

A speaker at a recent conference here suggested that electronics and aerospace companies may be more subject to such looting than their executives realize.

Although industrial espionage has been raised to a sophisticated level, he said, the quickest way to get a competitor's trade secrets is to hire knowledgeable employees or to buy the data from established "rings" or individual sellers.

Trade secrets or confidential "know-how" take various forms —perhaps a written formula that can be microfilmed, a bacterial culture, or simply knowledge in somebody's head. Those who sell them to outsiders, or hand them to new employers, may be scientists, engineers or technicians . . .

He cited the case of Dr. F., a former Lederle employee, and a half a dozen associates. Cyanamid has won a damage suit against them . . .

The Monsanto Company was startled several months ago by an order for a few pounds of an organic compound that it thought no outsider knew about . . . Investigation showed that a Monsanto chemist had been bragging innocently about the compound to former associates, probably over a "short beer" . . .

The New York Times provided another view of the situation in an article dated June 20, 1965. Note the last sentence:

CHICAGO
Criminal Offense Proposed
for Theft of Secrets

The rising tide of research espionage has attracted strong support for a pending Illinois Senate bill that would make the theft of trade secrets and technical formulas a criminal offense.

Many of the country's big research industries are centered in Illinois, and the enactment of a law to discourage such pirating is being pushed by such organizations as the Illinois Manufacturers Association.

In the past, thefts of trade secrets and other "intellectual property" have been difficult to prosecute in the absence of specific criminal law provisions. The new bill would amend the

Illinois criminal code to add trade secrets to the definition of property.

Pirating of trade secrets would be punishable under the new bill by imprisonment from one to 10 years if the value of the stolen property exceeded $150.

"Our ability to protect trade secrets is an important element in retaining and attracting industry in Illinois," said State Senator W. Russell Arrington, Republican majority leader and chief sponsor of the bill.

The need for trade-secrets legislation was dramatized in testimony at a hearing of the Illinois Senate Judiciary Committee by an officer of the American Cyanamid Company, which had some of its most valued research secrets stolen.

Lyman C. Duncan, vice president in charge of medical affairs, told how an international ring robbed the company's Lederle Laboratories division at Pearl River, N.Y., of formulas, cultures and highly developed techniques for the production of tetracycline antibiotics. Mr. Duncan set the cost of developing the stolen secrets and cultures at more than $10 million.

A former Lederle research scientist confessed that he had stolen the formulas and sold them through the spy ring to Italian companies. These concerns used the stolen research knowledge to produce the antibiotics cheaply and competed with Lederle and other drug companies in the United States.

Mr. Duncan said that the drug industry gambles more than $300 million a year on research in this country. The value of trade secrets stolen from United States companies exceeds $3 billion a year, according to one estimate.

A rather complete description of intelligence operations in the automobile industry appeared in *SAGA,* November, 1965, under the heading "Confessions of an Auto Spy" by Parke Boltwood as told to Al Griffin. Catching the mood of the moment in November, 1965, *The New York Times Magazine* presented an article by Lawrence Stessin, " 'I Spy' Becomes Big Business." The article presented a more restrained survey of the current business intelligence situation.

While we are considering the importance of business espionage, we probably should consider its use in international affairs. Various governments have for years used business espionage. In recent years, the Soviet Union has purportedly spied on many nations including the United States. As warfare has grown to encompass entire national systems and economies, business and economic data has become ever more important. A thorough analysis of this topic is, however, beyond the scope of this book, and would form the basis for many books. To aid the interested reader, a brief bibliography has been provided at the end of this chapter pertaining to general international intelligence and specific Soviet activities.

More serious articles in the press about flamboyant techniques also catch the public eye. Vance Packard contributed "The Walls Do Have Ears" to the staid *The New York Times Magazine* (Sept. 30, 1964), which surveys the use of eavesdropping devices. In the science section of *Time* magazine's issue of March 6, 1964, are the same topics under the title "Electronics." Both mention new microminiature devices such as cigarette-pack transmitters, olive-sized microphones and the like. As far back as the early 1920's the topic was a major theme in an interesting ad from the *National Geographic* for the Corona typewriter (see Fig. 1–2).

In a recent meeting of a marketing association, Ernest Emery, marketing consultant of El Cajon, California, told the following story about the training of a well-prepared intelligence man:

> One of our field agents was out playing golf with the president of a competing company last week and as they chatted back and forth around the 9th hole, the president looked around carefully and said in a soft voice . . . "Did you hear what our purchasing agent did last night?" Our man, eager for any information, said, "No, tell me!" "He beat his wife to death with a five iron," said the president. "Oh, no," said our agent, and then, thinking of his report in the morning, followed up just as he was taught. "How many strokes did it take?"

At the risk of making it appear that California is a hotbed

FIGURE 1–2

of business spying, other examples from the press of the area may be considered. The *Los Angeles Times* published an article in 1965 headlined "Business Use of Phone Monitor Devices Told" by a staff writer, Daryl E. Lembke. In the article it is stated that less than (but implying not many less than) 10,000 businesses use devices to listen in on employees conversations. Such publicity can backfire, however, for the article continues:

The practice was brought to light when the San Francisco Chronicle disclosed Wednesday that the telephone system in Brookside Hospital at San Pablo has been tapped by hospital administrators for the past four months.

It turned out that the Chronicle itself uses the device for checking on classified advertising employees' contacts with the public.

A rash of articles in July and August, 1965, arose from President Lyndon Johnson's awakening interest in wiretapping in general, some of it by agents of the Bureau of Internal Revenue and some of it by other agencies of the federal government.

More serious work in less exciting areas is also gaining attention. Several instructional courses have been presented on the subject. Al N. Seares, vice-president of the Remington Rand Division of Sperry Rand Corporation gave a talk entitled "Marketing Intelligence," in 1964 for the Department of Industrial Administration of Yale University and for the National Association of Manufacturers. Earlier, in April, 1959, Harold Tombach at that time of the System Development Corporation of Santa Monica presented a paper at a joint meeting of the Operations Research Society of America and The Institute for Management Sciences in Las Vegas, Nevada, attempting to establish a scientific and logical framework for the topic of business intelligence. A year earlier, 1958, IBM published in its journal, *IBM* (Vol. 2, No. 4, October, 1958), an article by H. P. Luhn called "A Business Intelligence System." Typical of earlier approaches the article described total data handling rather than dealing only with externally oriented data.

The *California Management Review* in 1961 included an article by John J. Beauvois on "International Intelligence for the International Enterprise," which was more practical and similarly related to today's definition of intelligence. The degree of attention given to business espionage by E. I. du Pont de Nemours and Co. was mentioned in *TIME* magazine (Vol. 84, No. 22, Nov. 27, 1964) in an article "The Master Technicians." It states:

> Du Pont showed as much savvy in testing and introducing Corfam as it did in developing it. First it piqued the curiosity of shoe manufacturers by sending them sample batches to make into test shoes. Du Pont inspectors went along and swept up the scraps to prevent them from falling into the hands of industrial spies . . .

Another instructional approach of the early group was an American Management Association seminar, March, 1958, "Business Intelligence and the Function and Application of Forecasting." Primary emphasis was on business forecasting from economic indicators and espionage was not even mentioned. Later in April, 1962, a Defense Industry Workshop of the AMA on "Market Intelligence in the Defense Community" was held.

R. M. Greene & Associates held two nation-wide conferences on Business Intelligence in Los Angeles in 1964, both well attended by representatives of top national firms.

One of the more recent of these quasi-academic approaches was a series of seminars in 1965 hosted by Industrial Market Research Associates at which John F. Lynch and Clyde N. Duber, among others, both involved in corporate intelligence work, spoke on "Business and Corporate Espionage."

The field seems to be maturing into a rational, planned and respectable part of normal business activity rather than a quasi-legal tricky stunt. E. M. Emory and Associates, marketing consultants in California have been integrating good intelligence-gathering techniques with modern PERT planning techniques for about five years. *Business Management* in January, 1966, featured as one of its "Emerging Ideas" series an article "Marketing Intelligence Systems," which started many people thinking about a more rational use of intelligence.

BUSINESS INTELLIGENCE—AN EMERGING PROFESSION

Certain steps seem to characterize the development of a profession, be it medicine, mathematics, business or teaching. These are listed on the following table.

Only steps 1 to 5 are now clearly established for this field. In a survey of major university business schools in 1965, R. M. Greene & Associates established that some 40 percent would establish a course on the topic, if a textbook were available. Further analysis of replies showed that in many ways the topic is being taught, but under different titles. The course titles may be in the fields of marketing, forecasting, planning, etc. Part of the reason for slowness in emergence as a profession lies in lack of definition. A real business intelligence expert is rare. Consider, for example, the topics which have been included within the definition as recommended in the 1964 Business Intelligence Conferences (Table 1–2).

These are but a few of the classes of data falling in this field! It is little wonder then that a true expert is a rare bird indeed.

CURRENT NATIONAL COSTS OF INTELLIGENCE

The cost of intelligence to the business or industrial community is anywhere from a few million dollars to many billions of dollars a year. It is impossible to build a cost estimate from the bottom up, starting with the expenditures of a firm. Most companies have not the slightest idea of their costs in this area. They can estimate the cost of their guard

TABLE 1-1

Steps in the Development of a Profession

Description

Step Title	Description
Internal definition	A company or person defines his work as being unique and not basically the same as any existing job title or function.
Irregular conference	People feeling themselves different (as above), but allied to each other either within a company or among companies, call infrequent meetings with exchange of ideas as their purpose.
Local formal organizations	People in the same line gather, elect officers, structure for themselves a purpose and a constitution, and start to hold formal meetings. Anyone interested is usually invited to attend and the only membership requirement is that the applicant is interested.
Independent education	People in the profession lecture here and there on their work. Gradually the topics of their lectures become a set part of some course in another field.
Publications	Informal publications start for members.
Ads	Advertisement for people with this specialized knowledge start to appear in newspapers, usually under some more well-recognized job title.
Formal regional organization	The organization grows in numbers, sets membership requirements and spreads to a larger geographic area. Special interest groups within the topic begin to form.

Independent educational
courses · · · · · · · · · · · · · · · · · A recognized college or university offers a course, usually starting in the extension school, on the topic. Later a minor for a Bachelor or Master's degree may be included in this new field. Even later, this field may become the major subject of a degree with basic and advanced courses. Finally, the topic becomes acceptable as a major academic field with instructors of its own, degrees of its own and regular graduating students.

Government recognition · · · · · · The various governments, usually preceded by the federal government, begin to recognize the field. The first step is to include it as a separately numbered item in the Dictionary of Occupation Titles (DOT). Then the Civil Service Commission and military issue a job analysis, using the field as a major heading.

Independent advertisements · · · Ads start to appear in newspapers for people in the field. They use the new field as the major heading.

Licensing · · · · · · · · · · · · · · · In many fields, licensing (such as law, medicine, etc.) is the last step in professionalization. Formal education and experience requirements must be met.

TABLE 1-2

TOPICS WITHIN BUSINESS INTELLIGENCE

Site location studies
Population shifts
Ethnic changes
Traffic patterns
Freeway planning

Competitive analysis
Who and where are they
Their plans
Their employees
Their wages
Their weaknesses
Their strengths
Their turnover
R & D
Reliability
Pricing basis
Mergers
Acquisitions

Counterintelligence
Others' marketing plans
Others' business intelligence
Penetration attempts
Evaluation of security

Market research
Consumer needs
Design-competitor
Pricing-competitive
Tie-in sales
Trends

Economic forecasting
GNP trends
Technology impact
Regional shifts
FRB actions
Interest rates
Stock and bond markets

Natural elements
Fire, earthquakes, etc.
Natural resources
Storms, floods, etc.
Geographic distances

Government
New taxes
Tariffs
ICC regs.
New programs
  poverty
  youth
  medicare
  crime
SBA activities
State and local govt.
Statutes
Zoning
Taxes
Hours of work
FEPC

World
Tensions
Tariffs
War potentials
Balance-of-trade
State dept. regs.
Overseas markets
Visas
Monitary equivalents

system and their burglar alarms, but the broader areas of acquisition of knowledge are rarely priced. Consider some of the details which should be included: the magazine subscriptions to both company library and individuals; the cost (part) of a sales trip during which data is also gathered; and the cost of hiring a competitor's engineer. Meetings, for example, to discuss data needed are rarely priced. In a survey of 20 aerospace firms in 1965, R. M. Greene & Associates found that the average intelligence group (often called market research, or market analysis) had four professionals and three clerical personnel. *Business Week* in its Oct. 31, 1964, issue estimates that between one million and four million dollars a year are spent just on electronic eavesdropping or bugging devices for business. Although we cannot estimate its cost, one thing is clear, it is a big field. Much effort is being expended in this direction, and the field is growing.

TWO BASIC TYPES OF SYSTEMS

It may help in thinking about Business Intelligence to conceive of two basic system designs, one we may call "reactive" and one "predictive." The predictive system is one in which you try to guess what data will be needed in the future. Normally you then keep tabs on a large list of topics, often clipping articles relating to these subjects. Files predominate and file searches are vital in this type of system. Your main problem is to guess correctly which data someone will ask for. Usually their request has a slightly different slant than the data collected.

The reactive system is one in which you build a capacity to react to a query. In this system one stores addresses of sources of data, not data. Files are smaller, communications costs larger, and sometimes time delay in gathering data is greater.

In a predictive system, for example, under "Jones, Tom,"

one would find a biography prepared by some public relations office containing his latest known employer, any articles about him which appeared in the public press, etc. In a reactive file would be his name and the following possible entries:

> Jones, Tom . . . See *Who's Who in the West,* 1954
> See *L.A. Times,* Nov. 24, 1953, p. 4
> Contact: Jay Fredrickson, field agent 6
> Contact: E. M. Jones & Co., 123 Market St.
> San Francisco, 887-3220

Similarly, a military organization such as the Space Systems Division of the U.S. Air Force or a particular logistic study group in the Pentagon would be indexed as:

> Army Special Logistic   Call Pentagon Locator
> Study Group . . . . Area Code 202, LI 5-6700
> See: Washington Field Office,
> Report, Nov. 24, 1964
> Contact: Lt. Col. S. S. Pierce,
> Army Logistic Command,
> Div. 24, Ft. Meade, Md.

The data retrieved by the reactive system is nearly always up-to-date, whereas much of that stored under a predictive philosophy is almost always out-of-date. Although most systems now in operation are primarily predictive, more use of the reactive principle may be foreseen in the future.

INTELLIGENCE AND PLANNING

The needs for intelligence differ according to the operation being run or planned. Companies may have long-range plans, tactical or short-range plans, and immediate operations, all of which require intelligence support.

Few companies budget, as part of expected expenses, the costs of collecting, collating, and presenting information on projects. Ernest Emery, a specialist in marketing planning, has estimated that in a typical defense contract-award bidding situation there are almost 200 common elements of data required. Standard major questions which arise include:

> Who is writing the RFP (request for proposal)?
> What is his (or their) background and interests?

Will there be a PDP (project definition phase)?
Who is on the proposal evaluating committee?
What are the pressures on them?
Will this be the sole source?
Which companies have done this work before with the
    issuing agency?
Was their work satisfactory?
If not, what went wrong?
Who is on the bidders' list?
What prices have been put on competitors' proposals?
What may Congress do with this line item at budget time?

Whole shifts in marketing emphasis, who is visited, what
is said, etc. can be brought about by intelligence items.
Proper intelligence prevents selling to those already sold,
permits time and energy to be spent on those who need selling, and identifies what will make the sale possible. It is
essential in all types of corporate planning, not just for goal
setting but for operational planning as well.

INTELLIGENCE REPORTS

Modern, well-managed marketing organizations keep their
staff informed of current events. For example, the following
is an extract from a leading firm's international intelligence
handbook on Saudi Arabia. It is a high quality area intelligence report.

SAUDI ARABIA

Population—8,000,000 (estimate)

Area—870,000 square miles

Capital—Riyadh (except the Ministry of Foreign Affairs which is
    located in Jidda)

Climate and Topography—

Saudi Arabia includes the most rainless portions of the Arabian
Peninsula and has one of the hottest summer climates in the world.
Only the western hills receive more than 10 inches of rain a year

and much of the country gets less than 5 inches. Most of this rain
falls from November thru April but in Asir the rain occurs in
summer. Daytime temperatures normally rise to 100° in summer and
may reach 115°. On the coast, humidity is high and the heat unpleasant. Winters are warmest on the Gulf coast with afternoon
temperatures of 65°. In the interior, particularly on the western
highlands, frost and snow may occur.

Saudi Arabia lies between the Red Sea and the Persian Gulf. Its
southern and eastern borders are fringed by a series of independent
sheikdoms or confederations of tribes, under British protection and
reach the Gulf coast only between Kuwait and Qatar. Saudi Arabia
consists of a block of old hard rocks, highest along the Red Sea
and tilted gently northeastward toward the Gulf. Layers of sandstones
and chalky limestones cover the old rocks although much of the
actual surface is sand. Almost all of the southeast, the "Empty
Quarter," is a great sand-dune desert, the Rub al Khali, linked by
a narrow sandy strip, the Dahana, to the central desert, the Nafud.
There is a narrow coastal plain (Tihama) along the Red Sea, below
the steep edge of the plateau. In the North (Madian) these steep
ridges reach 5,000 to 8,000 feet; farther south the ridges are lower
but in the south (Asir) they rise again to 9,000 feet. There are many
dry water-courses but no permanent streams. Underground water
rises near, or to, the surface in places and creates fertile oases. There
is very little vegetation except for scrub brush and palm trees near
these oases. Cultivation is possible only in the chain of oases in the
eastern part of the central plateau, in irrigated areas or on the western
plain or highlands. The prospects of turning water-scarce Saudi
Arabia into a highly agricultural country were immensely increased
by the recent discovery, near the capital, of a gigantic bed of water
covering 50,000 square miles at a depth of 400 feet. It is estimated
that this underground reservoir can supply the country with one
million gallons of water per day.

Languages—

Arabic, a Semitic language and the language of the Koran, was a
local dialect which has become the speech of the entire Arab world.
Most business and professional people speak and understand English.

Travel Information—

Banks—Branches of the Netherlands Trading Society, the Banque de
l'Indochine, the British Bank of the Middle East, the Arab Bank
(of Jerusalem) and the Banque de Caire are located in Jidda, Al
Khobar and Damman.

Cigarettes—Not available because of Saudi Arabian disapproval of smoking.

Courtesies—During the fasting month of Ramadhan, eating and drinking and smoking in public is prohibited between sunrise and sunset. Foreign visitors are served meals in their hotel rooms during the day. Restaurant service begins at sundown when the fast is broken.

Communications—Long distance telephone and telegraph and air mail services are available.

Customs Regulations—Saudi Arabian customs authorities have a long and variable list of prohibited and dutiable items. Check local Saudi Arabian embassy before departure. It is illegal to take liquor into Saudi Arabia.

Drug Stores—American type drug stores do not exist. Standard toiletries and cosmetics are available in larger cities including Al-Khobar.

Electricity—110 volts, 60 cycles A.C. is standard almost throughout the country. There is no problem except in some sparsely populated areas.

Laundry—Adequate laundry and dry-cleaning services are available but service is slow. Prices are reasonable.

Liquor—Not available. It is illegal to take liquor into Saudi Arabia.

Photography—Shops in larger cities stock film of all types, at a high price and a not too dependable quality. There is some service for developing and printing black-and-white film locally but quality is not high. Color film is sent out of the country for processing.

Religion—Almost the entire population is Mohammedan; the State religion is Islam. Roman Catholic, Episcopalian and non-denominational services are available in most larger cities.

Shops and Stores—Shops in larger cities have many useful items but prices are very high when compared to U.S. prices.

Time—Eight hours later than U.S. Eastern Standard Time.

Transportation—Other than private or rented cars, taxis provide the principal means of transportation. Since taxi rates are by zone rather than by meter, the frequent use of taxis becomes expensive. Roads, railroads and airlines are being developed at a rapid rate by the government.

Water—Safe in all larger cities. Bottled water is recommended in outlying areas.

Clothing—In general, the same type of clothing as is worn in the United States is acceptable although it should be of lighter weight. Standard summer wear for social occasions is white trousers, white short-sleeve shirt and black tie. For official formal occasions, black trousers, black shoes and stockings and black bow tie with white short-sleeved shirt is acceptable.

Monetary Unit—Riyal (United States equivalent: 22.2¢)

Gross National Product (GNP)—$1,002,000,000

Form of Government—Absolute Hereditary Monarchy

The Saudi Arabian government and administrative system is largely in the hands of the royal family. A constitution has existed since 1926 for the Hejaz. In 1932 it was proposed to provide a single constitution for the whole country, which really is a union of two countries—the Hejaz, consisting of many small chiefdoms administered by a viceroy, and the Nejd which is divided into five provinces. This constitution has only been partly implemented. It provides for the setting up of certain advisory councils, comprising a consultative Legislative Assembly in Mecca, the capital of Hejaz, municipal councils in each of the towns of Mecca, Medina and Jidda, and village and tribal councils throughout the provinces. The members of these councils consist of chief officials and notables nominated or approved by the King. In May, 1958, a "cabinet system" was instituted under which effective power was given to the President of the Council of Ministers. The religious law of Islam is the common law of the land, and is administered by religious courts, at the head of which is a chief judge who is responsible for the Department of Legal Affairs.

History of Government—

For most of recorded history the greater part of the country has been an unknown frontier region. Aside from small coastal areas, the country was not brought within the Babylonian, Egyptian, Persian or Roman empires. Ancient Arabia grew rich from the trade in spices and incense. The Arabian peninsula was the cradle of Islam (Mohammed was born in Mecca in 570 A.D. and fled to Medina in 622 A.D.) and of the Arab people. After Mohammed's death his followers spread the Islamic faith over the whole Middle East and established a great empire, based on his teachings and the military strength of the Bedouin Arabs. Once the center of this empire was moved to Damascus, it began to decline. From the sixteenth century the Ottoman Turks controlled the Hejaz, but never successfully held all of Arabia. About 1750 the Wahabis, a strict Mohammedan sect, began a holy war against other forms of Islam and at various times controlled most of Arabia. The modern kingdom of Saudi Arabia was created by the present ruler's father, Abdul Aziz Ibn Saud, traditional leader of the Wahabi movement, who profited from the breakup of the Ottoman Empire to make himself master of both Hejaz and Nejd between 1914 and 1925. Expansion to the east and southeast was stopped by British protection of the sheikdoms and the resistance of Yemen in the southwest. The boundaries with some of the sheikdoms are still disputed. Saudi Arabia is a member of the United Nations and the Arab League.

Head of Government—The King

The present King is King Saud Ibn Abdul Aziz Al-Saud and his official title is His Majesty King Saud Al-Saud. He was born Jan. 12, 1902, became Crown Prince May 11, 1933; Commander of Army in Asir, in 1934; Commander-in-Chief Saudi Arabian forces, in 1939; President of Council of Ministers in 1953; and King on November 9, 1953 on the death of his father, the late King Ibn Saud. King Saud, then Crown Prince, visited the U.S. in 1947 at the invitation of President Truman and again in 1957 at the invitation of President Eisenhower. In November, 1961 he came to the U.S. again for medical treatment at the Peter Bent Brigham Hospital in Boston. He has traveled extensively all over the world. As the late King Ibn Saud grew older, the Crown Prince became increasingly concerned with administration of the Central Government and the program of modernization initiated by his father. He supervised the building of highways across the desert, the development of agricultural resources with modern methods, irrigation through the construction of dams and canals, and the creation of modern communications facilities to link the agricultural areas with other parts of the kingdom. On Nov. 9, 1953, on the death of his father, the Crown Prince became King Saud Al-Saud of Saudi Arabia. The present Crown Prince is the Emir Faisal, brother of the King.

Governing Body—Council of Ministers

When the "Cabinet System" was adopted in 1958, the Emir Faisal was made President of the Council of Ministers. In Dec. 1960, the King assumed the Presidency of the Council of Ministers with a cabinet of his own nominees. This cabinet was shuffled on Sept. 11, 1961, and again on March 15, 1962, probably in order to appease the Emir Faisal who became Deputy Prime Minister and Minister of Foreign Affairs.

Cabinet Members—

President—King Saud
Prime Minister and Minister of Foreign Affairs—Crown Prince Faisal
Minister of Interior—
Minister of Defense and Aviation—H.R.H. Emir Sultan
Minister of Communications—
Minister of Health—
Minister of Education—

Minister of Agriculture—
Minister of Finance and National Economy—
Minister of Petroleum and Mineral Affairs—
Minister of Pilgrim Affairs—
Minister of Labor and Social Affairs—
Minister of Justice—

Defense Responsibility—

The King depends mainly on a small regular army in the Hejaz. In
1937 a Ministry of Defense and a training school for officers were
established. British Military and Civil Air Missions helped in training the Army and civil aviation from 1947–1951. The U.S. maintains
a Military Mission with an Air Force element.

Military Attachés—

1. United States Attachés Assigned to Saudi Arabia
   Address: U.S. Embassy, Jidda
   Phone: 2101, 2102
   Ambassador—Hon. Parker T. Hart
   Air Attaché—Maj. Clark S. Scott
   Army Attaché—Col. Joseph J. Jackson
2. Saudi Arabian Attachés Assigned to United States
   Address: 2711 Wisconsin Ave. N.W., Washington 7, D.C.
   Phone: 333-1284
   Ambassador—Sheikh Abdullah Al-Khayyal
   Armed Forces Attaché—Col. Ibrahim M. Al-Malik
   Asst. Armed Forces Attaché—Lt. Col. Hashem S. Hashem

Military Assistance Program Mission—

Mailing Address: Chief,
                  U.S. Military Training Mission to Saudi Arabia
                  APO 616
                  New York, New York
Chief—Col. W. W. Wilson (Air Force)
Deputy Chief—Col. S. E. Sacerdote (Army)
Chief, Army Service Section—Col. Elmer Schmierer
Chief, Navy Service Section—Cdr. J. E. Simone, Jr.
Chief, Air Force Service Section—Col. G. C. Whitley

Additional Government and Military Officials—

Maj. Gen. Abdullah Mutlaq—Chief-of-Staff of the Royal Saudi
  Armed Forces
Lt. Col. Akram Quaja—Director of Supply, Royal Saudi Air Force

Defense Organization—

1. Organization of Royal Saudi Air Force

   Headquarters are at Jidda. Director, Royal Saudi Air Force is Lt. Col. Assad Al-Zohair.

   The Royal Saudi Air Force (RSAF) dates from 1950 when a British military mission began reorganization of national forces and supplied several surplus Tiger Moths and Ansons. With the establishment of a U.S. transit base at Dhahran in 1950, a U.S. training mission took over with ten Temco trainers under MDAP. Also supplied were Douglas C-47 transports and North American T-6 basic trainers. Some RSAF pilots were trained in the UK and others in Egypt under an agreement which also resulted in Joint Armed Forces Command.

   First operational equipment, delivered in 1955, was three Douglas B-26 attack bombers, followed by another six at a later date. In 1956, four ex-Egyptian Air Force Vampire F.B. 52's were given to the RSAF. Following new Dhahran Airfield agreement on April 2, 1957, six Fairchild C-123B transports were given to RSAF and another transport gift in 1957 was a VIP Varsity to King Saud from King Hussein of Jordan.

   A request by King Saud for operational fighters resulted in the arrival, in 1957, of ten North American F-86F Sabres and a similar number of Lockheed T-33 jet trainers plus several Beech T-34 Mentors. Some RSAF pilots were trained in the U.S. and USAF advisors instigated a new training program before pro-Egyptian Emir Faisal took over much of the political power. The Northrop F-5A and the Douglas A4E are being considered as replacements for the F-86F in two or three squadrons.

2. Current Equipment of Royal Saudi Air Force

   Fighter-Bombers—North American F-86F Sabre, (10); de Havilland Vampire F.B. 52, (4).
   Light Bombers—Douglas B-26B Invader, (9).
   Transports—Fairchild C-123B Provider, (6); Douglas C-47.
   Trainers—de Havilland Chipmunk T.10; North American T-6 Texan; Temco TE-1A Buckaroo; Lockheed T-33A, (10); Beech T-34A.
   Miscellaneous—Avro Anson; Auster Aiglet; Vickers Varsity.

Commercial Airlines—

Saudi Arabian Airlines is a government-owned company managed by Trans World Airlines and operates regular internal air services, a three-times-a-week service to Cairo and a twice-a-week service to Beirut. Pilots are mainly Americans with a growing number of Saudi-Arabian co-pilots. Saudi Arabian Airlines has 6,049 unduplicated route miles and 2,500 employees. Equipment includes 9 DC-3's, 3 DC-4's, 9 Convairs and 2 Boeing 720B's. President of the airline is His Excellency Shaikh Ahmed Salah Jamjoom. The Director General is R. S. Al-Romaih. The main airports are at Jidda, Dhahran and Riyadh.

General—

The fact that the provision for economic development constitutes the largest expenditure in the Saudi budget is indicative that the foremost policy objective of the government is the economic development of the country. In 1957 the King arranged with the International Monetary Fund for a mission to examine the Saudi economic situation. A stabilization program was formulated which the Government announced in April, 1958. An Economic Development Committee was set up in July 1959. The International Bank for Reconstruction and Development was invited to send a mission to Saudi Arabia to study possibilities of economic development. A report was submitted in Sept., 1960 which recommended a comprehensive two-year survey on which a long range economic development program could be based. In July, 1960, a High Planning Council was established to handle problems of economic development. In 1932, the year of its unification, Saudi Arabia had no reliable source of income other than the money spent by pilgrims. It had no industry, very little trade in commerce, sparse argriculture, and a largely nomadic population. Today, the greatest single factor of economic importance in Saudi Arabia is oil, which accounts for most of its industry and 90% of its exports. It has about 19% of the world's known oil reserves. The first oil concession was given to Standard Oil Co. of California which later joined with other companies to form Arabian American Oil Company (ARAMCO). Oil was not discovered until 1938. During 1952 ARAMCO's total production of crude oil was 302,000,000 barrels; in 1962 it was 555 million barrels. Other minerals include gold, silver, salt, gypsum, iron ore and limestone. Until recently inland transportation was almost entirely dependent on the camel. Now, roads, railroads and airlines are being developed at a rapid rate with income derived from oil royalties. The ports of Jidda and Dammam are being widened and deepened and new dock facilities are being constructed at a total cost of $50 million. The 1962–1963 national budget was over $500 million, 90% of it obtained from oil revenues. Other sources of income consist of customs and import duties; taxes on companies, gold mines and trade. There is a Moslem tax on individuals which amounts to 2 1/2% of income and property and is used to finance a national form of social security. There is no national debt. In 1962 over 13% of the national budget was expended on education. In 1958 there were 600 educational institutions, 89,000 students and 4,000 teachers. All education is free to all Saudi citizens. The government selects students to study abroad, paying for their tuition in foreign universities. Medical services, like education, are free to all citizens. An auto mechanics guild has been formed and is the country's nearest approach to a labor union. Citizens can be arrested and charged with a criminal offense for smoking a cigarette. Saudi Arabia is a prohibitionist country and movies are forbidden. Many women still wear veils.

INTELLIGENCE QUALITY CONTROL

Just as one may examine the functioning of an intelligence group on three basic management parameters of cost, time and performance, the data produced also may be examined for quality. The first of these measures is timeliness, i.e., was the data required in the hands of the proper decision maker when he needed it? The second is quantity, i.e., was the data provided in enough depth or breadth to be useful, was there too much, or too little provided? The third measure is data quality. This is the most difficult to measure.

Data quality may appear to consist of two submeasures, validity and reliability. Validity means that the data correctly describes the real world. It is "correct" in the usual sense. Reliability refers to repeatability, or dependability of data in terms of consistency, which means that two or more sources, when queried about a topic, provide approximately the same answer. Intelligence data, however, can be reliable but invalid, and valid but not reliable. For example, at one time the rumors of Stalin's death went around the world, reprinted and rebroadcast by almost every news media. Everywhere one turned the word came "Stalin is Dead!" There was only one problem, he wasn't. Here is reliability without validity. Sometimes a very high degree of reliability may indicate an attempt at counterintelligence, i.e., planted information. If one were to rate validity and reliability on a five-point scale from most valid and most reliable to the least, Tables 1–3 and 1–4 might look like this:

TABLE 1–3

A FIVE-POINT JUDGMENT SCALE FOR INFORMATION VALIDITY

Score	Meaning
1	No relationship to reality, may by randomness alone be correct but this is most unlikely.
2	Probably untrue, only about 1 chance in 50 of being an accurate description of real life.
3	Possibly true, perhaps at least 1 chance in 10 of being correct if important, implies need for further study.
4	Good reason to believe this is true, definite basis for further study. 1 chance in 3 or 4 that the subject statement truly describes reality.
5	This statement exactly describes a known real situation precisely.

TABLE 1–4

A FIVE-POINT JUDGMENT SCALE FOR INFORMATION RELIABILITY

Score	Meaning
1	Data is a random input, bears no relationship to other data on same topic.
2	Rare agreement, perhaps 1 out of 25, among data sources.
3	Data agreement among various sources is fair, 1 out of 10 or so, requires further checking if important.
4	Almost all sources agree with a few exceptions.
5	All sources exactly agree.

SUMMARY

This chapter has given an overall picture of the field of business intelligence and espionage, providing some basic definitions and concepts, some examples, and a brief history of recent activities. On any one topic a great deal more could be said, but other chapters will deal with many of these ideas. The author hopes the reader has enjoyed this short trip into the area and will become a more productive, useful, and helpful executive to his firm as a result of reading this book.

BRIEF BIBLIOGRAPHY ON SOVIET AND
RELATED ESPIONAGE SYSTEMS

BEAUVOIS, JOHN J. "International Intelligence for the International Enterprise," *California Management Review*, Vol. III, No. 2 (Winter, 1961).

BENTLEY, ELIZABETH. *Out of Bondage*. New York: The Devin-Adair Company, 1957.

CHAMBERS, WHITTAKER. *Witness*. New York: Random House, Inc., 1952.

CHANDLER, LT. COL. STEDMAN, and ROBB, COL. ROBERT W. *Front-Line Intelligence*. Washington, D.C.: Infantry Journal Press, 1946.

DALLIN, DAVID J. *Soviet Espionage*. New Haven, Connecticut: Yale University Press, 1955.

DEANE, JOHN R. *The Strange Alliance*. New York: Viking Press, Inc., 1947.

DE TOLEDANO, RALPH. *Spies, Dupes, and Diplomats*. New York: Duell Sloan & Pearce–Little, Brown, 1952.

————, and LASKY, VICTOR. *Seeds of Treason*. New York: Funk & Wagnalls Co., 1950.

DEWHURST, C. H. *Close Contact*. Boston: Houghton Mifflin Company, 1954.

FINEBERG, S. ANDHIL. *The Rosenberg Case*. New York: Oceana Publications, 1953.

FOOTE, ALEXANDER. *Handbook for Spies*. New York: Doubleday & Company, Inc., 1949.

GISKES, H. J. *Spione über Spielen Spione.* Hamburg, D.R., 1949.

HARTEL, COL. GUNTHER E. *The Red Herring.* New York: Ivan Obolensky, Inc., 1962.

HIRSCH, RICHARD. *The Soviet Spies.* New York: Duell Sloan & Pearce–Little, Brown, 1947.

HOOVER, J. EDGAR. "The U.S. Businessman Faces the Soviet Spy," *Harvard Business Review,* Vol. 42 (January, 1964), pp. 140-46.

JORDAN, GEORGE R. *From Major Jordan's Diaries.* New York: Harcourt Brace & Co., Inc., 1952.

KRIVITSKY, W. G. *Ich war in Stalin's Dienst.* Amsterdam, Netherlands: Allert de Lange Verlag, 1940.

MASSING, HEDE. *This Deception.* New York: Duell Sloan & Pearce–Little, Brown, 1951.

ORLOV, ALEXANDER. *Handbook of Intelligence and Guerrilla Warfare.* Ann Arbor, Michigan: University of Michigan Press, 1963.

PILAT, OLIVER. *The Atom Spies.* New York: G. P. Putnam's Sons, 1952.

PURDY, ANTHONY, and SUTHERLAND, DOUGLAS. *Burgess and Maclean.* New York: Doubleday & Company, Inc., 1963.

ZACHARIAS, CAPT. E. M. (USN). *Secret Missions.* New York: G. P. Putnam's Sons, 1946.

Chapter Two

AN INTRODUCTION TO INTELLIGENCE SYSTEMS IN BUSINESS

Anonymous*

INTRODUCTION

IN THE LIFE CYCLE of a job, from proposal to delivery, access to the right information at the right time provides valuable assistance to management for decision making.

Time and again, the inputs of an intelligence group can make management more effective. The earliest application of intelligence to the cycle is to determine the general line of business through market research. Marketing management uses intelligence to determine customer desires, needs, purchasing capabilities, and supplier preferences.

Purchasing uses intelligence to find the supplier who offers the best product for the cost. Purchasing must also know and weigh such factors as the possibility of a strike, the likelihood of delivery shortages, and the probability of a competitor's action shutting off the source of supply.

Even for the last step of the job cycle—payment—business intelligence can help guard against loss by keeping

*The author of this chapter was unable to procure a release from his company, so sensitive is the topic of Business Intelligence. He is an operations researcher with a major scientific organization in the aerospace field.

management informed about the creditor's financial position. This chapter will serve as an introduction to the collection, storage, evaluation, and presentation of business information for the use of management.

THE ETHICS OF BUSINESS INTELLIGENCE

The goals of business intelligence are analogous to those of military intelligence, but this may not be true of methods. The ways of carrying out intelligence and espionage are often rejected, at least on the surface, by the business community. This is not just a matter of conjecture, for a few years ago, *Harvard Business Review*[1] distributed a questionnaire to 1,500 businessmen to establish their attitudes, at least their expressed attitudes, on how far they would go, or approve others going, to collect business information. The results, tabulated in Table 2–1 indicate the boundaries; and, as the reader can see, serious spying is strongly disavowed.

Besides being considered unethical, certain aspects of spying are illegal. In April, 1965, there was an incident of industrial espionage which matches any Fleming spy thriller. It involved a junior executive of a toothpaste firm and the firm's plans for marketing during the next year. The young man made contact with the leading competitor of his firm and offered to sell them the plans for $20,000. He arranged a meeting to carry out this transaction at the Kennedy International Airport in New York. The meeting took place on schedule in a men's room at the airport. The two sat in adjoining cubicles, as planned, and the money and plans were exchanged. The young executive took the other's trousers, to delay any possible pursuit, and fled from the men's room right into the arms of the FBI who had been tipped off by the competitor. The young man can be given up to ten years in prison.[2]

---

[1] E. E. Furash, "Problems in Review: Industrial Espionage," *Harvard Business Review,* November-December 1959.

[2] See *Time* magazine, April 30, 1965.

TABLE 2–1
SUMMARY OF RESPONSES BY TOP MANAGEMENT TO A QUESTIONNAIRE
ISSUED TO 1,500 BUSINESSMEN ON PRACTICES OF BUSINESS
INTELLIGENCE

Situation	% Approval
1. A retailer sends someone to "shop" in a competitor's store to get product and pricing information	96
2. An oil company establishes a scout department to watch the drilling activities of competitors	71
3. A company, learning of a competitor's test market, quickly puts on a special sale in the same location	64
4. A key employee is hired away from a competitor	59
5. Sales manager wines and dines his competitive counterpart, pumping him for information	47
6. Company representative poses as a prospective customer to get information from a competitor	32
7. A vice-president hires a detective agency to watch the proving grounds of a competitor	16
8. Design engineer steals the plans of a competitor's new model	4
9. Company president instructs his aide to secretly record conversations in a competitor's office	4
10. Production manager rewards a competitor's employee for certain process information	3
11. A company plants confederates in a competitor's organization	2
12. District manager wire taps the phone of his local competitor	1

Although spying and espionage are two techniques the modern businessman says he finds repugnant, there are other techniques of military intelligence he finds more comfortable. In background research techniques, business and military intelligence are almost alike and this example shows how similar they are:

After World War II, I interviewed the German Air Attaché who had been attached to the German Embassy in Washington, D.C. Before the United States entered the war, it had been his task to keep track of American aircraft production: the number produced monthly, the types, and the problems we were having, if any. Simply by following the "Help Wanted" columns in the newspapers of major aircraft producing cities and by reading the trade journals, he was able to chart production with most astounding accuracy. Some sources have indicated that his figures were as accurate as our own government's.

The use of publicly available documents to develop desired information is typical of techniques used by an astute businessman. He learns to infer changes from a few facts, often apparently unrelated. He must be on the alert for data from any source about his customers and about his competition. Some of this data comes to him without his instigation; i.e., a competitor gets high at a party and talks too much, an associate lets slip some data that was to be kept confidential, or a military man uses poor judgment and allows a businessman to see a competitor's proposal. Is it ethical to use this information? Here we will have to say that practice varies from verbal attitudes. Some firms would hesitate to take advantage of such valuable data. Most would not hesitate, justifying the act to themselves by saying, "Oh well, they really should have guarded their data better." This defense is a bit like the child of sixteen who, after murdering his parents, pleads with the judge for leniency because he is an orphan.

THE COST OF BUSINESS INTELLIGENCE

Two ways of approaching costs should be considered. The first is the standard costing technique; add direct labor, overhead, G & A, etc. The second is the cost of not having the system. If one can compare these, the justification for having or not having an intelligence system is clear. If your company bids on a project at the sum of $4,500,000, one might expect the profits to be somewhere between $40,000 (a little under 1%) to $400,000 (about 10%). If a competitor takes this contract with a bid of $4,400,000, from your bid, you may have lost money by bidding high. If the winning bid is $4,490,000 there is a difference of only $10,000 between bids. If business intelligence could have told you the size of the competitor's bid, you probably could have changed yours and not really risked losing anything. In a sense, not knowing your competitor's bid cost you the project which would have yielded a profit of between $30,000 and $400,000.

In some cases, lack of business intelligence can specifically be named the cause of a loss. In most cases, the cause is complex and cannot be so fixed.

Since there are times when a company's resources for collecting intelligence are limited, it is useful to have a procedure for determining if intelligence should be collected for a particular proposal or bid. In order to do this, we use expected values. We say that the probability of capturing a specific job multiplied by the expected profit from this job is the expected value of the job. We can estimate this expected value, assuming no use of business intelligence, and compare this figure with the expected value if business intelligence is to be used. The comparison provides a simple decision if no other factors are involved. Let us set up a procedure to establish the need for intelligence on a specific project.

Step 1. Estimate the expected profits for the particular project, if you win the award.

Step 2. Estimate the probability of winning the award, assuming business intelligence is not used.

Step 3. Estimate the cost of making the proposal or of bidding.

Step 4. Calculate the expected value of the project if business intelligence is not used:

EXPECTED VALUE = (STEP 1 $\times$ STEP 2) — STEP 3

Step 5. Estimate the cost of obtaining intelligence.

Step 6. Estimate the probability of winning the award if business intelligence is used.

Step 7. Calculate the expected value of the project if business intelligence is used:

Expected Value = (Step 1 $\times$ Step 6) — (Step 3 + Step 5)

Step 8. Calculate the expected value of using business intelligence on this particular project:

Expected Value = (Step 7 — Step 4)

The businessman can estimate the cost and effectiveness for several levels of intelligence effort. He can then choose the level for the particular project on the basis of maximum value or other criteria. He computes his return on investment for intelligence by the following equation:

$$\text{Return} = \frac{\text{Value of Intelligence (Step 8)}}{\text{Cost of Intelligence (Step 5)}}$$

Return on investment can be converted to rate of return by discounting for the time elapsed between the expenditure of money and its expected return.

DATA COLLECTION LOGIC

Because data can be processed to produce intelligence, and because an experienced intelligence man knows that small bits of data derived from widely separated points can suddenly bring a complex figure into focus, he has a strong drive not to throw away anything. One specialist characterized a good intelligence manager as a person who has "a chipmunk instinct with brains." Opposing this drive to retain is a drive to reject data or, as it is called by Fredrick[3] "purge" the files. This drive has several sources of motivation: knowledge that it is expensive to maintain files, knowledge that as files get larger, search time grows longer (there is more material to search through) and, finally, knowledge that in a larger file more material is out-of-date.

---

[3]See J. L. Fredrick's article, Chapter IV, page 82.

An interesting wartime example of the usefulness of a single bit of data follows:

During World War II, the Japanese lost a small air base to the Allies in the South Pacific. In a preliminary survey of this air base, a member of the intelligence team noted that the trash contained a number of identical aircraft motor parts. After going over their notes, the team decided that there were too many of these broken parts in the trash, considering the small number of planes that had flown from the field. The parts were sent to a laboratory for analysis and they were found to become brittle at operating temperatures, due to a lack of tungsten. It was known that the Japanese did know the correct percentage of tungsten to use, so the conclusion was drawn that Japan was suffering an involuntary shortage of tungsten. Based upon this, the Allied CINPAC decided to go after all tungsten sources available to the Japanese including mines, transportation channels, and storage locations of bars and ore. Later evidence shows the conclusions to have been correct and much inefficiency would have plagued the Japanese war machine had the war not been abruptly terminated.

One can evaluate files with what might be called a "selectivity ratio," which measures the competence of a file to satisfactorily fulfill data need. Such a ratio might be written:

$$\text{SELECTIVITY COMPETENCE OF A SPECIFIC FILE WITHIN AN INTELLIGENCE FILE SYSTEM} = \frac{\text{NUMBER OF SPECIFIC QUESTIONS ANSWERED SATISFACTORILY}}{\text{TOTAL NUMBER OF QUESTIONS ASKED}}$$

Ratios like this can give guidance on whether or not to collect data as has been done in the past. This kind of measurement is done at the "home office." Field agents should not be asked to evaluate specific bits of data because they do not have access to pertinent complementary data. The home office, having the broader view, is the better place to evaluate data and maintain files.

To provide guidance to field collection agents and others, one may prepare Topics of Interest lists or bulletins. (See Table 2–2.)

TABLE 2–2

Aircraft	Number produced by type
	Current proposals on. . . .
	R&D of new types of. . . .
	Weapons effects on. . . .
	Missile carrying ability of. . . .
Antiaircraft	Range of. . . .
	Types of current in production. . . .
	Number being produced. . . .
	R&D projects on. . . .
	Ground to air missile studies. . . .
	Concealment of. . . .
	Use of atomic weapons in. . . .
Plants	Number of and location. . . .
	Items produced within. . . .
	Studies to relocate. . . .
	Studies to build new. . . .
	Security used at each. . . .
	Number and types of employees. . . .
	. . . .

SOURCES OF DATA[4]

Table 2–3, following, indicates some useful sources of data and how frequently the data is available, i.e., daily, weekly, etc. In a reactive system (one in which a request for information triggers a search for data), the emphasis is on sources of data, i.e., government bureaus, people in various offices, books, etc.

With the file competence equation described earlier, one may examine sources statistically. Usually one finds that a small percentage of available sources provides a greater percentage of useful data. Making a practical check of this is difficult. The format implied by the efficiency ratio suggests, for example, that when a file is removed for use, that a check be added to the denominator value; and if the file is helpful and contains what is desired, a check be entered in the nu-

---

[4]See Chapter IX, by Howard Laitin, for more detailed information on data sources.

TABLE 2-3
SOME USEFUL SOURCES FOR BUSINESS INTELLIGENCE

Daily
  Aviation Daily
  Interavia Air Letter
  Missile/Space Daily
  Space Business Daily
  Spacewire
  New York Times, Los Angeles Times, Chicago Tribune
  Local papers from competitor city

Weekly
  Aviation Week & Space Technology
  California Institute of Technology (UCLA, MIT, etc.) Weekly Calendar
  Business Week
  Missiles & Rockets
  R & D Weekly (Federal Procurement Publ. Co.)
  Technology Week
  Time magazine
  EIA Weekly (Electronic Industries Assn.)
  Field Office Activity Summaries
  Newsweek

Biweekly
  Aviation Daily Index
  Moody's Industrials
  Space Marketing Intelligence
  Military Research Letter (Callahan publication)
  Underwater Defense Letter (Callahan publication)
  Space Letter (Callahan publication)
  Missile Ordnance Letter (Callahan publication)
  Forbes

Monthly
  Aerospace Management
  Army Research & Development
  Aviation Week & Space Technology Market Letter
  Business Cycle Developments
  DATA Magazine
  DMS Military & Civil Aircraft
  DMS Rocket, Missile & Spacecraft
  Dun's Review
  Industrial Research
  Interavia Air Letter Index
  International Science & Technology
  Labor Market & Employment Security
  Missiles & Space
  NATO Letter
  Research/Development
  Scientific American
  Space Log Index
  Fortune
  USSR
  Western Aerospace

Quarterly
  The Quarterly Review of Economics and Business
  Space Aeronautics
  Naval Logistics Quarterly

Other
  Field personnel trip reports
  House organs, customers and competitors
  Organization charts
  Telephone directories
  Biographies (*Who's Who*, etc.).
  Meeting calendars
  U.S. government documents, congressional hearings
  Books

merator. Similarly if cards are kept as files or even computer tape, a record can be made of use vs. usefulness.

One fallout of practical experience is this—before getting a full-scale intelligence study started, make sure you have completed a survey of your total organization. Pricing data of competitors may be found in your own pricing department, product information in your engineering offices, and biographies in your public relations files. In one case, a highly sought proposal prepared by a firm was made available through a staff member who had an outside business in printing and was reproducing it for a competitor.

Some data is available from the source company itself, for example, stockholder reports. It is common for an executive to own shares of stock in each of a number of competitor companies, just so he can receive the stockholder's materials. Data has been derived about vendor delivery and quality by calls to purchasing agents; about average wages by calls to the personnel department of a competitor by a personnel department employee and biographical data about top management and key employees from a competitor's public relations people.

In searching for published, open information, one should not overlook the local public library. The community library is a link in a system of libraries leading up to the Library of Congress. The local library may not have what you need, but by inter-library loan with larger libraries or with nearby university libraries, an amazing amount of material can be obtained. The reference librarian personally may be of help and, if approached properly, may give her time to help your company. Among her reference collection will usually be several sources-of-data directories.[5]

COLLECTING UNPUBLISHED DATA

Published information by its very nature is not current. Even newspaper articles are at least a half a day old by the

---

[5]See Marian O. Manley, *Business Information* (New York: Harper and Brothers, 1955).

time they hit the street. Usually, the really up-to-date information is in the form of oral inputs from organic sources.

In obtaining such data, we suggest attention to several simple ideas: learn how to ask questions, learn how to listen, and learn how to plan to get data.

The person who asks questions that seem pointed and likely to arouse suspicion is doomed in this work. Probing for data is a very ticklish task and a few courses in psychology would not hurt in preparing for this area.

Listening, too, is an art. Be alert for rumor, grapevine, and slips of speech. This does not mean that you have to accept as ultimate truth all that is heard, but rejection of some data and acceptance of other is best done when you have a good collection to draw from.

Planning to get data implies that you identify your "target," learn how to get to it, and plan your campaign. Here is an example of good planning in action.

A General is supposed to know when a certain request for proposal (RFP) is to be issued but has made it clear that he wants to hold back this information. One day he gets a call from an old buddy, now a Lt.-Colonel; the old buddy is in town and would like to lunch with the General, if possible. Upon checking with his secretary, the General finds that a long-standing luncheon date with some V.I.P. from Company X has just been cancelled.

The General and his old buddy meet and have lunch together. During the lunch, the buddy mentions that he knows the RFP is to be issued on such and such a date. The General, in passing, corrects him saying, "No, Bob, it is more likely to be a couple of weeks before that." No more was said about the matter.

Later, the Lt.-Colonel returns to his home base and reports the gist of the conversation to another friend of his. This friend thanks him for helping to establish the RFP date so he and his wife can plan their vacation.

The vacation story, of course, is not true. The "friend" immediately calls his home office and reports the RFP date.

The plan:

1. Find someone who can "get to" the General when he will have his guard down.
2. Make a luncheon appointment to reserve the General's time. Later it will be cancelled to let the "buddy" have more time with the General.
3. Our field man in (XXXXX) city will ask the aid of his good friend, who, in turn, is the buddy of the General. To find this inbetween, a search was made of the schools and colleges the General had gone to; these lists were then matched with a list of current and recently retired senior grade officers in the same service arm. Before this Lt.-Colonel was found, two others had been approached. It was assumed that people who are contacted for questionable activities usually will not report them, even if they are aware. This is almost always the case.

MEASUREMENT OF DATA USEFULNESS

In addition to examining file usefulness, it may be possible to attach to data some measures so as to evaluate its usefulness. In one case the following measures were developed, using a five-point scale to indicate the degree to which each was met:

1. *Subject.* The degree of relationship between the data and the current or proposed activities of the firm.

2. *Depth.* The amount of useful, nonredundant data on the topic, permitting analysis of what is the case, why, when, etc.

3. *Recency.* A measure of the up-to-dateness of the data. In systems in which no change is known to exist, old data may rate high. In situations of rapid change, only immediate data receives the highest score.

4. *Cost.* The estimated cost of collecting the data.

Neither validity nor reliability were measured because

TABLE 2–4

A TOPIC SUMMARY SHEET

Source	Title	Summary	Date	Reli-ability
		TOPIC: The ABC Company: Actions in System Training Programs.		
U.S. News & World Report	ABC company to offer system training as consultants	Describes plans based upon their experiences in army training. Three staff members, Ph.D.'s in psychology, are assigned as core. E. P. Jones, a VP, will head.	11/8/59	B
N.Y. Times	ABC appoints training chief	Photo plus 2 col. inches on the appt. of E. P. Jones as VP. He lives in Scarsdale, 2 boys, has EE from N.Y.U.	11/20/59	B
Spacewire	Bidders on AF system trng. for Project 165 L.	Lists 11 bidders on 12-million training program for 165L crews. ABC is listed.	12/10/59	B
Internal, friend of ABC Co. treasurer	Financial support of ABC Co. system training program	ABC budgeted $12,000 this year and will go to $45,000 next for promotion & personnel. Has no contracts yet. Lists as R & D.	12/27/59	C
American Psychologist	Help wanted	Ad for Systems Training Specialists run by ABC Co. offers 10K to 20K salaries to Ph.D. level psychologists.	1/6/60	A
Commerce & Business Daily	Contract awards	ABC Co. for System Training on Navy program ERAER . . . $150,000 for 6 months.	2/29/61	A
Standard Star newspaper	Deputy appointed in local firm	L. G. Sittaur, Ph.D., appointed deputy to E. P. Jones in ABC Co. system training, he will head up laboratories.	4/20/62	B

these arise from cross-data comparisons and cannot be attributed to the data itself.

A RUNNING DATA FILE BY TOPIC

It has been found useful, in some firms, to create a "topic sheet" and to enter data upon this, as it is collected. A typical topic sheet is provided in Table 2–4.

STORAGE AND RETRIEVAL OF STORED DATA

Files range from pure human memory to complex computer tape systems; sometimes they include a mixture within a single organization. The type of file to be used depends upon such factors as: frequency of referral after storage, amount of data to be stored, security classification, type of data stored, frequency of change to the stored data, access speed required, etc.

One useful tool for retrieving information is a moderately new technique, the permutation index. In this approach, the words of the title to a booklet or an article are permuted (rotated) so that if you can remember any one word of the title, you can find the whole title. This is illustrated in Table 2–5.

Advertising the data in the files is important, too. The number of requests for data received may well be a measure of the value of the intelligence group. Holding periodic briefings, publishing bulletins, and personal contacts with those that usually need intelligence information are but three of the many possible ways to assure that those who need the system are kept aware of its existence. One major aerospace firm had been keeping a biographical file for years although none of the marketing managers knew of it. This was a waste of time and caused a duplication of effort.

An actual file heading list from one of the nation's top aerospace firm's intelligence group is found in Table 2–6.

TABLE 2–5

How to Make a Permutation Index

1. List the Titles of Your Documents
   Auto Makers Too, Conduct Espionage.
   Business Espionage.
   Business Intelligence.
   Industrial Technical Intelligence.
   Measuring Business Changes.

2. Permute the Titles
   Auto Makers Too, Conduct Espionage.
   Makers Too, Conduct Espionage. Auto
   Too, Conduct Espionage. Auto Makers
   Conduct Espionage. Auto Makers Too,
   Espionage. Auto Makers Too, Conduct

   Business Espionage.
   Espionage. Business

   Business Intelligence.
   Intelligence. Business

   Industrial Technical Intelligence.
   Technical Intelligence. Industrial
   Intelligence. Technical Industrial

   Measuring Business Changes.
   Business Changes. Measuring
   Changes. Measuring Business

3. List the Permuted Titles Alphabetically
   Auto Makers Too, Conduct Espionage.
   Business Changes. Measuring
   Business Espionage.
   Business Intelligence.
   Changes. Measuring Business
   Conduct Espionage. Auto Makers Too,
   Espionage. Auto Makers Too, Conduct
   Espionage. Business
   Industrial Technical Intelligence.
   Intelligence. Business
   Intelligence. Industrial Technical
   Makers Too, Conduct Espionage. Auto
   Measuring Business Changes.
   Technical Intelligence. Industrial
   Too, Conduct Espionage. Auto Makers

TABLE 2–6

ILLUSTRATIVE FILE HEADINGS FROM A TYPICAL AEROSPACE
BUSINESS INTELLIGENCE FIRM FILE SYSTEM

AIR FORCE ASSOCIATES (of
  Gen'l Mgr.)
ACOUSTICS
AERODYNAMICS
ANTENNA
ANTI-MISSILES
ANTI-SATELLITE MISSILES
ANTI-MISSILE SATELLITES
ANTISUBMARINE WARFARE
Arms Control (*See:* Disarmament
  and Arms Control)
ASTRONOMY
Atmosphere (*See:* Space Environ-
  ment)
AUXILIARY POWER SUP-
  PLIES
    FUEL CELL
    NUCLEAR
    SOLAR
BIBLIOGRAPHIES
Bioastronautics (*See:* Life Sciences
  and Human Survival)
BIOGRAPHIES
    MILITARY
      DOD
      NAVY
      ARMY
      MARINE
      AIR FORCE
    CIVILIAN
      COMPETITORS
      CUSTOMERS
      SUPPLIERS
BUSINESS ECONOMY
CALENDAR OF EVENTS
CHEMISTRY
COMMUNICATIONS (General)
COMPETITIVE COMPANIES
    AEROJET
    ALLIS-CHALMERS
    AMF
    ARDE
    ASTRO SYSTEMS

COMPETITIVE COMPANIES
  (Con't.)
    ATLANTIC RESEARCH
      CORP.
    AVCO
    BEECH
    BENDIX
    BOEING
    Chance Vought (*See:* Ling-
      Temco-Vought)
    DOUGLAS AIRCRAFT
    DOUGLAS MISSILES
    DOUGLAS ASTROPOWER
    EMERSON
    GARRET CORP.
    GENERAL DYNAMICS/
      ASTRO
    GENERAL ELECTRIC
    GENERAL MILLS
    GENERAL PRECISION
    GRUMMAN
    HERCULES
    HUGHES
    ITT
    LEAR
    LEAR-SEIGLER
    LEE ELECTRONICS
    LING-TEMCO-VOUGHT
    LITTON D/S
    LITTON G & C
    LOCKHEED-CALIFORNIA
    LOCKHEED-GEORGIA
    MARQUARDT
    MARTIN (DENVER)
    MARTIN (ORLANDO)
    MC DONNELL
    MINNEAPOLIS-HONEY-
      WELL
    NORTH AMERICAN S &
      ID
    NORTH AMERICAN
      ROCKETDYNE

TABLE 2–6 (continued)

COMPETITIVE COMPANIES
(Con't.)
  NORTH AMERICAN LOS
  ANGELES
  NORTHRUP
  RCA
  RAYTHEON
  REPUBLIC AVIATION
  ROCKET RESEARCH
  RYAN
  RAMO-WOOLDRIDGE
  STL
  SYNCRON
  THIOKOL
  UNITED AIRCRAFT
  UNITED TECHNOLOGY
  WESTINGHOUSE
COMPUTER SYSTEMS
CONGRESSIONAL DOCU-
MENT LISTINGS
CONVERSION TABLES
CRYOGENICS
DICTIONARIES AND
  GLOSSARIES
DISARMAMENT AND ARMS
  CONTROL
EDUCATION AND TRAINING
ELECTRONICS
Escape Systems (see: Recovery &
  Escape Systems)
EXPANDABLE STRUCTURES
FACILITIES AND EQUIP-
MENT
  OUR COMPANY
  PMR, AMR (Kennedy)
  NASA
FOREIGN COOPERATION &
AID
  NATO
  SEATO
FOREIGN GOVERNMENTS
  FRANCE
  GERMANY
  ITALY
  JAPAN
  RED CHINA

FOREIGN GOVERNMENTS
(Con't.)
  RUSSIA
  UNITED KINGDOM
GEOPHYSICS (General)
Glossaries (See: Dictionaries and
  Glossaries)
GUIDANCE AND CONTROL
  (General)
HARDWARE
  BEARINGS
  CABLES
  SEALS
  VALVES
HYBRID PROPULSION
INDUSTRIAL INTELLIGENCE
INFORMATION STORAGE,
  DISPLAY AND RETRIEVAL
INFRARED
INSTRUMENTS (General)
Instrumentation (See: PMR,
  AMR-[Kennedy])
INTERNATIONAL ORGANI-
  ZATIONS
  COSPAR
  ELDO and ESRO
  ESLO
  UN
INTERPLANETARY EXPLO-
  RATION (General)
LABOR UNIONS
LASERS AND MASERS
LAW
LIBRARY BOOKS (Listed by
  Dewey Decimal System No.)
LIFE SCIENCES AND HUMAN
  SURVIVAL
LIQUID PROPULSION
Logistics (See: Space Operations
  or Systems Analysis)
LUNAR EXPLORATION (Gen-
  eral)
Magnetohydrodynamics (See: Elec-
  trical Propulsion)
MANAGEMENT SYSTEMS

TABLE 2–6 (continued)

MANPOWER AND POPULA-
TION
MANUFACTURING
MARKETING PROPOSALS
MATERIALS
MOTOR CASES
NATURAL RESOURCES AND
PUBLIC UTILITIES
NONPROFIT ORGANIZA-
TIONS
NOZZLES
NUCLEAR PROPULSION
NUCLEAR TECHNOLOGY
Oceanography (See: Underwater
Technology)
OPTICS
PHYSICS
Population (See: Manpower and
Population)
Procurement (See: Marketing Pro-
posals)
PROFESSIONAL ORGANIZA-
TIONS
RADIATION AND SHIELDING
RECOVERY AND ESCAPE
SYSTEMS
RE-ENTRY (General)
RELIABILITY
SOLID PROPULSION
SPACE ENVIRONMENT
SPACE OPERATIONS (General)
LOGISTICS AND
MAINTENANCE
RESCUE AND SAFETY
RENDEZVOUS AND
DOCKING
SPACE TECHNOLOGY
STRUCTURES
SYSTEMS
AIRCRAFT
GEM
HELICOPTERS
SST
TFX

SYSTEMS (Con't.)
AIRCRAFT (Con't.)
V/STOL
X-15
BALLOONS
ELECTRONIC SUPPORT
COMMAND AND
CONTROL
COMMUNICATIONS
DETECTION
TRACKING
GROUND SUPPORT
EQUIPMENT
MISSILES
ADVANCED ICBMS
ANTI-MISSILE & ANTI-
SATELLITE
ATLAS
BRITISH
BULLPUP
COBRA
CONDOR
DAVY CROCKETT
DERRINGER
FALCON
FRENCH
G.E.M.
GENIE
HAWK
HOUND DOG
LANCE
MAULER
MEDUSA
MINUTEMAN
Missile B (See: Lance)
MISSILE C
MMRBM
MOBILE ICBM
NIKE ZEUS
ORCA
PERSHING
POLARIS
RED-EYE
REDHEAD-ROADRUNNER
RUSSIAN
SERGEANT

TABLE 2–6 (continued)

SYSTEMS (Con't.)	SYSTEMS (Con't.)
MISSILES (Con't.)	SPACE BOOSTERS (Con't.)
SHILLELAGH	RIFT
SHRAM	ROOST
SHRIKE	RUSSIAN
SKYBOLT	SATURN (C-1)
SLAM	SATURN D (NUCLEAR)
SPARROW	SCOUT
SPRINT	SCRAMJET
TFX MISSILE	SEA DRAGON
THOR	THOR & THORAD
TITAN I	TITAN II
TITAN II	TITAN III
TITAN III	SPACE PAYLOADS
TOW	AASWS
UNDERWATER	ADVENT
RE-ENTRY VEHICLES	ADVENT II
CALORIE	AEROS
FIRE	AEROSPACE PLANE
LORV	ALBATROSS
MARK 12 & 13	ALOUETTE
TRAILBLAZER	ANNA
SOUNDING ROCKETS	APOLLO
ARCAS	ARIEL
AEROBEE	ARIES
AEROBEE HI	ASTRO
ARCON	BLUE CIRCUMOONSOON
ARGO E-5	BOSS
ASPAN	COMSAT
ASTROBEE-500	COURIER
SPACE BOOSTERS	DISCOVERER
ABLE STAR	DYNA SOAR
ADVANCED SATURN (C-5)	ECHO
AGENA	EMPIRE
ATLAS	EXPLORER
BLUE SCOUT	GEMINI
BLUE STREAK	HAVEN
CENTAUR	IMP
DELTA	INFLATABLE
DIAMANT	STRUCTURES
DIANA	LEM
FRENCH	LINGER
LITTLE JOE	MARINER
NOVA	MERCURY
PEGASUS	METEOROLOGICAL
PUTT-PUTT	SATELLITES

TABLE 2–6 (continued)

SYSTEMS (Con't.)
SPACE PAYLOADS (Con't.)
MIDAS
NEEDLES
NERV
NIMBUS
OAO
OGO
OSO
PAN
PHAETON
PIONEER
RANGER
REBOUND
RELAY
RITA
RUSSIAN
SAINT I AND II
S-4 B
S-27
S-55
SAMOS
SECOR
SHEPHERD
SPACE STATIONS
NASA
USAF
SURVEYOR
SYNCOM
TELSTAR
TETRAHEDRON
TIROS
TRANSIT
ULLV
VANGUARD
VELA HOTEL
VOYAGER

SYSTEMS ANALYSIS
TESTING
UNDERWATER TECHNOL-
OGY (*see* also: Antisubmarine
Warfare)
U.S. GOVERNMENT
BUDGET
AEC
DOD
NASA
USA
USAF
USN
CONTRACTS
GEOPOLITICAL
OPERATIONS
ORGANIZATIONS
AEC
DOD
FAA
NASA
NATIONAL SPACE
COUNCIL
PLANS AND POLICIES
AFSC
NORAD
NSF
SSD
USAF
USMC
USN
WARFARE
CBR
WEAPONS CAPABILITY
BIOLOGICAL–NUCLEAR
RADIOLOGICAL–CHEMI-
CAL

DATA EVALUATION

The five steps in intelligence development are: identification of data need, collection, storage, evaluation, and presentation. The process of evaluation, sometimes called analysis, should occur after storage, although the assessment of data itself is done before storage. This means that prior to placing information in storage it should be tagged with indicators such as:

1. Source organization and person.
2. Date obtained.
3. Date or period referred to.
4. Estimate of the completeness and probable bias present in the data.
5. Probable value of the source.

When retrieved from the file, bits of data are compared and part of the evaluation will depend upon these tags. If a fact that seems out of place has a tag indicating great reliability (e.g., data derived by discussion with a vice-president of a subject organization) and related bits of data on the same topic indicate a totally different conclusion, one may suspect the other data to be planted.

Other chapters in this text deal more fully with analysis.

PRESENTATION

Finally, our system must present information in a useful way. In some cases, the managers will want to know where you got your information and how you reached your conclusions. In other cases, they will simply want your conclusions.

Presentations must answer management's questions. If asked, "Where will Shoppers, Inc., place their next store?" we cannot come back with an answer like: "Shoppers, Inc., business is up 34%. They will hire two new assistant managers this year, they intend to try Hought meats starting in January and their next store is planned for May." It is amazing how often market research and business intelligence groups do just this; it is usually a sign that the group could not get the answer but wanted to prove itself adequate, anyway.

Presentations are formal (briefings, reports, bulletins) and informal (discussions, visits, notes). They may be regular, as in briefings, or irregular, as in replies to inquiries. No matter what the format or period, these rules are useful:

1. Answer the question if possible.
2. If you can't answer the question, say so.
3. Use visual aids only if they help put across complex ideas.
4. Make sure all materials can be read.
5. Permit, even encourage, feedback.
6. Label facts and opinions.
7. Be brief and unbiased.
8. Assure that the level of presentation and data is appropriate to the level of the recipients of the presentation.

Careful planning must be given the content and format of the presentation so that all the work discussed earlier in the collection, selection, storage, and evaluation of intelligence information does not go to waste.

Chapter Three

MILITARY AND CORPORATE INTELLIGENCE

CHARLES F. CARROLL*

INTRODUCTION

GATHERING DATA about one's environment is one of the oldest occupations. Examples of shrewd business intelligence work come to us in the Bible, in literature and in song from very ancient times. Marco Polo, Christopher Columbus, Lief Erikson, all were studying the environment for commercial reasons. Joseph's interpretation of the Pharaoh's dream and Daniel Boone disguised as an Indian to scout ahead, can both be seen as being related to this field.

Old as it is, intelligence is nevertheless on top of modern techniques too, for example, our satellites snoop for radiation and atomic bursts; our most modern electronics techniques use infrared sensors and snooperscopes to "see" in the dark; the CIA and military intelligence organizations have wonderously large computer systems. Each day over the teletype systems come many industrial intelligence newsletters, such as *Spacewire* and many others. Microminiaturization can produce an olive-sized transmitter. Armies of compara-

---

*Mr. Carroll served many years in top echelons of our government's intelligence community, and also has extensive corporate experience in design engineering management, design engineering, and system/operation analysis. He is an intelligence specialist and also is a Lieutenant Colonel in the U.S. Air Force Reserve.

tive shoppers mix with crowds in major shopping centers and at any given moment someone is carrying out a market study of consumer preferences in some city of our great nation.

What are they all doing? What is intelligence? It is the combination of several things, providing in the end an information service to a manager or a commander. It helps him anticipate situations that will require his decisions or action. Broadly, it comprises the functions of collecting raw data; processing it to provide a refined and ordered "concentrate" of raw data; interpreting, estimating, predicting, and disseminating the finished intelligence produced from this raw data; and then feeding guidance back to the collection system where further data is acquired. Presentation of data is the output of the loop. Success is measured by the timeliness and accuracy of the manager's or commander's anticipation of events and the effectiveness of his decisions.

THE INTELLIGENCE CYCLE

While the flow of events in the real world is fairly even and continuous, the collection of information about these events and the processing thereof is usually discontinuous or "batched." The groupings may be by time unit (daily briefing, weekly review, monthly summaries, and so on), and by topic (military, political, international, etc.), or by any other grouping that suits an organization.

The cycle starts with raw information collection, usually in response to a previously stated need. After processing, the analysts produce finished intelligence. In the development of a picture, certain gaps appear which identify requirements for new and more raw intelligence data and the cycle proceeds to collect it.

In addition to the major cycle above, there are usually many minor cycles, directives from commanders to assistants, from intelligence libraries to requestors, but these do not reduce the major cycle. Rather, they smooth it.

DATA COLLECTION

Raw data is collected in the field by any useful method. These methods range from the clipping, copying, and recording of data from available, published material to a wide variety of covert operations and the exploitation of opportunities and mistakes as they occur. Similarly, vast quantities of data are presented by readouts from advanced electronic and satellite reconnaissance systems. To be successful, data collection should be carefully planned. For example, priorities, suggested sources, methods and related data must be given to the field personnel when they are asked to provide data to the central office for evaluation.

This evaluation, in some schemes, is one of the more irritating system weaknesses of intelligence work. In some systems, sources are evaluated A to E and information itself is rated 1 to 6. In both of these cases the "I don't know" response is E and 6, respectively. Exceedingly good data and sources whose quality is not known beforehand would thus be rated as worse than false data and double-agent sources, only because the evaluator does not know with assurance where items belong. The "don't know" response should be in the center of these scales.

COUNTERINTELLIGENCE

In a major system, arrangements for the security of collection personnel, facilities and communications are so sensitive and vital that a separate staff often is assigned these tasks, called counterintelligence. In some cases, for example, after collection planners identify what is the best method to collect some particular data, they will purposely avoid this approach, under the assumption that the "enemy" has also figured this out and will be anticipating that approach and will be waiting like a cat at a mouse hole.

COLLECTION ORGANIZATION

Among the commoner ways to divide the tasks of collection personnel, their files and logic, is to deal with categories of raw information. Table 3–1 lists one such breakdown. It shows one national intelligence breakdown and possible corporate counterparts.

TABLE 3–1

CATEGORIES OF NATIONAL AND BUSINESS INTELLIGENCE

Basic Information:

Military	Corporate Equivalent
Geography	Market areas and their characteristics
Weather/climate	Weather/climate
Transportation	Shipping routes and storage
Telecommunications	Telecommunications
Sociology	Customer characteristics and preferences
Key personnel/biographical data	Competitors' management and key staff members' biographies
Military and civil leaders	
Economy/industry structure	Dun & Bradstreet type reports, location and relationship of plants and facilities
Politics/government structure	Corporate organization, informal power system, subsidiaries
Science and engineering	R & D and patent status, new products under development
Military	Sales force, strategies

Capabilities and Vulnerabilities:

Heavy and light industry	Own and subcontractor facilities, plus same data on competitors
Manpower and critical materials	Own and competitors' production capabilities
National objectives.	Company and competitor long- and short-range plans

Collection operations for information in these categories are like the input sensing devices of a complex electronic gear. Input sensing or transducing portions of servocontrol loops of many industrial processes resemble this collection step. Sources have to be competent and well placed and their communication links have to be high-rate, high-volume, and highly secure. For each success in penetrating an opponent's security screen and in developing invulnerability to his counterintelligence operations, an additional communication problem usually is acquired. Time lags and message garbles increase with the depth of penetration. For example, limitations in access or in freedom of movement will cause good information to have serious gaps and delays. These effects are analogous to dead time, delay, and noise in servo-loops.

FEEDBACK TO COLLECTION

If the corporation or nation has not yet experienced serious surprise in the tactical sense (i.e., it is not too late for effective action), the most effective response to fragmentary information is to identify the gaps and initiate high-priority collection operations for filling them, while processing and analyzing proceed on what is already in the data base. However, this urgent feedback to collection can have an adverse effect, due to the dynamic nature of the data base. Consider the overall data base as comprising these three major subdivisions:

a) Historic or past events, recorded but varying with each participant's interpretation and perception of history.
b) Real current events, being generated whether perceived by participants or not; i.e., the real world in real time.
c) Sensed current events, varying widely among participants due to their differing collecting and processing abilities and colored by their biases, prior convictions and relative values that affect their production of finished intelligence . . . the input that integrates into recorded history (a).

The sensed data base (c) will always lag behind and miss some of the real data base (b), and efforts to correct for such delays and gaps will cause results to oscillate about what could be nearly perfect intelligence, in much the same manner as a servomechanism with a dead space at zero error oscillates or "hunts" about its accurate position. Efforts to compensate for delays, errors, or omissions in collection, processing, or production will cause an overshoot. Estimates of the situation, typical items of (*a*), will miss a balanced presentation of all significant real events. Then, when the distortion becomes so gross as to be evident, corrective adjustment or damping is initiated, but can well cause an overshot in the opposite direction.

Both corporate and military staffs attempt to minimize such overemphasis and underemphasis for particular areas of intelligence. Their input to collection operations should be a controlled, well-modulated guidance, where self-control is as vital as external control down the chain of command. Management, by exception, often produces minimal interference with on-going functions. In this sense, over-centralized management or command risks aggravation rather than damping of this oscillation and can lead to instability or to rigidity of the system.

In this area management must remain on guard against the "self-fulfilling prophecy" type of activities, caused by feedback loop action rather than planning controlling system performance. For example, a company gets a "flash" on a hot, threatening situation. Management orders "get us more data." Communication lines get swamped with data requests to the field and with field replies and inquiries. Inputs on other important topics are decreased because the transmission facilities are becoming saturated. Management, not seeing data on other items coming in, assumes that much action is taking place in the real world on the "hot" item, and orders more and more data, thus possibly sealing off completely any other inputs. Another similar hazard is in planning where, at first, only fragmentary data is available. Plans are centered on that data, because that is all you have. The presence of plans then makes you call for more data to support what is being planned. This rapidly develops into the classical vicious circle that tends to block consideration of other input data or response to other needs for planning and action.

PROCESSING RAW INFORMATION

The initial processing of raw information is closely associated with collection operations. Reports must be sanitized or desensitized to protect sources and communications. False or inaccurate data, if known, must be removed and the useful "concentrate" must be collated into subject categories or classes that facilitate its storage, retrieval, and analytical study. After such processing the data is still no more than raw information. This point in the intelligence function would be illustrated by an exaggerated yet fitting analogy:

A capable information processor puts his output folder on the chief's desk and says, "I don't know what this data means concerning Soviet nuclear weapons, but all available information on that subject is here, correctly classified and cross-indexed."

The raw data is impersonal, cold and without meaning. Significant interpretations and conclusions are no more than latent within the data and do not stand out. Considerable effort is required to produce a finished product.

It should be noted that often the removed material is not thrown away without specialized scanning, because experience has shown that completely new, wholly unexpected developments usually are first encountered in the "obviously useless material that should be discarded." A few of the more imaginative and speculative analysts should study such data. The occasional discovery of a vital item more than repays the effort.

Flow of data into storage for later utilization ranges from development of a library (static data, dynamic questions) to sampling or monitoring of the incoming flow to check for answers to certain predetermined questions such as the indicators of imminent hostilities (dynamic data, static questions). Library services dominate when time and adequate information both are there, but when raw data is sparse or available commander time is short, scanning incoming raw data is often resorted to. The analogy of the stock market investor trying to make a quick killing and searching the tape comes to mind; the large corporate investor with more time and less pressure will look at books and charts about the potential stock.

The need in more pressing areas, national defense among them, for selective scanning of data flow will probably lead to automated situation recognition programs in which raw data is processed and subprograms such as pattern recognition, profile matching, ergodic frequency or distribution, and multiterm association will produce finished intelligence from the dynamic flow.

PRODUCTION OF FINISHED INTELLIGENCE

When first collected, raw intelligence data is as useful to managers and commanders as crude oil fresh from the well is to the ultimate consumers of petroleum products. Raw information must be processed and distributed before being useful. Finished intelligence is produced on three levels: interpretation that sifts and sorts raw data to reveal significant relationships and patterns already evident in that data; estimates of future situations; and predictions which usually lead to identifying the other data which, if collected at some future time, would confirm the prediction as the true course of events.

DISSEMINATION

Identifying who should get what data, when and how, are major problems the intelligence director has in an organization. There are situations requiring briefings, newsletters, personal telephone calls—all sorts of methods of input to management, only partially resting upon the importance of the item. The commanders' wishes determine, too, how he gets his data.

The level of detail is another presentation variable which has been hard to crack. If you present too much, you bore people and they ask for higher level material. If too little, then they walk out satisfied that they understand, when they do not, or they ask for more detail.

On the commander-manager's side, there are the human problems of accepting and examining bad news, no matter how reliable or well presented. In past empires, messengers bearing bad news were frequently tortured and killed by an upset emperor or consul. Today the consequences are just as fatal to political, corporate, or military careers; they just take longer and are less bloody. In a corporation, the resistance is sometimes called "not pulling with the team," and on the military side, the staff member with bad news raises the "commander credence" problem. Very important intelligence is rarely other than bad news. A national or theater commander or a top manager in a company may all undergo agonizing reappraisals. New courses of action must be planned and it is natural to resist all this, but those who wait until the situation is unambiguously certain usually wake up dead.

Automation might help; the data is less personal. It seems to be unbiased and may make credence easier but it is still easy to say "the program goofed."

ROADBLOCKS TO GOOD INTELLIGENCE

Certain errors or roadblocks to good intelligence arise in studying a large number of intelligence systems. These are:

1. Not recognizing that the side effects or after effects of a recommended action can create problems worse than the original problem.

2. Excessively generalized studies usually cover everything but handle nothing.
3. Lots of good, expensive, well-collected data on the wrong topic.
4. Problem well defined, and therefore considered solved.
5. Cook-book development, "putting roller skates under buggy wheels."
6. Failure to see a real advance as helpful, often because it "isn't the way we did it before."
7. Overly optimistic development of plans, i.e., planning a system on monies or breakthroughs which may not occur.
8. Definition of the problem never achieves closure on specific boundaries for a problem to be handled.
9. Ideas and descriptive concepts, but no reduction to practice.
10. Theoretical work, vigorous pure research, discovering unexpected breakthroughs with no foreseeable applications and then searching for some problem to fit the new solution, rather than attacking problems requiring solving.
11. Use of undertrained or mistrained intelligence personnel, for example, using military intelligence retired officers for commercial business intelligence systems.
12. Falling for "knowledge is power" line and attempting to be managers rather than serve managers in decision making.

When properly designed and monitored, when adequately supported and understood, the intelligence function in business or in the military can provide a rational basis for decisions. Without support and understanding, it can do harm by inputting erroneous data. Successful units and organizations usually have successful intelligence groups.

Chapter Four

PLANNING AND ADMINISTRATION OF THE BUSINESS INTELLIGENCE GROUP

J. L. FREDRICK*

INTRODUCTION

THE PRACTICAL business intelligence (BI) group administrator directs an organized ethical operation that is usually not too well understood and, often, offers few rewards.

Management doesn't care about intelligence sources, nominal costs of collection, or clever filing techniques; they want answers to questions, and they want the answers promptly.

This kind of pressure calls for a smoothly functioning group. This chapter describes how to form such a group, plan its activities, staff it, and mesh it with the rest of the organization.

PLANNING

Whether starting a new group, or relating to the annual operation of an established group, planning must occur. Two

---

*J. L. Fredrick holds several degrees in Aeronautical Engineering. He was, for a long time, the branch manager of Market Intelligence in the Missiles and Space Systems Division of the Douglas Aircraft Company, Inc. He is now in Advance Systems Planning. Mr. Fredrick has been active in professional societies in the Los Angeles area, including the American Marketing Association and the American Institute of Aeronautics and Astronautics.

types of planning are required: organizational, in which we plan for the BI group itself; and operational, in which we plan for the group's operations. I have surveyed many different techniques, but I have yet to find one better than a properly organized PERT/Cost System. This type of system functions well in both organizational and operational planning.

Although several sources of PERT planning techniques are available, I recommend B. J. Hanson's *Practical PERT* (Washington, D.C.: America House, Division of American Aviation Publications, 1965).

The plan should state who will do what, and when and how it should be done. An appendix can show why, and also can give details on goals and on decision logic imbedded in the plan. Cost data can also be appended to the plan. A single plan stretching to an indefinite future will probably be more effective than separate short and long-range plans. The plan should provide answers to the following questions:

1. What type of business intelligence group is required, and should it function under a predictive or a reactive concept? (See Chapter I by R. M. Greene for further discussion on this dichotomy.)

2. Who should lead it, what should his background be? Should this be a permanent or temporary assignment?

3. How many personnel of what type should be assigned? Should they be recruited from inside or outside of the organization?

4. What kinds of security clearances will be required? What physical security arrangements are needed?

5. What will be the group's functions? What equipment is required? How can their output be measured? To whom should the group report, and how often? What should be the general contents of each report?

6. Where should the group be attached to the organization? What are its interactions with marketing, library services, and other groups in the company?

7. What must be done to prepare the company for this new group?

8. What meetings should group members attend? What forms will be available or needed to start work? What counter-intelligence is necessary?

Preliminary thinking must be done concerning the degree of centralization of BI, and the extent of the initial efforts. Centralized, by way of definition, implies only one BI activity in the company, with all units feeding and being supplied by that group; decentralized implies possible BI groups within marketing, engineering, or proposal staffs in the various plants or geographic divisions. In my own experience, I have found strongly centralized BI groups most effective. Table 4–1 indicates a few factors that are typical of centralized and decentralized groups.

Experience has shown that within the overall plan, a set of subplans or alternate plans are useful. In one sense, these are like failure plans, they specify what services will be rendered by the BI group under different budget approval levels. It is frequently helpful to management, themselves under budget squeeze, for the BI director to be able to say, for example, "If we get $10,000 we can do A, B, and F, if we get $50,000 we can add services C and D, and if we get $100,000 we can sponsor program E and provide bulletin G, etc."

ORGANIZATIONAL LEVEL

It is a natural tendency for everyone to want to report directly to the boss. Most staff members think their functions deserve attachment to the president's office. BI is no exception; however, experience has shown that a highly ranked BI group produces gainful output, while a group that is seated low on the organizational chart is disregarded and dwindles. If the BI group is located fairly low on the chart, perhaps reporting to the market research director, the usual problem is communications upstream through the organization. This can be overcome in some cases by creating a BI advisory board or steering committee comprised of some members of top management.

TABLE 4-1

Alternate Methods of Structuring a Business Intelligence Group

Structure	Characteristics	Problems	Benefits
Tightly centralized	Chief of group is "Mr. B.I." for the company, all report directly to him. Group has reproduction, library, file, and other services within it. Group determines projects, has own budget, own field agents.	Tendency to lose contact with company needs. Hard to assess, close knit, defensive. Must get work by asking departments. Agents sometimes don't know enough about department activities.	Easy to assign BI responsibility. High efficiency and morale if well run. Hard to penetrate with counterintelligence. Speedy response.
Functional centralization	Chief of BI is really only a co-ordinator. Staff provides reproduction, library, and file functions but field agents report elsewhere. No daily control over agents unless they are assigned by a department head. Cannot select agents. Small BI central budget. Each department has a BI budget line item.	Usually departments don't see eye-to-eye on projects, no way to schedule agents as their time belongs to another group. In money shortage, BI suffers since its budget is overhead on various departments, and they do not see it in the mainstream of their work. Agent turnover causes training problem.	Spreads out responsibility, sometimes interest, too, because of wider involvements. Spreads costs of BI operations, keeps activities in the open and slows "empire building."
Totally decentralized	Each department in the firm has its own BI group, has own files, uses central reproduction. Each department puts BI in its overhead. No centralized BI head. Projects totally decided by department chiefs.	Duplication of studies, files, books, etc. Most files inadequate because no one department can afford to generate a good one. Difficult to assess BI quality. Easy to penetrate with counterintelligence. Lack of close cross-checking of data leads to acceptance of bad data.	Department's questions may be answered faster, no fight for priority. BI cost is spread. No expensive central file or reproduction build-up. BI specialists in department can become real experts on department topics.

Reports from the BI group are of two types—the intelligence reports themselves and administrative reports of the group. It is usually a good idea for both reports to be reviewed by the person to whom the director of business intelligence reports. This is because there is a close relationship between administrative expense and activity and BI output. In several cases, important data have been lost to a company because a trip exceeded a travel budget, or a request to reproduce a document was turned down by a decision maker who was a comptroller rather than someone in the direct chain who could assess the value to the company of the proposed actions.

BI PERSONNEL MANAGEMENT

BI personnel are subject to several unique hazards. Often those who volunteer or are assigned to this field are well educated, intelligent, and willing workers, but quickly fall prey to morale problems which can plague even the best BI groups. Their own colleagues in the firm may speak of them as "snoops." They are sometimes regarded by management as a necessary skeleton in the company's closet. Employees of other firms may avoid them and brand them as "business spies," when in reality they are market researchers or statisticians.

To counter such negative attitudes, should they occur, one step is to give the group a more acceptable name, such as "business information" or "information research," rather than "business intelligence." Another method is planned development of the company employee esteem by creating an attitude of professionalism in the BI work. Holding open houses with guided visits to the BI group area, including planned discussions of each person's work and the use of the equipment, are other ways of improving image. Occasional attention from supervision is, of course, useful in maintaining morale but, for the BI group members, feedback on how their work helped the company is vital, not only to improve morale, but also because of the need for better business intelligence. Guidance on what has been helpful and what has not is useful.

We sometimes see people in BI groups who feel that they have reached a "dead end" professionally. They meaningfully point out that their specialty is relatively unknown since it is only employed in certain firms, that they are not protected or enhanced by being a professional group (or by having a professional organization to speak for them), and that there are relatively few openings in this field that can provide opportunities for advancement.

The first step to overcome this problem is to create grades or steps within the group, preferably before the group even starts, so that good work can be rewarded by increases in title and pay. A two-level group (director and analyst) does, in reality, have built-in problems. But when analyst positions can be broken down into several grades, and growth through these depends upon education, experience, and recommendations by supervision, then we have a way to motivate the worker.

Also, it is useful to see the BI group member as growing into other areas such as market research and planning, field sales, advertising, public or personnel relations.

Elsewhere in this book, there are comments on the field of business intelligence growing toward a profession. Later in this chapter, training is discussed in more detail.

POSITION ANALYSIS AND DESCRIPTION

As in any other organization, to avoid unnecessary internal overlap and conflict, the BI group should have stated job descriptions. An example of such a set has been appended to this chapter.

The position descriptions should describe actual tasks, salary levels and ranges, possible sources of candidates for the positions and any special requirements in experience, physical properties, and education. These types of inputs promote good employee reviews, but they cannot be cast in concrete for, with the passage of time, certain changes will become necessary. Because of the nature of BI work, system training concepts (concepts based upon treating the group as a system of people rather than a gathering of individuals) will be useful. Position descriptions, then, are a starting point for productive work. Good supervision, emphasis on getting the job done at minimum cost, with adequate rewards and feedback structuring, will carry the group from there.

TRAINING BI PERSONNEL

Experience has proved that cross-training is useful so, within the bounds of intellectual or educational capability, I usually recommend that all BI personnel have certain areas of common training. These areas are as follows:

Quantitative. The ability to make meaningful statements about many facts providing basic statistical treatment to express central tendencies, dispersion, and reasonable future expectancies, e.g., behavioral probabilities.

Technical. The ability to manipulate mentally with full cognizance the basic technical vocabulary (jargon) of the work in which the company is engaged.

Collection. The ability to collect data with skill and without danger of compromise.

Reporting. The ability to prepare vocal and written reports that make sense, are as brief as possible, and are unbiased.

Management. The knowledge of organization, planning, and business-in-general to provide smooth guidance in his internal company contacts and external researches, both in terms of planning what to do on a collection program, and knowledge as to where and how to contact sources.

To achieve these goals, a program that could be structured into a curriculum for business intelligence at a local university is given in Table 4–2.

In planning this program, it is assumed that the business

TABLE 4–2

REQUIREMENTS FOR A CERTIFICATE IN BUSINESS INTELLIGENCE—
COURSE CURRICULUM

Year 1:	Year 3:
Written English	PERT/Time and
Basic data processing	PERT/Cost Systems
Public speaking	Public relations
Systems and procedures	Basic statistics
	Sensitivity training
Year 2:	Counselling interviews
Marketing	
Psychology (basic and indus-	Year 4:
trial)	Operations Research
Corporate planning	Statistics II
Economics	Business forecasting
Library science	Market intelligence
	Business law

intelligence specialist already holds a basic degree, such as
Business Administration, Engineering, or the Humanities.

SIZE AND BUDGET FOR A BI GROUP

No set rules can relate the size of a business, or its nature
or its products, to a specific size BI group. We can only work
from known data, and Table 4–3 compiles staff size data,
salary costs, probable overhead, and space requirements as
well as what one might expect to spend on source data such
as printed material, booklets, etc. The table should be used
as an idea generator rather than specified requirements.

BI GROUP OPERATIONS

An early step in planning a BI group is to determine the
needs of management. These needs fall into two general
classes, those that existed before the BI group was planned
(which stimulated management to have such an organization
formed), and those that arise when it becomes known that
there is such a group. We do not ask management what it
wants, we ask management what it needs. Those who have

TABLE 4-3

Staffing Recommendations for Various Size Corporations in Business Intelligence

Company Size in Personnel	BI Staff Title	No. Required	Costs (1) Salaries	(2) Overhead	(3) Data Sources†	Total	Space in Sq. Ft.‡
0-50	Manager of BI (part time)	1	$ 3,300*	—	$ 300	$ 3,600	—
51-100	Manager of BI	1	$ 7,000	$ 5,000	$ 700	$ 12,700	100
101-500	Manager of BI	1	$ 8,000	$ 6,000	$ 1,200	$ 24,200	175
	File clerk	1	5,000	4,000	—		
501-1,000	Manager of BI	1	$10,000	$ 7,000	$ 2,000	$ 36,000	250
	File clerks	2	10,000	7,000	—		
1,001-5,000	Manager of BI	1	$11,000	$ 8,000	$ 2,400	$ 52,400	350
	BI analyst	1	7,500	5,100			
	File clerks	2	11,000	8,000			
5,001-10,000	Manager of BI	1	$12,000	$ 9,000	$ 4,000	$ 90,500	600
	BI analysts	2	16,000	11,000			
	File clerks	3	18,000	12,000			
	Secretary	1	6,000	4,500			
10,001-25,000	Manager of BI	1	$14,000	$10,000	$ 6,000		1,200
	BI analysts	2	17,000	11,500			
	File clerks	3	18,000	12,000			
	Editor	1	8,500	5,000			
	Reproduction clerk	1	6,000	4,000			
	Secretary-steno	1	7,000	5,000		$124,000	

*This salary is estimated on the basis of one-third time of a $10,000 executive.

†This represents subscriptions in excess of those the company library may be allotted, and does not include library books, or items available in the public library. If the firm cannot easily assemble existing subscriptions, or cannot use a large nearby library and has no major library of its own, this figure should be doubled.

‡See Greene, Richard M., *Space Analysis for Management*, SP 76 (Santa Monica, Calif.: System Development Corporation, 1959).

had the experience of asking management what it wants have usually wound up with a "laundry list" of just about everything, not all of it useful. To determine needs, BI group representatives may attend management meetings, management personnel may be interviewed, previous BI personnel may be quizzed as to what they did, surveys of personnel may be made with questions like: Where do you now get data on . . . ?" or "What trade publications do you now get and why?" etc.

Another early step in setting up a BI group is to start a cross-reference file of terms, so that questions on "SAGE" can be related to data on the "AN/FSQ-7 Computer," and data on "General Funk" can be related to the "SSD-USAF," and so on.

Other early files often will include a biography file, a file of clippings and data about key products, and a file or listing of organic and inorganic sources of data in general.

Developing inorganic data sources such as journals, papers, letters, organizational charts, etc. is usually the second major step. In this operation, it is wise to check duplication with other employees in the company; in some cases the same magazines may be distributed to a dozen or more different people in the same division of the company. Clipping services should also be investigated. In this respect great care should be used in defining the areas of interest carefully, and in closely monitoring the input until several months have established that the service is productive.

The files should be purged periodically to eliminate duplication, remove "dead" items, and help keep costs of maintaining files and space down. Rather than having this assigned to lowest level personnel, with the assumption that it is a housekeeping task, one should consider assuring that a top-level person participates in purging because, if not done properly, much previous work may be wasted, needed information may not be retrievable, and valuable data may be lost. On the other hand, when done too superficially, data will be retained that should have been removed, thus cluttering the files, costing extra search time and creating unnecessary space and file maintenance costs.

ORGANIC SOURCES

People provide by far the best sources for business intelligence. By the time something is committed to paper, it already may be obsolete. Only people can be relied upon to produce up-to-date source material. But handling people has its problems. For example, for a person in one company to pass along data to someone in another company for personal gain, with knowledge that what is being done is revealing business intelligence, a strong motivator must be available to overcome the natural fear of discovery and possible punishment.

Most of the BI gathered today in the nation is not of this nature. It is chance remarks, planned conversations, and implications drawn from comments. It is probably quite rare that anyone has to resort to "buying out" another person.

Among the motives that have been used in the field of intelligence are; money, fear of revelation of some abnormal or improper behavior, loyalty based upon past work with another company, dissatisfaction with the present company, a desire to get revenge for some imagined or real wrong, and a desire to be considered for a high-level job in a different firm.

It is beyond the scope of this chapter to discuss in detail the various motivating techniques and psychological approaches that develop good organic sources. It might be mentioned, however, that many organic sources provide excellent research and planning material, either because they are trying to sell the company's products, as they have a public relations function, or because they are part of a counterintelligence unit. Many times a company places no restrictions on what may be discussed with outsiders, often because they do not feel threatened competitively, or because the

employee is trusted and it is left to his "good judgment" as
to how much of the company's operations can be revealed.
In general, it can be stated that rewards and motivations to
organic sources rarely take the form of outright gifts. A flow
diagram showing how data is procured and purged is given
in Fig. 4–1.

FIGURE 4–1
Intelligence Information Cycle

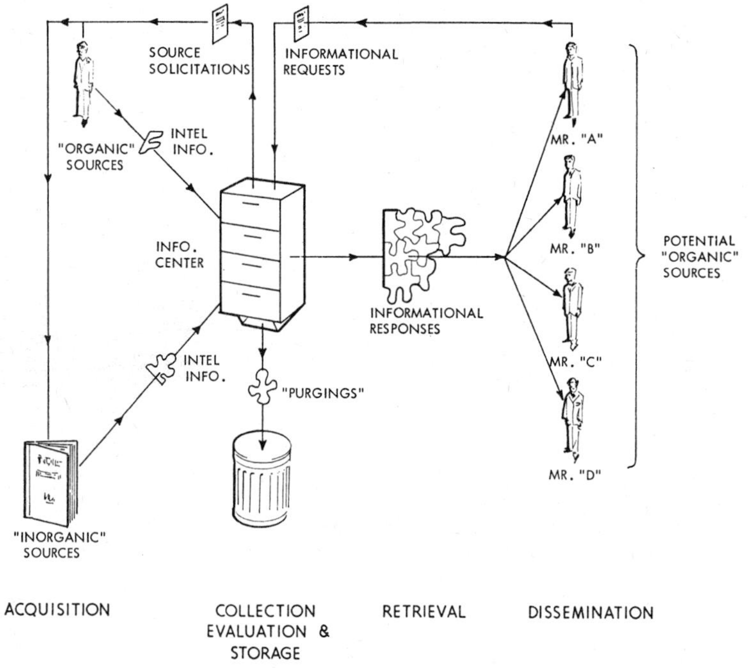

| ACQUISITION | COLLECTION EVALUATION & STORAGE | RETRIEVAL | DISSEMINATION |

THE BI GROUP MANAGER

In addition to hiring, training, supervising, discharging,
and the other normal personnel functions of a manager, the
BI group manager must relate his organization to other
groups and departments within the company, try to feel the
pulse of management with regard to its intelligence needs,

watch for counterintelligence from competitors, and assign priorities on searches and tasks. This last requirement is often complicated by office politics, which may play even a bigger role than logic.

Presuming high morale, each requester of data thinks his work is the most vital of all, and that he should receive his answers first. The earlier the manager can evolve a rationale, such as a decision-assistance matrix, to help him determine proper choices among simultaneous requests for service, the easier his job will be.

One of the methods he can use in helping him to assess the usefulness and the image of his group is to check if all BI requests are being directed to the group. If BI-type requests are being directed to other departments or individuals, he should know that something is wrong with intercommunication, or with his organization itself.

Another key achievement that marks the successful business intelligence leader is the amount of cooperation he commands from others. In some cases others in the organization will assist in periodic data purges. In many cases field engineers, sales and other field personnel will volunteer to act as a BI data source. He can also spread his effectiveness by training, such as by having the internal training department arrange BI lectures for all new personnel, and as a part of the executive development program.

When a member of the group receives an assignment, good leadership will assure that the assignment is carefully planned and that instructions are fully detailed. The procedures recommended are similar to those of the Dynamic Management Systems. They are:

a) List requests and tasks, both externally and internally generated.

b) Place competing requests in a decision matrix that assists in the evaluation of all pertinent factors.

c) For those that pass with highest scores, prepare detailed plans of execution.

d) List activities called for by the plans.

e) List all critical items and items that require assistance from next higher level supervision.

f) Meet periodically to review plans and status.

A task of leadership, sometimes overlooked, is to know when to call a halt to work. As costs of a specific intelligence project mount, with negative results, the supervisor may well have to establish a cutoff point. The skill of knowing when not to throw good money after bad is a valuable asset in any manager. An 80 percent completed study can be worthless without a specific piece of critical data, the cost of which might be unreasonable compared to benefits. Skill is also required in knowing when to reject a proposed project because the data provided by the requester is too vague. When, because of a requester's position, political problems become involved, a great deal of interpersonal skill is needed not to discourage the requester, but to firmly train him to make adequate requests.

Supervising an active BI group is a challenging task that calls for high management skills and solid knowledge of the jobs to be done.

SELECTED POSITION DESCRIPTIONS FOR A TYPICAL
BUSINESS INTELLIGENCE GROUP

Position Description—Sample 1

MANAGER/DIRECTOR OF BUSINESS INTELLIGENCE

Alternate Titles:

Coordinator (manager), business information
Coordinator (manager), business intelligence
Manager of marketing information (intelligence)
Director, business information research

Duties:

To direct a staff performing tasks of collection, review, storage, analysis, and reporting information about the business and related environment, ranging from detailed technical/engineering type data to broad information and statistical data of an economic or sociopolitical nature.

Reports to vice-president of marketing.

His group may provide briefings, newsletters, bulletins, statistical studies, and reports (including personnel reports) to top management of the company.

Background:

Education. A degree in Engineering, Operations Research, Physics or general science preferred.

An advanced degree in Business Administration and/or the Social Sciences will be helpful.

Education should include Statistics, Business Organization and Forecasting, and Data Processing. (Military intelligence education may be helpful if firm engages in defense contracts.)

Employment. A number of years of successful management of a marketing research staff, or business information library, will be required.

Must have planning, supervision, and research experience and have demonstrated ability to get along with others in a complex and demanding environment.

Personal:

Should be a logical thinker and a hard worker, possessing high verbal abilities.

Position Description—Sample 2

BUSINESS INTELLIGENCE ANALYST

Alternate Titles:

Intelligence specialist
Business information specialist
Business librarian
Market research associate
Market analyst

Duties:

To review and examine data from multiple sources, collect and collate facts and information, and prepare written and oral reports on complex situations.

To prepare statements predicting the outcome of events and trends, and to identify additional data required to complete a picture of a situation.

To provide statistical and nonstatistical analyses to management, to give briefings, and write reports and studies.

Background:

Education.   A broad education with at least two degrees, preferably in different fields, including such scientific topics as engineering, and physics, as well as basic courses in statistics.

Economics and business administration training are essential with some emphasis on market forecasting and sales analysis.

Employment. Employment in several firms in different areas of work, including, at least, marketing and/or market research or forecasting.

Experience in planning, data processing, and field sales will be helpful.

Personal:

A logical thinker, patient, tenacious, with the ability to digest a large amount of data and rapidly find common roots or topics.

An ability to communicate well both orally and in writing.

Position Description—Sample 3

BUSINESS INTELLIGENCE FILE SPECIALIST

Alternate Titles:

Data storage and retrieval specialist
Information librarian
Business information system clerk
Market research librarian

Duties:

To develop and maintain the files of the business intelligence group, including books, periodicals, punched card storage, microfilming, computer tape storage, document filing and storage, etc.

To establish the logic of retrieval, prepare cross-references, plan storage techniques and requirements with technical specialists inside and outside of the firm.

To periodically purge the files, developing logical rules therefor, and to supervise file clerks.

Background:

Education. A degree in Library Science and a technical degree would be preferred.

Education in systems and procedures, business organization, marketing, office practice, and data processing will be helpful.

Experience. Several years experience as a team leader or supervisor in a library or filing organization.

Experience in file search, storage and retrieval problems with computers, and in systems design are also preferred.

Personal:

Willing and able to carry out detailed file searches, provide motivating supervision to file clerks, and motivated to pursue personal education in areas of computer processes and storage techniques are important characteristics.

Chapter Five

DEVELOPMENT OF INTELLIGENCE FROM FIELD OFFICE PERSONNEL

E. M. EMERY*

INTRODUCTION

ALL MANAGERS could make 100 percent correct decisions if they had *all* the data surrounding the problem. Getting data from one's own plant is often difficult and when answers must be obtained from customer's or competitor's organization, the process becomes extremely complicated. In fact, the acquisition of vital data from a competitor's office is often thought to be so difficult that it is not seriously considered as a valid source of business information. Yet information exists in a competitor's firm which, for example, might cause management to make a diametrically opposite decision regarding the development of a new product. While this chapter does not advocate industrial spying (principally, because it is not necessary), the example does serve to illustrate that large amounts of vital data influencing the success of management's decisions do rest with sources that are not under

*E. M. Emery is director of Emery Associates, Management Systems consultant and general manager of Delta Design Incorporated. He has been West Coast marketing manager for a division of The Whittaker Corporation and president and general manager of several firms. He consults to large aerospace corporations on marketing.

91

the direct authority of the management group. Hence there is the need for a formalized business information gathering process.

This chapter deals with the problems involved in acquiring business information through the use of field office personnel. A recommended program for the achievement of an effective business information gathering system is also presented.

BUSINESS INFORMATION

What is business information? It is the "what," "where," "who," "why," "how much," "how true," "who says," "when," and even the attitude of the man gathering the answers to these short sharp probes which express the critical need of management trying to get part of the vital data it needs to make intelligent decisions. Analytically, the business intelligence problem can be examined by dissecting it into six components.

The first is the definition of the business information re-quirement. It is the very foundation of successful business intelligence function and, correspondingly, mishandling dooms any business information process to failure.

Suppose that the man in the field is not aware of management's need of specific data and he receives this request: "Please forward all information relative to WS—117M, sub task of WS—117L, include analysis of companies which might compete with our capabilities. Reply TWX ASAP, Signed 'MBK.' "

If the field man can decipher the request and does discover that the home office is asking about the "Samos" program, then he will try to reply as soon as possible; he may still think the requesting party's initials "MBK" really stands for "must be kidding" when he discovers that there are at least 26 major firms already involved in the program and who knows how many subcontractors with capabilities which compete with those of his own company. The response to this request will undoubtedly be: more questions from the field man for clarification; procrastination, hoping the request was not really a requirement; or total frustration at the insurmountable task requested of him. None of these reactions will supply the information management was hoping would follow upon its request.

While it may appear that the above example is an extreme case, be assured that it is a typical request as determined by a recent survey of business information requests conducted in several aerospace firms. Other typical examples of questions were:

1. How much money does ARPA have for the remainder of FY '65 UPSTAGE?
2. What will our main competitor offer as capability for diversification?
3. What is the status of our recently submitted centrifuge work statement at NASA/Houston?
4. When will the MOL RFP be issued?
5. When will General "X" retire and who will replace him at AFSC?
6. Will MIRV/MK 12 be a competitive or directed procurement?
7. What will the probable effect of the President's October budget review be on the Space Agency budgets?

To receive an effective response from a field man, the request for information must contain the following ingredients:

1. What Is to Be Learned?

The data should be expressed with the full use of the common language of both parties communicating, defining specific areas in which information is required and supplying pertinent facts which are already known by the home office.

For example: "Please forward information relative to the present status of the Samos satellite system, U.S. Air Force

WS—117M (sub task of WS—117L). Home office understands that fiscal funding for fiscal year 1965 has been de-
layed for six months. Also determine if our Agena umbilical
tower will be compatible with requirements of this program.
Agena umbilical tower specifications and drawings have
been forwarded to you under separate cover." Now the field
man has some idea of management's interest. They do not
really want to know "all information relative to ——." They
are principally interested in funding. And as far as competition, they are really concerned only with the umbilical tower.
This cuts the task down to size.

2. Where Does the Home Office Think the Information Is Available?

Tell the field man where to get the answers if it is known;
don't make him guess. "We understand that cognizance for
this program was recently moved from directly under the
Secretary of the Air Force to a special staff in the Pentagon.
Suggest you start with the Secretary's Office . . ." Now the
field man can quickly check out the home office lead. If it is
right, management's information is on the way back; if not,
at least the field man has started on the right trail and the
data will be available in much shorter time than if the field
man were conducting a guessing game.

3. Who Has the Information?

If it is known, give the name of the office aide who may
have the data or can direct the field man to the proper
source. Tell the field man all you know about the information request; it may make the difference in his recognizing the data when he hears it or it may provide him with an
air of knowledge which will inspire those with the information to take him into their confidence.

4. Why Is the Information Needed?

If the field man understands the ultimate use to which the information will be put, it will influence his action regarding effort exerted, time spent, thoroughness of search and other matters of judgment. Continuing the example: "If our umbilical tower appears compatible with the program requirements, a company-sponsored program will be undertaken to modify our Agena Prototype tower for demonstration to the Samos people." From this, the field man understands that company funds will be spent or saved according to the information he sends back. Certainly this will influence the quality of his effort.

The first step to effective business intelligence acquisition is definition of the requirements by stating clearly in a common language, without abbreviations or colloquialisms:

1. What is needed?
2. Where can it be found?
3. Who has it?
4. Why is it needed?

The second component of the Business Information Request deals with the quantity of data required. A reply to some of the typical questions stated above could well occupy the whole economic analysis department of a "RAND" corporation for an indefinite period of time. On the other hand, an unimaginative or busy field man may reply with one sentence.

The management of a medium-sized aerospace company decided to compete for some of the work in the Apollo program about a year after the program had been initiated. Having made this policy decision, the company began to organize its marketing program and sent this message to its field offices: "Find out all about the Apollo program." At this stage in the development of the Apollo program, 52 major tasks had been identified and some 82 major contractors had been selected and were working on as many major contracts with an indeterminable number of subcontracts and subtasks in process. Figure 5–1 in the Appendix of this chapter presents a partial listing of the tasks and firms involved in the program.

Now, it is not implied that it was too late for this medium-sized aerospace company to participate in a share of the contract work, for their particular capability was vital to the program and they were a highly competitive firm. Rather, it was even more essential that the firm define the business information request specifically and clearly spell out *how much* of this vast mountain of data that is available is required for the company's decisions. All too often the field man is completely overwhelmed at the potential size of the business information reply that he could supply. In many cases, the field man knows so much about a government facility that he literally does not know where to begin in telling the home office about it and, without specific direction, he won't know where to quit. A simplified "Request for Intelligence Data" guide is included in Figure 5–2 on page 106.

The second step in effective business intelligence acquisition is to determine how much data is needed and to cut it off when it has been secured.

The third component of the business information request deals with the quality of the information. How good is the answer? Can we depend upon it? "Well, everybody is saying it." O.K., it's repeatable information (often labeled reliable); that is, no matter which source is checked, one still gets the same answer. Remember when Secretary of Defense McNamara was going to resign his post? Everybody had the same rumor; it was repeatable, hence reliable, *but not valid.* It was not true.

The quality of a reply then consists of two ingredients:

1. Validity, pertaining to the truthfulness.
2. Reliability, its repeatability by multiple sources.

The major cause of invalid responses to business information requests are inaccurate questions. Inaccurate questions usually result from lack of knowledge of the program about which data is sought. This resembles the chicken and egg routine! The solution, of course, is iteration of the questions and answers, building question upon answer until the questions become specific and accurate enough to produce valid answers. This is a technique which requires the close cooperation of the field man and the home office.

Frequently, the preliminary design group is involved in second guessing technical designs, and it may require management participation in a role-playing action to develop the probable decisions in the target company. Some companies go so far as to have whole teams representing the other competing companies, often drawing upon former employees of the other company for personnel. Finally, when valid answers seem to be coming into the home office, one must remember to feed them back to the field office for future reference, signalling a halt to the cycling, and permitting peace of mind.

The third step in effective business intelligence acquisition is in the determination of the quality of the data. Is it valid or just reliable?

The fourth component of the business intelligence request deals with interpretation of data. Taking an information theory point of view, we may examine the anatomy of the typical information request/response cycle, as shown in Table 5–1.

Note that if the home office requester goes out to the field, he eliminates some six steps in the cycle but considering the cost, one doubts if the tradeoff is worth it.

Over a number of years of consulting experience, several suggestions have become standard to alleviate the probability of error in the process of fact gathering. Among these are: (1) get the home office man to know the field personnel personally so he can calibrate their responses; (2) standardize the

TABLE 5–1

Detailed Steps in the Information Request/Response Cycle

Location	Action (Voluntary or Involuntary)	Description
1. Home office	Recognize need for information	Problem arises which requires the acquisition of information from sources outside of the plant.
2. Home office	Interpret	The request is expressed, in prose or illustration, to a data gatherer or home office representative of field personnel.
3. Home office	Filter	Request is filtered by the understanding and mental biases of the second party.
4. Home office	Coding	Depending upon transmission method, the request is drawn, typed, TWXed or in some other way prepared to go outside.
5. En route	Transmission	Message travels, subject to channel noise, random and other noises.
6. Field office	Decode	Interpret for reading in English.
7. Field office	Filter	Interpretation in English is filtered by mind of field agent and reflects his biases.
8. Field office	Select source of data	Sort through various persons and organizations, as well as methods, to obtain data.
9. Field office	Contact source and extract data	Obtain referrals as may be required.
10. Source	Filter	Source reports data as he understands the question and may insert extraneous or inaccurate data as part of counterintelligence or to disguise his role.
11. Field man	Filter	Field man hears reply from source in terms of his own needs and understandings, experience, technical limitations, etc.
12. Field office	Code	Prepare reply according to the transmission method to be used.
13. En route	Transmission	Exposure again to noise.
14. Home office	Decode	Listen or read.
15. Home office	Filter	Message interpreted in terms of needs and understandings of reader/listener.
16. Home office	Collate and transmit	Prepare for others, relate data to other data, make up report.

information request form, working "eyeball to eyeball" with the field men until the form can substitute for personal interaction; and (3) know sources (who says so) in attempting to interpret and evaluate data. Is the data your field man's best guess or interpretation, or is it strictly what was said to him? Sometimes it may be best to have him transmit each separately, his ideas and the source's quoted comments.

The fifth component of business information requests is timing. These are the "whens," i.e., when is the data needed, how long will it take to collect, when will it be evaluated, to what time period does it pertain, when will it no longer be useful? The field personnel naturally are concerned that a request for data arrive in sufficient time to carry out the search. In addition to lead time, the request should be properly timed with regard to the availability of the data and, finally, when the need for data has been fulfilled or no longer exists, then the field people should be pulled off the job.

The sixth and perhaps the most important component of the business information request is the attitude of the field man. Here we mean his attitude toward business intelligence in general and, in specific, the request which is before him. Generally, field office personnel put intelligence gathering rather low on their priority of things to do. The indifference is understandable when we consider the reward-punishment pattern in this area.

Typical management, responsible for operations of field offices, rewards personnel on the basis of their ability to get new business (measured by dollars of new contracts contributed per person or per office per unit time), and/or miles traveled, or number of visits to potential customers—in general, "the ability to actively get around." This attitude on the part of field office management is clearly perceived, and discourages careful and repeated cultivation of an intelligence source. The field man who does so would probably be obliged to explain his inactivity and justify its substitution for "getting around" to "customer contacts."

There is no easy way to measure intelligence inputs and little work has been done to develop an objective measure thereof. It is natural then for him to emphasize those parameters which his superiors measure for salary review purposes and he neglects those things not rewarded or that are actually punished.

This indicates that the firm desiring to improve its quality and quantity of intelligence input or to improve responses to requests for information must elevate that activity on the emotional/time/promotion perception ladder in the eyes of the field representative. Identifying intelligence inputs, measuring them, and rewarding their production is a step toward improvement of a firm's intelligence posture.

The System Formula

We have been examining the system design aspects of business intelligence functions concerning field personnel. One may use a simple formula to establish the impact of these system design parameters upon the output of the intelligence group. The formula is:

$$S \cdot P = O$$

(THE SYSTEM USED TIMES THE PERSONS INVOLVED = OUTPUT OR RESULTS)

The six system components discussed are:

1. Definition
2. Quantity
3. Quality
4. Interpretation
5. Timing
6. Attitude

Procedures and aids can be designed to accomplish the aim of each component. The use of check lists such as the "Request for Intelligence" form (see Figure 5–3), is an example. Attention to business intelligence as a function will raise it in the eyes of participants.

The second part of the formula, the person, is also vital. As much care must be spent on designating who will be part of the intelligence function, or training those who are automatically involved, as is spent in system design. The steps in training, communicating, and motivating are discussed.

Training

One aspect which immediately comes to mind is sensitivity training, an awareness of the impact you have on others. In addition, training in understanding others, if necessary through formal interviews, is vital. Understanding here includes nonverbal communications, evidences of blocking and inhibition. Technical familiarity is most useful, but the possession of the vocabulary would suffice. It is not necessary for field personnel to be experts in everything, but to be able to report complex technical conversations correctly.

Communicating

Close consideration of the request/response cycle, which was previously discussed, will show the key problems that hamper quality communication. To make improvements may involve the following steps: (1) mapping of the company's particular request/response cycle, (2) review of this with home *and* field office personnel *together,* (3) design efforts to reduce the steps to a minimum, (4) frequent interaction between field and home office personnel, and (5) separation of field office personnel reports into opinion and verbatim accounts.

Motivating

Improvement in this area can be achieved by (1) assuring rewards for intelligence work; (2) showing evidence of man-

agement interest and support of this work; (3) providing
rapid feedback to field men ("Your report received, notify
you by TWX Monday p.m. if further data needed"); (4) providing of information on on-going programs so the field man
knows what to report on, how, and to whom; (5) cutting off
a data search at the earliest possible minute to avoid dupli-
cate data discovery; (6) rewarding individuals for work well
done; and (7) assigning field people to specific programs, so
that each can learn to identify with his program. A field man
who represents ten systems at once can hardly be expected to
give adequately motivated intelligence inputs on all of them.
His attention should be focused (program 6 matures next
week, program 7 is not due until August, and so on). Evidence that inputs are being used is another reward for field
personnel.

SUMMARY

By careful consideration of the role and capabilities of
field personnel, and upon provision of carefully designed
training and procedures, management can, through its own
strong support, create an effective team for intelligence
gathering.

Collecting such data is not enough, we must be aware of
motivational, organizational and administrative factors related to this process.

FIGURE 5–1

Major Contractors and Their Area of Involvement in
the Apollo Program

An example of the overwhelming quantity of data available to
answer the business information request: "FIND OUT ALL
ABOUT THE APOLLO PROGRAM."

NASA HDQRS
  MSC

    COMMAND MODULE

COMMAND MOD GUIDANCE & NAVIGATION	NAA S & ID
EQUIP	RAYTHEON
	MIT
	KOLLMAN
	AC SPARK PLUG
REACTION CON-TROL	MARQUARDT
CHECKOUT (ACE)	GE
EARTH LAND SYSTEM	NORTHRUP
ENVIRONM CONT SYST	AIRESEARCH
LES	LOCKHEED PROPLUSION
STAB & CONTROL SYST	MINNEAPOLIS-HONEY-WELL
HEAT SHIELD	AVCO
ANTENNAS	AIRBORNE INSTR LAB
	MELPAR
ELECTR SYST INTEG	RCA

    SERVICE MOD

SERVICE MODULE	NAA S & ID
FUEL CELL	PRATT & WHITNEY
PROPULSION MOTOR	AEROJET
REACTION CON-TROL	MARQUARDT
SPACECRAFT INTE-GRATION	NAA S & ID

  LEM

LEM	GRUMMAN AIRCRAFT ENG
DESCENT ENGINE	STL
	NAA ROCKETDYNE
ASCENT ENGINE	BELL AIRCRAFT

FIGURE 5–1 (continued)

REACTION CON- TROL	GRUMMAN MARQUARDT
FUEL CELL	PRATT & WHITNEY
GUIDANCE SYST	MIT

KSC

KSC MSFC GOSS LAUNCH INFO EXCH FACILITY	AT & T

LC 39

LUT	PAUL SMITY CONSTR- INGALS IRON WORKS
CRAWLER TRANSP	UNIVERSAL MARION CORP
VAB	MORRISON-KUNDSON- PERINI-HARDEMAN U.S. STEEL BLOUNT BROS
LAUNCH OPS SUPPORT	CHRYSLER DOUGLAS AIRCRAFT HAYES INTL BECHTEL BROWN ENGR
OPS & C O BLDG	P. HARDEMAN & MORRI- SON KNUDSON

GOSS

LAUNCH INSTR	IT & T
LAUNCH CONTROL CENTER	VARIOUS

SATURN V

S-IC STAGE

S-IC STAGE	BOEING
F-I ENGINE	NAA ROCKETDYNE
DUCTING	ARROWHEAD
COMPONENTS FAB	AVCO
FLEX LINES	FLEXONICS
STRUCT COMPO- NENTS	REPUBLIC
FAB & WELDING	PROGRESSIVE WELDERS
GORE SEGMTS	RYAN
SUPPORT-STRUCT	LOCKHEED

FIGURE 5–1 (continued)

S II STAGE
   J-2 ENGINE   NAA ROCKETDYNE
   S-II STAGE   NAA S & ID
S-IVB STAGE
   J-2 ENGINE   NAA ROCKETDYNE
   S IVB STAGE   DOUGLAS AIRCRAFT
IU
   GUID COMPONENTS
      IBM   IBM
                        BENDIX

GSE
   COMPUTER   RCA
   ELECT C O   REYNOLDS ELECTRIC
   TEST SUPPORT   VITRO
   R & D SUPPORT   ARING
   ENGINEERING SER-
      VICES   SPACP
                        HAYES
                        BROWN ENGINEERING

SATURN V LAUNCH H   BOEING
VEH SYST ENGR
SR & T
   STRUCT SYST STUDY WHITTAKER CORP
   ENVIRON CONTROL   MIDWEST RES INST
      STUDY
   STAB & CONTROL   GE
      STUDY
   STRUCT SYST STUDY REPUBLIC
   STRUCT SYST STUDY LOCKHEED
   PARTICIPATING
   AGENCIES   US AIR FORCE
                        US ARMY
                        CORP OF ENGINEERS
                           MAPPING
                        ATOMIC ENERGY COM-
                           MISSION
                        US NAVY
                        DEPARTMENT OF STATE
                        DEPARTMENT OF DE-
                         FENSE
                        FEDERAL AVIATION
                         AGENCY
                        US COAST GUARD
                        FED COMMUNICATION
                         COMM

FIGURE 5–2
A BI Collection Request Form

REQUEST FOR INTELLIGENCE DATA

TO: Field Office: ————————————————————————

        Attn: ————————————————————————

From: ————————————————————————————

Date Issued: ——————— Suspense Date: ———————

General Topic: ——————————————————————

———————————————————————————————

Specific Data Required: ————————————————

———————————————————————————————

———————————————————————————————

———————————————————————————————

Send to: ——————————————————————————

Address: —————————————————————————

———————————————————————————————

   Method of Sending: ————————————————

   Classification: ——————————————————

Suggested Sources: ——————————————————

———————————————————————————————

———————————————————————————————

Limitations on Search: ————————————————

———————————————————————————————

———————————————————————————————

Use Reverse for Notes & Continuations. See Over _____

FIGURE 5–3

REQUEST FOR INTELLIGENCE	SUBMITTED BY:

DATE REQUIRED _____

TELEPHONE EXT.:

VERBAL O.K. _____ WRITTEN _____ SEE OVER-SIDE _____   DATE: _____

DELIVER TO: _____

DATA REQUIRED:

_____

_____

_____

_____

_____

_____

SUGGESTED SOURCES:

_____

_____

_____

_____

NOTES:

_____

_____

_____

Chapter Six

PRIVATE INVESTIGATORS IN BUSINESS INTELLIGENCE AND ESPIONAGE

A. D. JOHNSTONE*

FANTASTIC AS IT SEEMS, many reliable sources estimate that the loss to business by theft, stealing of secrets and purposeful, willful destruction of property for business reasons runs over one billion dollars annually.

Major industries, which seem to be a focus for theft of business secrets, are pharmaceutical, chemical, electronics, and aerospace. This information is not new to those who have been keeping up-to-date. There are many articles written on lax security, espionage, and how to improve security programs. These appear in various sources. The federal government issues periodically an industrial security letter and there are a number of guard and security-force oriented magazines such as *Security World*.

Security from these losses, some of which cause business

*Mr. Johnstone is managing director of the Crest Detective Agency which has, in over twenty years of experience, brought him into contact with industrial security problems of some of our nation's largest firms. Crest, located in Santa Monica, is utilizing modern techniques such as electronic eavesdropping as well as traditional techniques and is a sample of the more advanced firms in private investigation work. Mr. Johnstone was educated at Electrical Sound Projection Engineering School, Southwestern University; Santa Monica Junior College and the University of Southern California.

failure, is a product of management's interest. Often management will call upon private investigators to evaluate a situation which should not have come up if there had been adequate internal security. Costs for such studies have run from hundreds to thousands of dollars.

As we will note later, there are areas in which the private investigator is better equipped or more appropriate for this work than normal plant security. Much of the cost of loss of stolen ideas, drawings, methods, and related items would never even be considered for removal from premises if the plant security was adequate, both in fact and employee image. Evidence of this is easily seen in the recent studies of shoplifting in places which have installed TV cameras. Although, the public does not know if they are real or if they are loaded with film, many retail outlets have reported a 50 percent drop in shoplifting just because a camera-shaped object was placed in a visible area and appeared to move, sweeping the store regularly.

Nothing inhibits an engineer from taking a set of drawings more than the thought that he will probably be caught by a gate guard. In most companies, however, the gate guards become unmotivated. Their search for pilfering becomes a boring routine which results in an ineffective search. One major aerospace firm has, inside its buildings, key-card access areas where the installation of doors and their controls costs hundreds of dollars per door. Loss of employees' time and inconvenience due to key-card opening doors also may be assessed as a cost factor. Close watch is being kept on visitors to the area; yet, at the main guard gate, the only form of inspection for a person carrying a box, briefcase or bundle is to say, "nothing classified," and he is waved through. Such erratic attention so often seen is one sign of an inadequately planned security program.

The independent private investigation agency has a special position, however, which permits it to play a unique and useful role in a company's total Industrial Security/Business

Intelligence program. First, the staff of private agencies is usually not known to individuals in a firm while security guards or those who were former security guards may be known. Second, there is almost always a strong possibility of a leak that security is "on to something," especially when there are discussions of the case in the industrial security office. Secretaries, top key staff people, who overhear conversations and others may well give away the fact that security is "in-the-know." In dealing with an outside agency, conversations on the topic are held at the outside agency offices and only a minimum amount of paperwork need be kept inside the firm. Third, techniques and contacts are often available to the private investigator which are not available to a firm. For example, in a recent case a large firm wanted close surveillance of a certain employee. This included his home and business phone calls. A private investigator was employed although the company's own security people knew how to do the job. Why? Because of the negative publicity which might have come up were electronic equipment discovered. Imagine the company's loss of face with headlines like "XYZ Company Eavesdrops on Home of its Own Engineering Chief," or "Company Probes Bedroom of Key Employee." A fourth reason may be the expertise of the private investigator, who, after all, works with these techniques full time. To many firms, such things as investigations are side issues and quite infrequent. The art of total surveillance is an advanced one: from knowing how to gain access to premises and where to put a bug, if eavesdropping is the topic. All these require skill. Incorrect placement of a microphone will at best result in no useful tape, too soft voices or similar. At worst, wrong placement may lead to discovery.

In many cases, a private investigator is employed to discover evidence of intent to commit a wrongful act. For example, when a group of engineers left a large firm, it was necessary to establish that they intended to manufacture a product almost identical to a new product developed by the company. The thousands of dollars invested in research and development would have been wasted had this new firm gone into competition. The private investigator collected the necessary data and a court took action by issuing an injunction to prevent the sale of almost identical products.

If, in such a case, management were to take legal action against employees, or others, without investigation and collection of evidence, they may be putting themselves in jeopardy of numerous suits for such things as defamation of character, libel, and slander.

We also have numerous cases in which a trusted employee has taken money or valuables, often over a period of years. Here, again, the contacts of the private investigator in credit checks, financial and income estimates may help establish the crime itself. Then we often are asked to play another role, i.e., to garner evidence so that the employee can be confronted and coerced into repayment. Often, the private investigator does all the in-between work and confrontation. Under his hopefully wise guidance, the offender's properties may be sold off, transferred in title or restoration made otherwise. Thus, instead of sending the culprit off to jail, the company winds up with a fair amount of its losses recovered.

Similarly, if it is discovered that an individual is leaking data, the discovery of evidence permits a confrontation which may permit false data being sent in the future—a form of retribution. The employee is told, "You had better send this data off or we shall use this evidence to prove to a court that you have been leaking data."

Another major advantage a private investigator has over a plant's own security forces in a special area is provided by the fact that he, the private investigator, is independent. This gives him an advantage. For example, he may play a role in training a plant's security forces by lectures or by exercises. He brings independent experience and knowledge to the lectures. In exercises, he especially shines for he can attempt to penetrate the plant's security and keep security on its toes.

In a smaller or different setup, where the plant itself has people attempting to violate security, too often the word of the test leaks out and the test is negated. One well-meaning secretary, I recall, thought she was doing a group of guards a favor when she would call and "tip them off" that the boss, a Lieutenant, was coming their way. If the testing agent were a private investigator, his secretary, located remotely, would usually have no motivation to protect the guards, but on the contrary, would help detect sloppy security.

Ethical private investigators will not undertake any activity which is illegal or improper. Several requests are received now and then to "mingle with my employees and see how they feel about our management" or "test the loyalty of my top staff." Normally, there must be a specific expected or known crime or violation identified and a clear indication that the work of an investigative nature is to prevent or solve the crime or improper act by another.

Properly utilized the private investigator may be of great help to the firm's intelligence and espionage program and should not be overlooked as one resource for those responsible for management of the firm's business intelligence efforts.

PART II

Techniques

Chapter Seven

USING MARKETING INTELLIGENCE AND INFORMATION TO WIN DEFENSE PROGRAMS

PHILLIP L. OSTER*

EXECUTIVES IN THE DEFENSE INDUSTRY can no longer afford to rely heavily upon their overall technical superiority to win contracts. In the last 20 years industrial diversification of products accompanied by labor mobility has outmoded the corporate "technical monopoly." Today each company in the defense business has ease of entry and accessibility to a trained labor market. As a result of this "technical standoff," government contracts have been awarded on more diverse criteria. These new evaluations may range from advanced multicorrelated "trade offs" to simple geographical selection.

Obviously every company submitting a proposal will have given attention to most of the government's evaluation criteria in varying degrees of detail. The company which can learn the most about the degree of influence possessed by each of the factors will stand the best chance of winning the contract. In fact, the survival of the company is contingent

*Mr. Oster is in the Market Analysis Group of the Missiles and Space Systems Marketing Department of the Douglas Aircraft Company. Prior to this he was with Hughes Aircraft Company in a similar position. He holds the B.S. in Industrial Management and an M.S. in Quantative Analysis in Business from University of Southern California. His Ph.D. work has been in marketing and management controls.

117

upon the information about the attitudes and bias of the awarding agency and the accuracy of their strategy. Competition in this market requires accurate forecasting, good planning, a knowledge of one's own company, its capabilities and limitations, an equally accurate knowledge of one's competition, and of course, knowledge of the activities, and philosophy of the Department of Defense.

The best method of assuring that each of the selection criteria has been evaluated and approached with the best possible strategy is to develop a marketing operations plan.

THE MARKETING OPERATIONS PLAN

A good marketing operations plan should consist of four major areas, each section requiring a great deal of information input. First, a plan of customer actions or milestones on a time base; secondly, an anticipation of the competition's strategy to satisfy the customer's requirements; third, an external marketing plan for the company, countering both the customer and competitive actions; and last an internal plan for implementing the marketing strategy and preparing a proposal.

These sections are most effective when set up on a time base, indicating the cost of pursuing each of the milestones charted. This allows management to review the cost of marketing a program against the action items already accomplished and those which must be undertaken prior to contract award. It also is a management tool for use in allocation of budgets among various programs. This marketing operations plan is primarily developed from marketing information.

MARKETING INFORMATION DEFINED

Marketing information can be defined as that data on which the basic marketing operations plan and strategy is developed. It is generally comprised of second source data, such as publications, or interviews with personnel drafting the requirements. Normally companies keep data banks in which they accumulate and disseminate this type of information to the various internal organizations requiring such data. Background information will be used in the primary pre-program planning stage to answer questions such as:

1. What is the current program name, and previous names?
2. What agencies are involved in procurement, in system or design specification, and in proposal evaluation?
3. Who are the individuals responsible for customer technical qualification, who personally will sign the contract?
4. Which Hitch (Charles Hitch) package is it in, and what are the other elements of that package, its future projections, and its relationship to other current packages?
5. What justification has been given for the program, what was the response of Congress, has it any adversaries in Congress or DOD and who are they? Why are they against it? Who is pushing for it?
6. Who will use it, and where?
7. Who prepared the RFP (request for proposal)? Has any other company been involved in this program? How?

In addition to the information obtained regarding the program specifically there are internal questions which must be answered prior to the active pursuit of a program that would be categorically classified as marketing information such as:

1. Do we want a primary, major contractor contract or a sub-contract? If it is to be a team, with whom can we team? With whom should we team?
2. What leadership and support personnel are we going to assign? What are the budget requirements? Where will they work? What will happen to the work they were doing?
3. How does this program relate to our company goals? How about our image?
4. What other programs are expected to mature just after this one? Will all our best people be tied up? Which is more valuable to the company?

5. What are the internal political implications of this if we win it?
6. Do we have the resources to carry out this work? Have we the necessary skills to present our capability? Are skills available?

After the development of this marketing information into a comprehensive marketing operations plan the real job of marketing intelligence begins.

MARKETING INTELLIGENCE DEFINED

Each of us has at some time seen people stumbling through great stacks of periodicals attempting to get a late start in education on some current program. While this constitutes information, it does not fall under the category of what is classified as intelligence. Intelligence is an action word and only has value when related to decisive situations, therefore, the use of the term marketing intelligence will signify any data acquired which alters a preconceived strategy. Intelligence also has overtones of timeliness, which in effect follows since strategy cannot be altered unless there is time.

The anticipation of actions upon which a marketing strategy is based will generally identify several key events, or pivotal decisions that precede the selection of our alternative decision of sequence of actions by the customer. Intelligence is concerned with identifying these key events and keeping an ear to the ground for their occurrence.

Intelligence is also concerned with any competitive action which would alter your basic strategy; these competitive actions should be identified in the market operations plan and monitored by the intelligence section. Success in market intelligence is measured by the lack of "blind alley expenses" and smoothness of the marketing operation.

It is important that one understands the basic role of intelligence and information in the marketing operations plan so that expensive and talented personnel expressly on the payroll for their ability to gather intelligence are not used for the clerical task of developing information.

In summary then, the marketing operations plan is developed from both intelligence and information, and this plan is used to convince management that they should spend funds to pursue the program and to act as a guideline to market the program. Because most of the applications of marketing technique have been directed toward the customer, we will discuss at length the "in-house sell."

ACCOMPLISHING THE "IN-HOUSE SELL"

Marketing can and should establish the parameters of planning, strategy, and tactics required for the capture of a program. The most general problem encountered by the marketing department, however, is not the customer-orientated presentation but the "in-house sell."

Management requires that the marketing department present to them an accumulation of information and intelligence sufficiently arrayed in a presentation of strategies to warrant the risk of capital in attempting to win the program. This presentation generally takes on grand statements about "our edge," future astronomical sales, our buddy at the Pentagon, and a gross underestimate of the cost of pursuit. With today's management and the numbers of program opportunities which are available, this type of internal sell, dubbed the "golden throat orator approach" is on its way out and is being replaced by comprehensive risk evaluation ratios.

AIDS TO THE "IN-HOUSE SELL"

In many industries, including the aerospace industry, the number of active competitors for specific requirements has narrowed over the past few years. Due to this reduction in numbers, it is possible to know a great deal about the other firms who may be planning to compete on a program opportunity. What do we want to know about them? We want to know at least as much as we know about ourselves; for example, prime technical areas of strength, administrative skills, "ins" with the customer, costs, overhead rates, etc. If possible, we should be able to practically write their proposal, and indeed this has been attempted several times. Aerospace company "A" has a group of employees, some of whom may have been with competitor "B," and their task is to prepare a proposal exactly as the company "B" staff will. Naturally, a good deal of business intelligence goes into such an operation. The pricing, markup or profit percent may well rest upon a very simple cost technique of "B" and be a critical issue in a contract award, therefore, no gimmick should be overlooked. With the growing equivalence of competence, price differentials become extremely inflated in value.

There are several methods currently employed in competitive evaluation. One of the uses of marketing information is in the evaluation of a competitor's system by the "black box" approach. In this analysis you collect your competitor's brochures on specific products over a period of time, and as he sells this equipment to the government, you collect the prices he puts on these products. When a new system is to be procured and you meet this competitor in the marketplace, your technical staff can assemble your competitor's products (for which you have prices) in such a manner as to solve the system problem, leaving only those "black boxes" without prices which the competitor will have to design. A cost estimate of the "black boxes" is made and added to those components which you have already priced, thus giving your management the competitor's "ball park" system price. Marketing intelligence as to specific details can then be utilized to specifically tie the price on the "black boxes" down within acceptance limits.

Another useful method of competitive analysis has to do with an automation factor, applied burden rate, and purchased parts evaluation. By studying a competitor's pricing structure through employee interviews, stockholder reports, independent surveys, your own purchasing department records, public statements by competitive officials, and just good "marketing intelligence," you can evaluate the competitor's fixed costs; allowing your management the edge of only having to evaluate a competitive position in terms of variable costs which can further be sophisticated by weighting the automation factor or advantage from special equipment.

The best overall method of competitive evaluation, and the most comprehensive management tool is "matrix evaluation." In this method you rank the competition on the "Y" axis in relation to the government's selection criteria on the "X" axis, further improving the system if you wish by weighting the selection criteria. The ranks assigned obviously must be supplied by the marketing information available.

Comparative ratings of capability are important because they will provide your management with goals for development or hire. We must know why we are "third best in mechanical ability," "second best in delivery," etc.

A popular risk evaluation method which is currently sweeping the defense business is the assessment form. There are many permutations of this basic idea and each has different connotations. The main theme, however, is to assign to a program a quantitative percent of capture "probability." Good assessment forms also attempt to identify areas where improvement can be made.

Any quantitative tool by which you can evaluate risk for management will enhance your probability of obtaining funding from management to pursue that program. The proper utilization of marketing intelligence in risk analysis will obviously maximize your chances to win the related program and minimize the cost of program capture.

INTELLIGENCE AND ITS DISSEMINATION

With any sizable company one has enormous amounts of information availability of both the critical and noncritical type. One of the major problems of the intelligence team is to identify sources, and establish validity, prior to dissemination among the decision makers. The determination between fiction and fact may well be the key to success on any program since a common strategy is to let your competition believe information about yourself which is untrue. Many a healthy competitor has ceased effort on a program because he was led to believe that it (the program) was "wired" for someone else. After the validity check on information has been made, you must get the information to the appropriate people.

Most firms don't have a well-planned information control system; therefore, available information which is not specifically asked for or pursued as a specific item, has a difficult time in getting to the proper decision makers. If unsolicited information could be posted in a control center, we might rest assured that all concerned would see and note it. Unfortunately, it works otherwise. A man brings in an important item about a program and he doesn't know what to do with it. If a proposal is being worked on, he hasn't met the people in the engineering department working on it, or may not know which of the several marketing sections has been assigned, and much of the potentially interesting data goes down the drain. A firm today has fantastic opportunities for gathering data, if it uses its personnel, provides clear channels for accumulation, and gets the data to the proper personnel.

The point to be made is this: intelligence systems don't just grow, someone has to sit down and give thought and planning to the internal workings of the system. During the proposal writing phase, one might say it is the task of market planning and intelligence to provide each person who helps write the proposal with information so that each sentence and phase of the proposal can meet a need of someone on the evaluation committee as well as clearly accomplishing the entire contract task. In addition, they must act as a clearinghouse for validation and establish the system design of information dissemination.

SUMMARY

There can be no specific statement as to what is and is not of value when evaluating information inputs. Creative use of everyday information along with sparsely acquired intelligence may easily win a program when confronted in the marketplace with unorganized or nonsystematic competition.

In many ways the average firm suffers from the same intelligence problem as Axis nations in World War II did prior to the classification of information; there was just too much data available to identify the critical information.

In your own organization it is imperative that your information not necessarily be of great volume, but pertinent, concise, timely, and valid.

Chapter Eight

A MODEL FOR RFP EVALUATION

R. E. BECKWITH, Ph.D.*

IN MANY OF TODAY's business situations, an organization must decide whether or not to commit the manpower and money to bid on a proposed project, especially in the defense industry, where a single company can receive several RFP's (requests for proposals), in a single day and where the preparation of the documents necessary for a winning proposal is a costly process. Accordingly, the process of deciding to pursue an RFP is one of paramount importance. To be sure, many RFP's can be rejected following a cursory inspection; they may not coincide with the company's interest or they may be significantly beyond the company's capability. They then are excluded from consideration. Others, however, present considerably more difficulty; they may lie within the realm of interest and they may be well within the production capability. The problem is, then, to separate those RFP's which have a high probability of being won from those with a lower probability of being won, and to suit the response to the probability of winning.

There are two actions available for responding to an

---

*Associate Professor in the School of Business, University of Southern California; specialist in Operations Research; member of R. M. Greene & Associates and also an independent consultant to business and industry throughout the nation.

RFP: the first involves the hasty assembling of a proposal from bits and pieces of available documentation and submitting it to the awarding agency with little work being done on it. Although this method does not require large expenditures of time and money, it seldom wins contracts; whenever it does win, those who submitted it find that the hastily assembled costing information, production time, etc. are unrealistic, and may lead to subsequent embarrassment. The second approach requires that varying degrees of care and detail be utilized in the assembly of a proposal. This latter type, although more costly than the previous, is usually the type of proposal which wins contracts. Obviously, should this latter type fail to win the contract, the cost of its preparation becomes a nonproductive addition to the corporate overhead; the ideal organizational response pattern to RFP's is one where no detailed proposals have been nonwinners, with the possible exception of deliberate nonwinners which are prepared to keep an organization on a specific bidder's list.

This chapter is concerned with a method which is valuable in assessing the chance that a given response to an RFP would have in winning a contract. Associated with this method is a measure called the proposal's *capture probability*. If this measure is implemented adequately and if it is, itself, successful, the *capture probability index* will provide management with a means of selecting only the most promising RFP's for response. The method, itself, is predicated on the assumption that men who are experienced in the state of the art of the preparation of proposals are available to the organization to assess certain critical factors: those relevant to the job itself, those relevant to the contracting agency, and certain social and political factors which may affect the award of the contract. If these criteria are filled, the time and effort spent on nonwinning proposals would be minimized. Additionally, the model could be used to indicate how and where the organization's resources should be strengthened in order to enhance the *capture probability*.

NATURE OF THE REQUIRED INFORMATION

An RFP model could include variables both of quantity and of classification; in fact, many models do contain both, but the general dearth of quantitative data available to an organization about its probable competition suggests that a more realistic approach would be a model based upon classification data. Whenever quantitative data are available, they should certainly be included in any responsible model, particularly when specific costing information is to be provided. But, in general, a strict classification model will provide the most realistic approach to the problem of evaluation.

There are three areas of information which are required for the model and which are presumed available to the organization. The identity of the probable competition is the first area. This information is generally available to experienced organizations considering a bid on a significant technical project. This list should consist of a standard number of most probable competitors. Knowledge of the particular factors that will influence a contract award constitutes the second area of information. This second area consists of the items specifically delineated in the RFP, together with other factors whose influences are suspected or indicated on the basis of political and geographical considerations, and from the findings of the industrial espionage system. Finally, the ranking of the subject organization and the probable competition relative to the influential factors constitute an area of information which will reflect the skill and objectivity of the marketing and preproposal staff in assessing the relative positions of the probable competitors in terms of the pertinent factors in the second area of information. Obviously, the assessment must be objective and such dogma as "our organization leads the field in all respects" will do nothing more than undermine any attempt to win the contract.

An example of the specific influential factors can be seen in the compilation below:

$F_1 =$ Technical capability (perhaps two or three components may be required, or a weighted average of several components).

$F_2 =$ Organizational structure or management quality for the proposed task.

$F_3 =$ Performance record on past jobs for the agency releasing the RFP.

$F_4 =$ Experience in the execution of similar jobs.

$F_5 =$ Geographical factors (for example, is DOD currently favoring the Boston area?).

$F_6 =$ Political factors (for example, how long has it been since this area has been awarded a contract by DOD? Does this organization have an influential contact within DOD?).

$F_7 =$ Proposal quality relative to that expected from the competition.

$F_8 =$ Price or profit margin.

RANKED DATA

Let n organizations, O_1, O_2, O_3, ..., O_n, be ranked with respect to each factor in the group, $F_1, F_2, F_3, \ldots \ldots F_n$. Assuming no ties, this means that there is an integer from the set, $\{1, 2, 3, \ldots n\}$, associated with each organization. For example, consider the jth organization, O_j; the sequence (X_{1j}, X_{2j}, ..., X_{ij}, ... X_{mj}) of positive integers, each being at least 1 and at the most n, i associated with O_j. X_{ij} is the ranked position of organization O_j, with respect to factor, F_1, where "1" indicates the highest position *in* the ranking, and n the lowest. Associated with the ith factor, F_i, is the sequence (X_{i1}, X_{i2}, ..., X_{ij}, ..., X_{in}) which is the permutation of the integers (1, 2, ..., n). This sequence ranks the n organizations with respect to capability regarding factor F_1, as judged by the evaluating group.

Sometimes, an absolute judgment cannot be made; sometimes, ties between the rankings will exist. To resolve this situation, assign each member of a group of tied organizations a ranking, possibly a noninteger, which is equal to the average value of the ranked positions were they untied and in consecutive order. For example, two organizations tied for second place would each be given the "rank" 2.5 with the next organization in ranked order being assigned the rank 4; or three organizations tied for third place would each be assigned the rank 4 with the next organization in ranked order being assigned the rank 6.

Statements made by the awarding agency, and the implications of those statements during a debriefing session held after the contract award, can help to check the correctness of the rankings made prior to the contract award. Various technical tools, such as the theory of precedence matrices and rank correlation, can assist in this task. Correctness is used here to denote agreement between the estimated rankings forming the basis for action by the contract awarding agency, assuming that such actions are rational and that the debriefing statements are truthful and relevant.

THE MODEL

Although the model presented here is tentative, its details suggest those which might be found in a final version.

Consider a fixed group of factors, F_1, F_2, ..., F_n; with respect to each of these factors, organizations O_1, O_2, ..., O_n are ranked in decreasing order of excellence for a particular job with the appropriate adjustments for ties having been made. Define the capture probability, $p_{ij} \geq O$, for O_j obtaining the contract award by the linear function of its ranked positions.

$$p_j = \sum_{i=0}^{m} a_i x_{ij} \geqslant 0 \tag{1}$$

for $j = 1(1)n$, where $X_{0j} \equiv 1$ for all j. Require also that

$$\sum_{j=0}^{n} p_j = 1 \tag{2}$$

where $p_0 \geq 0$, which is determined from (2), represents the probability that the contract is awarded to an organization not included in the selected set.

The theoretical model follows from the supposition that the actual award of the contract is a multinomial process with parameters, p_j, varying with the X_{ij}. That is, the contract is awarded to an organization O_j with a probability p_j, $J = 1(1)n$, and to an unlisted organization with probability p_0. The p_j are estimated through ranking information which are generated internally by the subject organization after the coefficients, a_i, have been estimated by a suitable method from historical data which is supposed to have been produced by the hypothesized process.

PARAMETER ESTIMATION AND DATA COLLECTION

The statistical problem is the estimation of the parameters, $a_0, a_1 \ldots \ldots, a_m$ and p_0, from data histories. These parameters are connected by the relationship

$$\sum_{i=0}^{m} a_i = \frac{2(1 - p_0)}{n(n + 1)} \tag{3}$$

which follows from (2) and the observation that the sum of the ranking numbers of the n organizations for any factor is a series with the sum $n(n + 1)/2$.

The mathematical problem of estimating the above parameters in the presence of the indicated constraints will not be treated in this expository paper. Data for such estimations will consist of the ranking by factors of the selected, probable competitors as well as the actual disposition of the contract by the awarding agency.

The data for estimating the parameters can be designated as the pair (X_k, S_k); the equation, $k = 1(1)N$ is an index which includes information from the RFP's in the data history. X_k is the *ranking matrix* and is given by $X_k = (X_{ij}^{(k)})$, and S_k is an index that records the actual award. To be more precise, $S_k = j$ denotes that the contract was awarded to the organization numbered j in the listing sequence of the kth ranking matrix. If $j \neq O$, while $S_k = O$, the contract was awarded to an unlisted organization. The actual identities of the listed organizations in any ranking matrix are unimportant; different organizations may occupy different listed positions in different evaluations. The salient item is the *indexed position* in a particular evaluation.

IMPLEMENTATION

The purpose of this model is to create a mechanism for synthesizing the contract-awarding process to at least the point of statistical equivalence. The user must be prepared to establish and maintain an organization for producing, accumulating, and processing RFP ranking histories; this organization must also obtain actual contract disposition information, and acquire and disseminate follow-up intelligence to improve the quality of the competitor identification process and the internally generated rankings. With these data the numbers $a_0, a_1, \ldots , a_m$, and p_0 will be estimated for each major contract-awarding agency. Experience in carrying out this ranking procedure will reveal methods by which the subject organization can carry out this task with reduced error, thereby improving the model.

Comparing the multipliers, a_i, for each major contract-awarding agency may result in the merging of different sets, thereby simplifying the data-processing requirements and improving the model's predictive accuracy. All historical data used in estimating the multipliers, a_1, should be sufficiently current to capture the essence of the contract-awarding agency's present thinking and behavior pattern. These multipliers should constantly be tested for currency and they should be updated whenever necessary. The number of data histories necessary to estimate the multipliers, a_i, with a proper balance between precision and the cost of acquiring the data, and the specific nature of the statistical tests designed to check for model currency are topics that will be dealt with in a more technical paper.

The factors, F_1, ..., F_m, should be selected with care and the list standardized. It would be helpful, although not essential, if each ranking were conducted with the same number, n, of listed and anticipated serious competitors, including the subject organization, for the contract award. Experience in selecting competitors, and experience in producing the ranking information will help to produce standardized techniques, and will help the user to recognize which types of information and data are most useful in the production of rankings that are highly correlated with those made by the contract-awarding agency.

USES OF THE MODEL

Suppose that the characteristics of a particular contract-awarding agency have been "captured" by the multipliers, a_1, appearing in the model, and suppose that good agreement between prediction and fact has been established, then whenever a RFP of potential interest is received by the subject organization, O_1, a panel would decide on the identities of the probable competitors, O_2, ... O_n, produce the ranking matrix, X, and compute the numbers, p_0, p_1, ..., p_n, from (1) and (2). The number, p_1, is the probability that the subject organization will win the contract award if it produces a proposal in accord with its ranked specifications in those factors, F_i, relevant to the proposal effort of O_1. The number, $(1 - p_1)$ is the probability that the subject organization will fail to win the contract. If p_1 exceeds p_2, p_3, ..., p_n, then Max $(p_2, p_3, ..., p_n)$ is the probability that the contract will be awarded to its closest competitor in the listing. The number p_0, interpreted as the probability of the contract's being awarded to an unlisted organization.

If the cost of the proposal's effort is estimated to be A dollars, and the profit to be gained from the award of the contract is B dollars, then the action represented by the preparation of the proposal and its submission has an estimated, expected profit of $Bp_1 - A$ dollars. If this quantity is negative, then a loss is to be expected from the action of preparing a proposal. The estimated standard deviation for the above is $B\,p_1(1 - p_1)$ dollars.

If odds for success, p_1: $(1 - p_1)$ are not sufficiently favorable to justify the proposal's effort, then an inquiry into the manner available to O_1 to improve its contract's winning ability is most pertinent. For each of the factors, F_i, the minimal effort, which improves the ranked position of O_1 *by one,* must be determined and priced. Each improvement, considered separately, increases p_1, unless the rankings in that factor are negatively correlated with proposal winning success, a highly unlikely possibility. The largest increase in p_1 will result from a unit improvement in the factor associated with the most negative a_i in model (1), but the most efficient improvement will depend upon which factor-improvement yields the greatest improvement in p_1, and therefore in the estimated expected profit, *per dollar.* Certain tactics to improve the subject organization's ranked position, such as the hiring of a distinguished scientist, engineer, or administrator from a listed competitor, should not be overlooked. Such an action can simultaneously improve the ranked position of the subject organization and degrade that of the competitor, thereby producing a twofold improvement in the subject organization's relative posture.

Repetitive application of the above process, which encourages the exercise of latitude and inventiveness in the tactics proposed for factor-ranking improvement, will yield a sequence of marginally efficient actions that can be taken by the subject organization to improve its contract-winning posture for a specific RFP. A trade-off curve for expected profit vs. proposal preparation cost, plus the cost of posture improvement, for example, can be prepared from this sequence. Consistent use of such curves as this will stimulate the objectivity of the proposal selection and preparation process, and will permit a standardized and rational treatment of RFP's.

Chapter Nine

DATA SOURCES AND THEIR EVALUATION

HOWARD LAITIN, Ph.D.*

IN DISCUSSING THE HUMAN MEMORY, a famous computer scientist once said that he thought man's ability to forget was more amazing than his ability to remember. "Without this power to forget," he said, "a single glance around a small room would overwhelm the nerve cells and mind for a lifetime."[1] Today, of course, it is a commonly held point of view that nothing is really forgotten. Everything sensed and thought is entered into the brain's storage, but when recall is required, it is not all scanned. Computers and files, however, do not have this capability; they easily reach the limits of their storage capacity and it becomes vital for someone to separate the wheat from the chaff so we store only useful data.

In this chapter, I will present thoughts about specific useful sources of information, some ideas on relating their value to their cost, and, as a service to readers, provide reproductions of two articles on data sources.

---

*Dr. Howard Laitin is manager of Systems Analysis of the Aeronautical Systems Division of the Hughes Aircraft Company, a consultant to the Institute for Defense Analysis and the the U.S. Army as well as the Southwest Foundation.

[1]See Isaac Asimov, *The Human Brain, Its Capacities and Functions* (Boston: Houghton Mifflin Co., 1964).

THE LOGIC OF PLANNING DATA SOURCES

We have just so much time to study, read, and listen to news of the world about us. It may be well worthwhile to sit back a moment and plan this data input in terms of our personal lives and interests. As indicated by Figure 9-1, it may best serve our needs to progress from the general to the specific. First, as human beings, we are interested in the world as a whole; wars, conflicts, trade, population, politics, and major developments of the day which may have impact upon us. Because it is so large a topic, we scan this lightly and pick up only the most critical trends.

FIGURE 9–1

VIEWING PERSONAL DATA INPUT FROM GENERAL TO SPECIFIC NEEDS

DATA ABOUT WORLD AFFAIRS

Wars Economics Politics Balance of Gold International Trade Laws
Physical Geography UN International Bank SETO NATO

DATA ABOUT NATIONAL AFFAIRS

Politics Federal Actions New Laws Stock Market Market Shifts
Fair Trade Excise Taxes Import Business FAA NASA
Navy Army Air Force DOD Congress Farmers
Computers IRS FDA

DATA ABOUT BUSINESS

Stocks & Bonds Federal Reserve Actions Carloadings Housing Starts
Personal Income Levels Population Shifts Excise Taxes
Business Taxes Local Taxes Legal Decisions
Cost-of-Living Index Defense Market
Business Forecasts Pricing
R & D Developments

DATA ABOUT BUSINESS DECISIONS TO BE MADE

Then, as citizens of a nation, we look for things happening in our country, politics, floods, new state laws, federal doings, defense matters, and so on. One of the areas of interest is business, illustrated by the stock market, bond markets, Federal Reserve Board, and other actions.

Within business, we then gather data on our business, for there are many in which we haven't the slightest interest. We look to our economic factors, competitor actions, and potential market shifts.

Thus, as illustrated, we funnel our data and interests to have a balance, and also an ever-narrowing progression so each day we may be well informed. Note that the ultimate purpose of all this is to come up with the data necessary for decision making.

SPECIFIC PERSONAL SOURCES

Let's start then with sources for the world news. With no special order implied, we can start with *Time* magazine, The *New York Times,* Sunday edition, and *The Wall Street Journal*. These plus morning or evening newscasts will provide concise summaries with relatively little bias, on the world news. Moving toward the business area, next we take up *Fortune*, the *Harvard Business Review* and *Business Week*. When time permitted, some rather specific sources have been helpful to me, for example, *Commerce and Business Daily* provides useful information about government contract awards as well as general economic indicators. The stock and bond houses put out bulletins of interest, for example *Dun's Review* and the *Kiplinger Report* letters. These organizations and the larger banks such as Chase Manhattan or Corn Exchange, will provide special studies on topics such as foreign nations, and import taxation.

In January, 1965, American Heritage Publishing Company started a new publication, named after Albert Gallatin (1761-1849), a Swiss-born financial genius and diplomat who served as U.S. Secretary of the Treasury under Jefferson and Madison. The publications are a book, *The Gallatin Annual of International Business* and a newsletter, *The Gallatin Letter.* The annual contains statistical and descriptive data about nations, people, trade, international finance, and related data. It is quite complete. The cost is $300 a year and inquiries may be directed to Mr. Willet Weeks, Publisher, at 551 Fifth Avenue, New York City. This material alone well covers much international marketing data.

PERSONAL BUSINESS SERVICES

Several well-qualified personal business services bring to the busy executive information he may need about taxes, business, federal laws, and similar topics. Often organized by job there are specialized services for personnel managers, company lawyers, and others. One general service worth noting is produced by the Institute for Business Planning, Inc. of 2 West 13th Street, New York, N.Y. 10011. Ranging from tax planning, both personal and corporate, their material gets into personal financial planning, family financial planning, and real estate programs. It includes sample forms and procedures, the latest laws, and tips for managers.

To really dig into a topic one may go to monographs published by universities or by technical societies. Journals, too, provide detailed analysis, one of which is the *Journal of Economic and Social Implications of Science and Technology,* and another by the Econometrics Society is called, aptly enough, *Econometrics.* In searching out specifics, the *Harvard Business Review, California Business Review,* and other similar journals from universities may help. The Federal Reserve Bank *Letters* are useful for economic studies.

By now we have passed through world and national affairs and should be ready for our own area of business. There are thousands of publications in the hundreds of business areas which exist today. I will cover only two, the aerospace industry and the topic of marketing.

AEROSPACE DATA SOURCES

Starting with research and development (R&D) and new business, let us look first at a newsletter published by the Small Business Administration called the *Products List Circular*. Published monthly, it averages about 40 pages and tells of government-owned patents which are available on a royalty-free and nonexclusive basis, information about patents owned by individuals or corporations which may be used after negotiations for license or sale, and contains other unclassified information about R&D programs. It costs but $1.50 per year and may be obtained from the Superintendent of Documents, GPO, Washington, D.C. 20402.

A second source of new products, processes and technical improvements is the *U.S. Government Research and Development Reports,* popularly called *USGRDR*. Published by the Clearinghouse for Federal Scientific and Technical Information, it appears twice monthly and describes some 3,000 new unclassified and publically available reports of government-sponsored research and development. Among the contributing agencies are DOD, NASA, and AEC. Each issue is indexed by subject, author, corporate source, contract number, and accession report number. USGRDR costs $15.00 for a yearly subscription.

For those involved with overseas R&D developments, there is *TT, Technical Translations,* also by Clearinghouse and published twice a month. *TT* draws from hundreds of sources including the Library of Congress, Special Libraries Association and the European Translation Center. Thousands of complete translations and abstracts of articles and books of European, Slavic, Oriental and other sources are included. Annual subscriptions are $12.00, available through the Superintendent of Documents, GPO, Washington, D.C. 20402.

In April, 1965, Clearinghouse began publishing a master R&D index, called *Government-Wide Index to Federal*

Research and Development Reports, which is the result of a
number of years of studies in the field of coordinated indexing of widespread government programs. Available at $10.00
a year, this publication includes reports from *Nuclear Science
Abstracts, Scientific and Technical Aerospace Reports* (a
NASA publication), *Technical Abstracts Bulletin* (of the
Defense Documentation Center) and *USGRDR* itself.

Moving now to more general DOD data, beyond the
R&D area, we often want to remain "on top" of military
planning and thinking. Some sources of interest in this area
are periodicals such as the *Army Digest* which discusses current and possible future tactics and strategies, the *Military
Review,* an outlet for heavy thinkers who are often powerful
influences and may clarify coming trends, and *Naval Institute
Proceedings.* Of course, there are books written by recently
retired high military officers which deal with broad scope
strategy, among them recently books on our foreign policy,
on why we should maintain manned bombers, on our in-
volvements in NATO, etc. Scanning the *New York Times
Book Review* will keep one up-to-date on better books of this
type.

Biographical materials, on our customers, clients, and
competition, all may bring insight to a current or portending
action. Classic sources are *Who's Who* by Marquis which is
divided into *Who's Who in the East, Who's Who in the West,
Who's Who in Commerce and Business,* etc. Likewise, in
science there is a well-maintained tome: *American Men of
Science.* Public relations officers in companies and in government are fine sources of biographies and a call indicating an
interest may bring forth photos, speeches and other data beyond a biographical sketch. For longer surveillance of people
and companies, clipping services are helpful although expensive.

Naturally our previous readings of newspapers will provide
foundations for major military policy changes, such sources
as *The Christian Science Monitor* and *The Wall Street Jour-*

nal tending to provide excellent background analyses of current events.

SOME AEROSPACE INDUSTRY SOURCES

One useful data source of the aerospace industry is *Spacewire*, published daily and teletyped (or mailed) to the customers' offices at an annual rate of $125 (plus transmission costs). *Space Marketing Intelligence*, also put out by *Spacewire* publisher Peter G. Moosmann, is published twice a week and costs $200 a year. Sample pages may be obtained on request by writing Moosmann at P.O. Box 90456, Airport Station, Los Angeles, California 90009 (Figure 9–2).

Typical of a number of directories, but better than most, is MacRae's *Blue Book*, a four-volume industrial directory put out at 18 East Huron Street, Chicago, Illinois 60611. This lists more than 45,000 manufacturers alphabetically, over 50,000 product headings and some 60,000 trade names. Such materials frequently run between $50.00 and $500.00.

Some of the same data, but with geographic and demographic emphasis, is to be found in a new service offered by Rand McNally & Company called the *City Rating Guide* and *City Rating Map*. For about $15.00 (paperback) one can get a good deal of information on census type data, cities, locations, and business-oriented map materials.

For special events, fairs, exhibits, etc. Graphointer, 4, Stadiou Street, Athens (133), Greece, puts out an annual *International Directory of Fairs and Exhibitions*, some 400 pages on 1,000 events in 54 countries. Priced at $5.00, this is a satisfactory international listing.

Overseas data on electronics is keyed through EID, *Electronics Intelligence Digest*, which for $75.00 a year will provide data on the electronic industries of the United Kingdom and Europe. Arrangements to see or buy this service require contact with their business manager, Heywood & Co. Ltd., Drury House, Russell Street, London W.C. 2. Issued fortnightly, each issue is about 18 pages of information in the electronics field.

Typical of domestic products is *Western States Electronics Directory and Buyers' Guide* available through P.O. Box 5005, Bendix Station, North Hollywood, California, for $5.00 per copy. Typical of some of its contents are manufacturers, laboratories, testing firms, government research centers, divisions of major companies, geographical indices, addresses and names of purchasing agents, etc. Some 2,200 manufacturers and laboratories are listed.

Appended are two reprints, "A Bibliography of Sources for Defense Information" from *DATA* Magazine, and "Where to find Marketing Facts" from the *Harvard Business Review*. Both are reprinted with permission.

Additional sources not listed in these or above are as follows: *Air Traffic Control; Army Reservist; Space Business Daily; The Air Reservist; ASTIA Index; Interavia; Commerce and Business Daily; Defense Marketing Service; Congressional Hearings; AEC Reports.*

EVALUATION OF SOURCES

We have indicated but a few of the hundreds of data sources which exist. Naturally, few would be able, even if they wanted to, to buy all of these. This raises the issue on evaluation, i.e., how can we evaluate these many data sources so as to select that which portends to be most useful and productive at least total cost?

Let us try a simple decision grid. First, on a grid, the competing data sources are listed across the top. The factors which must be considered are listed down the side of the grid, as in (Figure 9–3) on page 146.

Each factor is to be scored for each alternate source. The scores run from one to five, and should be treated as if on a normal curve. This means that one and five, being extreme values, should appear very infrequently. Two and four ap-

FIGURE 9–2

SPACE MARKETING INTELLIGENCE

P.O. BOX 90456 AIRPORT STATION ■ LOS ANGELES 9 ■ CALIFORNIA
PETER G. MOOSMANN, PUBLISHER ■ SPRING 2-4123 ■ SPRING 2-3367

Volume 4	Number 2	Monday, July 26	1965

COMMENTS ON MK 17 RV COMPETITIVE OUTLOOK AT AFBSD

As the three-way evaluation draws to a close for the award of modified PDP contracts for the Minuteman-2 Mk 17 re-entry vehicle, it has been generally confirmed that one of the three contenders failed to submit a completely responsive proposal. As noted in SMI July 22, the competition centers among Avco, Chrysler and General Electric, which responded to the AFBSD RFP, and the following comments are noted:

1) Several sources have indicated that one of the proposals--actually a portion thereof--was not responsive to the statement of work. Unconfirmed reports tend to center upon either Chrysler or General Electric submittals.

2) East Coast sources intending to monitor the contractor selection as it is forwarded from AFBSD up the chain of approval tell SMI that considerable question arose during the early phases of the evaluation whether the entire proposal should be rejected on the basis of the non-responsive section. Following liaison with East Coast staffers who would review the recommendations at a later date, it was decided to continue evaluation of the proposal, however not to award rating points for the specific section.

It appears to many observers that selection of two contractors for a PDP-type effort may be forthcoming in the near-term future. The Mk 17 will be deployed in a mix with the Mk 12 (General Electric) RV aboard the siloed Minuteman-2 force.

- -

REDEYE SECOND SOURCING REPORTS GROW STRONGER

Despite the lack of official confirmation from the Army Missile Command, industry reports increasingly point toward an anticipated second sourcing of the Redeye system. In general the following two major phases are foreseen for the system in the not-too-distant future:

--SECOND SOURCE: SMI has previously reported that the AMC has elected to pursue the second source route for Redeye. It has been unofficially indicated that the move will be handled in a manner similar to the current Shillelagh, i.e., that a small production order would be placed with a qualified firm other than General Dynamics/Pomona whereupon a further decision could be made regarding the selection of one, or both firms to continue large-scale production. It is noted that considerable impetus exists to make Redeye available operationally on a wide scale.

--UPRATING REDEYE: It is believed that following the second source competition and subsequent resolvement, that an effort will be initiated to uprate the system--with emphasis in the area of propulsion. Sketchy input thus far strongly suggests that much concentration will be directed toward (1) higher impulse propellants, and (2) a modest

FOUNDERS OF: SPACEWIRE ● SMI NEWSLETTER ● SPACE MARKETING ASSOC.

SPACE MARKETING INTELLIGENCE IS PUBLISHED TWICE WEEKLY TO PROVIDE MARKETING INFORMATION AND ANALYSIS FOR COMPANIES PARTICIPATING IN ALL ASPECTS OF CURRENT AND FUTURE SPACE AND DEFENSE PROGRAMS. SUBSCRIPTION RATE: $200 ANNUALLY. FURTHER INFORMATION AVAILABLE BY TELEPHONING SPRING 2-3367 -- SPRING 2-4123 IN LOS ANGELES (AREA CODE 213) OR TWX 213 326 3125

pear more frequently, and three, the average value, appears most frequently.

Number one implies a very bad, undesirable situation. For example, if the source is quite unreliable, or very expensive or poorly edited. Number five represents the best possible, for example, an expert opinion, a very reliable guide, or very inexpensive.

FIGURE 9–3

EVALUATION DECISION GRID FOR ALTERNATE DATA SOURCE SELECTION

Factors	Alternate Data Sources							
	Aerospace Daily	Space News	Missiles and Rockets	DMS Reports and Letters	Spacewire	Aerospace Management	Aerospace Engineering	etc.
Cost/year								
Value								
Breadth of Defense market coverage								
Readability								
Overlap with already available data								
Etc.								
Total score								
Actual cost per annum								
Budget Limitation								

The following curve illustrates the frequency of use facet:

```
Times           |          1
used in a       |          1
sample of       |     1    1    1
10 ratings.     |1    1    1    1    1
                 ‾‾‾‾‾‾‾‾‾‾‾‾‾‾‾‾‾‾‾‾‾
                 1    2    3    4    5
```

Although these will have to be defined more closely for any specific use, let us examine as examples, cost and value. One may lay out a table as follows:

Cost of Source Yearly	Score for Evaluation
$0-20	5
$21-100	4
$101-300	3
$301-1,000	2
Over $1,000	1

Or, in the field of value, defined thus: The number of times per 100 look-ups (or percent of times) that the source contained a satisfactory answer to the business intelligence question. The table for scoring might look like this:

% Successful Look-ups	Score for Evaluation
0-15	1
16-50	2
51-75	3
76-90	4
91-100	5

An arithmetic sum of the scores will permit differentiating among sources. A minimum score permissible may be established if desired. With the addition of an actual cost line (see Fig. 9–3), and by ticking off amounts from a budgeted sum, one may establish which sources may be purchased in any one budget period.

The useful exercise of defining factors, researching the sources, scoring and retesting the procedure will help support budget requests and tends to improve the objectivity of business intelligence group management.

A BIBLIOGRAPHY OF SOURCES FOR DEFENSE INFORMATION†

by Ed Richards, Thiokol Mkt. Research Mgr.

The following alphabetical listing indicates those magazines, periodicals, organizations, which to a lesser or greater extent, supply information relating to the defense industry. While the list may be found to be not all-inclusive, it does represent most of the regularly published, and generally available publications, which deal in any sense, with the defense establishment. Business and financial publications which publish economic data related to the defense industry, or studies of companies engaged in defense activities, are also included as sources of background information. A simple code was utilized to indicate the general type coverage of the field covered by each publication.

Code Description

G = General coverage of newsworthy events within various industries, countries, etc. Can be either general coverage of a specific industry (usually indicated by title) or general coverage of the general economy.

T = Technical descriptions of new equipment, new methods and techniques, systems, etc.

M = Marketing information including description, cost, quantities, delivery schedules, etc., covering equipment, components, systems utilized within, or by the defense establishments.

Where two code letters are used, the first indicates primary and major interest (at least 75% of publication), and the second letter indicates secondary and minor coverage. The absence of any letter indicates either unfamiliarity with the publication, or a situation difficult to classify.

The date in parenthesis, following the publication title, is the first year of publication of that magazine or series.

---

†Reprinted from DATA Magazine, September 1961.

T   **Aero Space Eng. (I.A.S.)**   (1934)
     2 East 64th Street
     New York 21, New York
     Monthly—$10.00/yr.
Technical articles on components and systems of aircraft, missiles, rockets, satellites, spacecraft. Extensive review and bibliography of articles, books published both in the U.S. and abroad.

MT   **Aerospace Management**   (1958)
     Chestnut & 56th St.
     Philadelphia 39, Pa.
     Monthly—$10.00/yr.

Formerly **Aircraft & Missiles.** Both technical and general articles covering military and commercial missiles and rockets. Primarily a marketing aid.

M   **Aerospace Year Book**   (1919)
     1001 Vermont Avenue
     Washington 5, D. C.
     Annual—$6.00/yr.

Statistical compilation of aircraft production broken down into numerous different categories, commercial aviation details, private flying, etc. Descriptions of aircraft.

MT   **Air Facts**   (1938)
     90 Nassau Street
     Princeton, N. J.
     Monthly—$4.00/yr.

Descriptions of commercial aircraft, statistics, airport facts, new equipment and procedures.

G   **Air Force Times**
     2020 M Street, N.W.
     Washington 6, D. C.
     Weekly—$7.50/yr.

Especially for military overseas, timely coverage of Air Force topics of general knowledge.

MT   Air Lanes   (1936)
340 W. 57th Street
New York 19, New York
Monthly—$3.50/yr.

General coverage, including some technical descriptions of commercial flying, components, aircraft, operating characteristics and statistics.

MG   Airlift   (1937)
1001 Vermont Ave., N.W.
Washington 5, D. C.
Monthly—$5.00/yr.

General coverage primarily of non-military flying. Features sections devoted to commercial and private sectors of the aircraft industry. Descriptions of aircraft and operating characteristics.

G   Armed Forces Management   (1954)
1001 Vermont Ave., N.W.
Washington 5, D. C.
Monthly—$3.50/yr.

Self improvement, philosophy, "how to" articles, new developments, organizations, etc.

T   American Rocket Society Journal   (1930)
500 Fifth Avenue
New York 36, New York
Monthly—$18.00/yr.

Primarily technical articles on missile, rocket and space components and systems.

G   Army (AUSA)   (1956)
1529 18th St., N.W.
Washington 6, D. C.
Monthly—$5.00/yr.

General coverage of new Army developments, equipment, mission and role discussions,

GT   **Army Aviation**
    1 Crestwood Road
    Westport, Connecticut
    Monthly—$3.50/yr.

General coverage for both military and non-military flyers; also aviation writers.

GT   **Army Information Digest**
    U. S. Government Printing Office
    Washington, D. C.
    Monthly—$2.25/yr.

Primarily general articles concerning missions, roles and philosophy of the "Modern Army."

G   **Armed Forces Journal**   (1962)
    Weekly—$10.00/yr.

Merger of Army Navy Air Force Journal and Army-Navy-Air Force Register, effective 17 March 1962; general coverage of all services in regards to legislation affecting service personnel, marriages, promotions, pay scales, duty assignments.

G   **Army Times**   (1940)
    3132 "M" Street, N.W.
    Washington 7, D. C.
    Weekly—$7.50/yr.

General newspaper coverage of appointments, marriages, unit deployment. Primarily "people" coverage.

MG   **Missile/Space Daily**   (1939)
    1001 Vermont Ave., N.W.
    Washington 5, D. C.
    Daily—$220/yr.

General non-technical coverage (contract awards, new developments, legislative developments) of both the defense establishment and commercial aviation.

M   **Aviation Directory of Canada**   (1959)
341 Church Street
Toronto, Ontario
Annually—$5.00

Statistical compilation and descriptive details of primarily commercial aviation activities in Canada.

M   **Aviation Facts & Figures**
1001 Vermont Ave., N.W.
Washington 5, D. C.
Annual—$2

General statistical coverage of military and commercial aircraft and missile industries. Production figures, manpower, dollar volume, etc.

GM   **Aviation R & D Issue**
330 W. 42nd Street
New York 36, New York
Annual—$1.00/yr.

General coverage of R&D in aviation field, with some technical aspects. Regular delivery as issue to subscribers.

MT   **Aviation Week**   (1947)
330 W. 42nd Street
New York, New York
Weekly—$7.00/yr.

General coverage of both commercial and military aviation, missiles, space. Contract awards, descriptions given. Some technical articles on new developments in components and systems.

M   **Aviation Week Buyers Guide**

Listing of products, systems, manufacturers, within the aircraft and missile industry.

M   **Aviation Week Inventory of Aerospace Power**

Statistical and descriptive coverage of the aviation and missile industry. General review and forecast of the aircraft-missile industry.

G   Banking   (1908)
         12 East 36th Street
         New York 16, New York
         Monthly—$15.00/yr.

General coverage of the banking field. New products, methods, etc., development for banking utilization. Financial news, mergers, corporate happenings, etc.

G   Barron's   (1921)
         50 Broadway
         New York 4, New York
         Weekly—$15.00/yr.

General coverage of business and industry. Describes new products and developments of various companies in various industries. Complete listing of N. Y. stock exchange happenings for previous week.

G   Business Week   (1929)
         330 W. 42nd Street
         New York 36, New York
         Weekly—$6.00/yr.

Very general business, government, economics coverage. All types of articles on all facets of commerce-business.

GM   Commercial and Financial Chronicle   (1839)
         Box 958, Church St., Annex
         New York 7, New York
         Semi-weekly—$65.00/yr.

General business coverage, financial news, corporate happenings. Special feature is a complete listing of New York ship movements.

GM   DATA Magazine   (1956)
         1808 Wisconsin Avenue, N.W.
         Washington 7, D. C.
         Monthly—$12.00/yr.

General coverage of the defense establishment. Primarily concerned with "which organization does what" and who to see within an organization. Contains organizational charts of various government agencies. Defense Marketing Section gives functional material on various aspects of defense marketing.

GT   Datamation   (1957)
141 East 44th Street
New York 17, New York
Bi-monthly—$5.00/yr.

General and technical coverage of new methods, equipment, developments, connected with data handling, processing and computing activities.

M   Defense R&D Report
P.O. Box 150
Long Island 1, New York
Weekly—$90.00/yr.

Contract awards, descriptions, new developments in research and development efforts concerned with the defense industry.

G   Dun's Review   (1893)
99 Church Street
New York 22, New York
Monthly—$5.00/yr.

General business coverage, corporate news, new procedures, products, etc. Emphasis is on financial details.

TG   Electronic Design   (1952)
850 Third Avenue
New York 22, New York
Bi-Weekly—Qualified circ.

Primarily technical descriptions of new products, equipment, systems. Some general industry-wide coverage.

GT   Electronic Industries   (1942)
Chestnut & 56th Streets
Philadelphia 39, Pa.
Monthly—$10.00/yr.

General coverage of all aspects and segments of the electronics industry. Includes technical articles concerning new equipment and systems.

TM   Electronic News   (1957)
     7 East 12th Street
     New York 3, New York
     Weekly—$3.00/yr.

Technical coverage of new product equipment techniques. Considerable general coverage and marketing type information and news.

MT   Electronic Procurement
     1 East First Street
     Duluth 2, Minnesota
     Monthly—$10.00/yr.

Technical and general information concerning production and procurement of electrical equipment on government contract, within private industry, and in research among both.

TM   Electronics   (1930)
     330 W. 42nd Street
     New York 36, New York
     Weekly—$6.00/yr.

Primarily technical coverage of equipment and systems with some contract award information, new plant description, general news articles.

M   Electronics Buyers Guide
     (With subscription to "Electronics")

Product and manufacturer directory of all electronic products.

M   Electronic Specifying and Purchasing   (1962)
     2775 South Moreland Boulevard
     Cleveland 20, Ohio
     Annual—Controlled circ.

Directory of manufacturers and sales offices of electrical equipment—"Who s Who in Electronics."

M   Federal Subcontracts Weekly
           46-05 Vernon Blvd.
           Long Island City 1, N. Y.
           Weekly—$40.00/yr.

Contract award coverage of all weekly major awards, by agency and industry grouping.

G   Financial World   (1902)
           17 Battery Place
           New York 4, New York
           Monthly—$15.00/yr.

General news of financial interest. Discussion of corporate news, financial details. Almost anything which might affect the financial position of a company appears.

G   Flight Magazine   (1934)
           1901 McKinney Avenue
           Dallas 1, Texas
           Monthly—$3.00/yr.

General coverage of aviation industry, including equipment descriptions.

G   Forbes Magazine   (1917)
           70 Fifth Avenue
           New York 11, New York
           Semi-monthly—$5.00/yr.

General coverage of commerce and industry with emphasis on finances and financial details. New products described, company structure discussed.

G   Fortune   (1930)
           Rockefeller Center
           New York 20, New York
           Monthly—$10.00/yr.

General coverage of commerce & industry. Description of specific companies and management. Philosophical discussions.

MG   **Ground Support Equipment**   (1959)
Sheffield Publishing Co., Inc.
644 Washington Bldg.
Washington 5, D. C.
Bi-monthly—Controlled circ.—free

General coverage of new products, companies, developments
in the ground support equipment segment of the defense industry.

M   **Industrial Marketing**   (1916)
740 North Rush Street
Chicago 11, Illinois
Quarterly—w/subscrip.

Listings of market details, magazines and other periodicals
covering industry, sources of marketing information, advertising
information, etc.

TM   **Inventions Wanted by the Armed Forces**
National Inventors Council
U. S. Dept. of Commerce
Washington 25, D. C.
Semi-annually—Free

Listing of inventions and developments sought by the various
Armed Forces. Includes brief description of current status, plus
forecasted requirements through 1970.

G   **Industrial Research News Letter**
Armour Research Foundation
35 W. 33rd Street
Chicago 16, Illinois

General coverage of new developments in research and development activities.

G   **Magazine of Wall Street**   (1907)
120 Wall Street
New York 5, New York
Bi-monthly—$20.00/yr.

General coverage of various companies is listed on the New York Stock exchange, primarily financial emphasis. Discusses individual companies, future prospects, etc.

GT   Mechanical Engineering   (1907)

345 East 47th Street
New York 17, New York
Monthly—$7.00/yr.

General coverage of products, methods, processes, equipment of interest to mechanical engineers. Technical articles as well as more general type articles.

T   Microwave Journal   (1958)

1330 Beacon Street
Brookline 46, Massachusetts
Monthly—$10.00/yr.

Technical articles relating to new products, equipment, plants, etc., concerned with microwave transmission.

M   Microwave Engineers' Handbook and Buyers' Guide
(1961)

1330 Beacon Street
Brookline 46, Massachusetts
Annual—$3.00/yr.

Technical information concerning procurement and installation of radar, missile guidance, missile tracking, telemetry, communication, and similar equipment . . . listings of companies engaged in production of microwave products.

TG   Military Systems Design   (1957)

845 Ridge Avenue
Pittsburgh 12, Pa.
Bi-monthly—Qualified Circ.

Technical descriptions of new equipment, methods and systems, within the military electronics segment of the defense industry.

MT   Missiles & Rockets   (1956)
      1001 Vermont Ave., N.W.
      Washington 5, D. C.
      Weekly—$5.00/yr.

General coverage of the defense industry with emphasis on the missile & rocket segment. Some technical articles on new developments, much information on contract awards, etc.

TG   Missiles and Space   (1956)
      Engineers Building
      Manhasset, New York
      Monthly—$10.00/yr.

General timely information directed toward procurement officials in missile and space vehicle construction and government research and development agencies.

MG   Missile/Space Letter
      1722 Wisconsin Ave., N.W.
      Washington 7, D. C.
      Twice monthly—$90.00/yr.

General coverage of the defense industry. Contract awards, new product and system descriptions, "who to contact," etc.

G   Nation's Business   (1912)
      1615 H Street, N.W.
      Washington, D. C.
      Monthly—$6.00/yr.

General coverage of all phases of business and industry. Articles on corporate leaders.

GT   Naval Research Reviews
      U. S. Govt. Printing Office
      Washington 25, D. C.
      Monthly—$1.50/yr.

Information on basic research in the Navy. Mostly concerned with "pure science" within Office of Naval Research (ONR) scope.

G   **Navy Times**   (1951)

2020 M Street, N.W.
Washington 6, D. C.
Weekly—$7.50/yr.

General news of Navy personnel, installations, regulations, marriages, social, etc.

TG   **New Equipment Digest**   (1936)

Penton Building
Cleveland 13, Ohio
Monthly—Qualified Circ.

Technical-general coverage of new equipment, services, products, used or produced within general industry.

G   **Newsweek**   (1933)

444 Madison Avenue
New York 22, New York
Weekly—$6.50/yr.

General coverage of industry, government, economics, etc. Regulations affecting business are discussed, trends are reviewed.

T   **Nuclear Science & Eng. Journal**   (1956)

111 Fifth Avenue
New York 3, New York
Monthly—$39.00/yr.

Primarily technical coverage of nuclear power for the military and industry.

TM   **Nucleonics**   (1947)

330 E. 42nd Street
New York 36, New York
Monthly—$8.00/yr.

Primarily technical articles relating to the use of nuclear power by the government and industry. Describes new plants, reactors, etc. Some contract award information.

GT   Ordnance (1920)

708 Mills Building
Washington 6, D. C.
Bi-monthly—$5.50/yr.

General coverage of ordnance developments in the various military services. Technical descriptions of new ordnance developments, etc. Contract awards are indicated.

GM   Presidential Economic Advisers Report

U. S. Govt. Printing Office
Washington 25, D. C.
Single Copy—$1.00

General coverage of the state-of-the-economy, including recommendations as to what should be done to correct deficiencies.

T   Proceedings of I.R.E.

1 East 79th Street
New York 21, New York
Monthly—Assn. dues

Professional papers of the Institute of Radio Engineers, written at high technical level.

T   Product Design and Development (1946)

Chestnut and 56th Streets
Philadelphia 39, Pennsylvania
Monthly—Controlled circ.

Technical data concerning production, design and engineering with some general purchasing, military and civilian.

GT   Research & Development (1950)

201 N. Wells Street
Chicago 6, Illinois
Monthly—$10.00/yr.

Technical and general coverage of new equipment, methods, scientific discoveries, in non-defense scientific investigations.

TG   Scientific American   (1845)
415 Madison Avenue
New York 17, New York
Monthly—$6.00/yr.

Technical articles and general coverage of new discoveries, scientific project reports, personnel happenings, etc. Primarily "pure science" reporting.

T   Signal   (1946)
1725 Eye Street, N.W.
Washington 6, D. C.
Monthly—$7.00/yr.

Technical coverage and general coverage of electronics developments within the defense industry. Primarily emphasis is upon Army Signal Corps equipment.

G   Skyways   (1942)
1001 Vermont Avenue, N. W.
Washington 5, D. C.
Monthly—$7.00/yr.

General coverage of private and commercial flying. Statistics given, new products described, important legislation discussed.

TM   Space/Aeronautics   (1943)
205 E. 42nd Street
New York, New York
Monthly—$10.00/yr.

General coverage of the "space" industry with primary emphasis on technical descriptions of new products, theories, developments. Contract award information, significant developments are given.

T   Space /Aeronautics R & D Technical Handbook (1957)
205 East 42nd Street
New York 17, New York
Annual—Qualified circ.

Technical information concerning materials and purchasing

in the aeronautical field; directed toward government aeronautical research agencies, prime contractors and manufacturers.

MG   Space Age News   (1958)
> 160 S. Robertson Blvd.
> Beverly Hills, Calif.
> Monthly—$12.50/yr.

General marketing type information on contract awards, new products and developments, defense budget news, etc.

M   Statistical Abstract of U. S.
> Supt. of Documents
> U. S. Govt. Printing Office
> Washington 25, D. C.
> Annually—$3.50/yr.

Statistical compilation of population, income and expenditures, industry, government, etc. Most charts and tables include historical background figures.

G   Survey of Current Business
> Dept. of Commerce
> Supt. of Documents
> Washington 25, D. C.
> Monthly—$4.00/yr.

Status and trends of the various segments of the U. S. economy. Where we are and where we are going, general economy.

M   Synopsis of U. S. Govt. Proposals Procurement, Sales & Contract Awards
> U. S. Dept. of Commerce
> Office of Field Services
> 433 W. Van Buren Street
> Chicago 7, Illinois
> Daily—$10.00/yr.

Daily listing of contracts awarded, bids requested, by each of the various government agencies, including the military services with special emphasis on those items biddable by small business.

G   **Time**   (1923)
Time & Life Building
Rockefeller Center
New York 20, New York
Weekly—$6.00/yr.

General news coverage of significant happenings in government, industry, international politics, sports, medicine, etc.

MG   **Underwater Defense Letter**
1722 Wisconsin Avenue, N. W.
Washington 7, D. C.
Twice monthly—$90.00/yr.

Marketing type information specifically covering developments connected with underwater warfare.

TG   **Undersea Technology**   (1960)
Sheffield Publications
640 Washington Building
Washington 5, D. C.
Bi-monthly—Controlled circ.—Free

Mostly technical information on such things as transducer
wave patterns, torpedo propulsion, etc. Formerly **Underwater
Technology.**

G   **U. S. News & World Report**   (1933)
2300 N. Street, N. W.
Washington 7, D. C.
Weekly—$5.00/yr.

General coverage of business, industry, government, economics, etc. Important happenings which effect business discussed.

GM   **Wall Street Journal**   (1889)
44 Broad Street
New York, New York
Daily—$24.00/yr.

General coverage of the business world. New products, equipment, methods are discussed, and all significant financial news is reported. Contains prices on main stock exchanges.

TG **Western Electronic News** (1953)
10373 W. Pico Blvd.
Los Angeles 64, Calif.
Monthly—$5.00/yr.

Technical and general coverage of the electronics industry in the western United States. Describes new equipment, components, contract awards, etc.

M **World Aviation Directory** (1940)
1001 Vermont Ave., N. W.
Washington 5, D. C.
Twice Year—$20.00/yr.

Statistical issue which gives pertinent figures for all phases of flying, including product and manufacturers listings, and airport directory.

New Publications

Listed below are publications covering the defense industry, which have started publishing since 1957. Numerous letter type publications have also been started in recent months. However, many of these letter publications are just an abbreviated rehash of the news and contract awards, and at the same time are much more expensive. Many of these publications will have short lives and are, therefore, not included in the following list:

Publications Started Since 1957

Aerospace Management	1958
Astronautics	1957
Datamation	1957
Electronic News	1957
Ground Support Equipment	1959
Microwave Journal	1958
Military Systems Design	1957
Space Age News	1958

Sample Reading Lists

Following below are two sample reading lists. The first listing indicates a basic minimum subscription list for a general, broad, overall picture of the defense establishment and the defense industry. The second listing includes all of the publications on the first list, plus additional publications which will give a fuller, more complete picture of the total defense establishment and industry.

Both of the listings are basically non-technical in nature. To these lists should be added those publications which specialize in those segments of the industry, in which there is particular interest. This would add another $15-$20 to the total.

Basic List ($42/year)

Aviation Facts & Figures	$ 2
Aviation Week	$ 7
DATA Magazine	$12
Electronics	$ 6
Missiles & Rockets	$ 5
Space/Aeronautics	$10
	$42

Supplemental Listing ($300/year)

All on basic list	$ 42
Air Force & Space Digest	$ 5
Aerospace Management	$ 10
Army	$ 5
Aviation Daily	$220
Business Week	$ 6
Ground Support Equipment	Free
Missile Design & Development	Free
World Aviation Directory	$ 12
	$300

Many of the various publications also publish as supplements to their magazines, special studies, reports, directories, summaries, newsletters, etc., some of which are included in the magazine subscription price.

WHERE TO FIND MARKETING FACTS††

by Steuart Henderson Britt and Irwin A. Shapiro

SOME GENERAL SOURCES

Any important library offers a wealth of information. But you can save yourself time by quickly locating the right books, documents, periodicals, and other materials.

Where can you find marketing data that will help you to keep abreast of current marketing developments?

A. PERIODICALS

The first answer consists of periodicals that contain numerous articles on marketing, such as *Advertising Age, Business Horizons, Fortune, Harvard Business Review, Industrial Marketing, Journal of Advertising Research, Journal of Marketing, Media/scope, Printers' Ink,* and *Sales Management.*

Some journals in the social sciences, such as *Human Organization, Journal of Applied Psychology, Journal of Communication, Public Opinion Quarterly, Social Forces,* and *Sociometry* may be of interest to marketing men, too. In addition, of course, there are hundreds of excellent specialized publications for specific fields.

B. INDEXING SERVICES

Second, there are several indexing services.

Reader's Guide to Periodical Literature indexes the contents of most of the nation's popular magazines.

Business Periodicals Index is a reference book similar to the *Reader's Guide,* but covering approximately 120 periodicals in accounting, advertising, banking and finance, general business, insurance, labor and management, marketing and purchasing, office management, public administration, taxation, and the like.

The Bulletin of the Public Affairs Information Service is a selective list of the latest books, pamphlets, government publications, reports of public and private agencies, and periodicals re-

---

††Reprinted from *Harvard Business Review,* September-October 1962.

lating to economic and social conditions, public administration, and international relations.

The Wall Street Journal and *The New York Times* publish indexes listing all articles that have appeared in these publications.

The Agricultural Index, The Engineering Index, Psychological Abstracts, and *Sociological Abstracts* are examples of other indexes for specific areas.

C. TRADE SOURCES

Your own trade sources are, of course, invaluable. This is especially true in fields characterized by fast-moving technical development. Product research or technical research is conducted or coordinated by some of the more active trade associations; and most of the associations collect basic data on costs, sales, stock-turnover rates, bad-debt losses, collection ratios, net operating profits, and similar factors.

Even though you may know of the principal trade associations in your own field, it might be advisable to check the *Directory of National Associations of Businessmen,* published by the U.S. Department of Commerce. (See item III B 2 in the listings that follow.)

There are, of course, a number of other general business associations and bureaus, as well as foundations, which may have data for your special purposes. Note also the bureaus of business research in many leading universities.

D. GOVERNMENT

The U.S. Department of Commerce is a valuable purveyor of information and maintains excellent reference libraries in its 33 field service offices in major cities. Also, the Small Business Administration assists with business problems and maintains field offices in 54 cities. State and local governments also provide considerable data.

*   *   *

The 46 basic sources of marketing facts and figures we shall turn to now are divided into five categories: (1) guides to reference sources; (2) selected marketing bibliographies (topical and current); (3) directories (of business organizations, of associations, of marketing and advertising organizations, and of media); (4) geographical market and population data (from government and nongovernment sources); and (5) business and economic statistics.

In selecting the sources of information, we have tried to make sure that:

1. The publications all emphasize prime data or lead to other sources which can be used to locate more detailed data.

2. The material is of general interest to all marketing people, regardless of field of specialization.

3. The list is brief enough to be actually read and used, rather than just filed.

I. GUIDES TO REFERENCE SOURCES

The seven items listed in this section are detailed sources of marketing facts and figures. All are excellent "finding guides" in their respective areas.

1. *How and Where to Look It Up,* by Robert W. Murphey (New York, McGraw-Hill Book Company, Inc., 1958, 721 pp., $15.00).

This is an exceptionally useful up-to-date guide to standard sources of information.

Part I explains how to use reference works in general, including how to use libraries and how to prepare a research report.

Part II discusses the major varieties or categories of reference works, listing and describing items such as encyclopedias and almanacs, guides to periodicals, guides to directories, and guides to governmental and commercial sources of information.

Part III is a guide to *specific* sources of information and is the most valuable part of this book. The bulk of Part III consists of an alphabetical listing by subject heading of standard reference sources on 481 topics. Thousands of specific reference and guide books are described in a well-classified arrangement. Although intended to be a general reference work, its coverage of business sources is comprehensive. Cross-referencing and indexing are excellent and detailed, yet not cumbersome.

2. *Information for Administrators,* by Paul Wasserman (Ithaca, Cornell University Press, 1956, 375 pp., $6.00).

A guide to publications and services for management, this book was prepared by the Librarian of Cornell University's Graduate School of Business and Public Administration.

It provides an organized introduction to where and how to locate authoritative information on business trends, statistical data, marketing research sources, legal problems, government regulations, industrial research, management services, local areas, international conditions, and many other subjects of concern to marketing management.

3. *Current Sources of Marketing Information,* by Edgar Gunther and Frederick A. Goldstein (Chicago, American Marketing Association, 1960, 119 pp., $4.00; $2.00 to members).

This is a classified annotated bibliography of primary reference sources of marketing data published during the six years from 1954 through 1959.

It is the most valuable source book on specific marketing information currently available. It includes almost every item in the present article, plus many more specialized references.

Arranged from the general to the specific, this publication begins by covering basic sources of information; then tells where to find national economic and population data, regional and state data, data on specific industries; and concludes with listings of data on consumer surveys, advertising, and distribution.

4. *Activities and Services of the Federal Government in Distribution Research* (Washington, D. C., U.S. Department of Commerce, 1957, 60 pp., 40¢).

This is a guide to the major statistical studies of the federal government, economic analyses and industry studies, and government research studies.

The data source and frequency of issue are listed for each item. An extensive appendix also lists major statistical publications of the federal government that are useful in marketing, and briefly describes each.

5. *Sources of Information on Foreign Trade Practice* (Washington, D. C., U.S. Department of Commerce, 1959, 47 pp., 25¢).

This pamphlet lists publications dealing with operational aspects of foreign trade, including guides, handbooks, pamphlets, and magazines published by the U.S. Department of Commerce and other government agencies, as well as private organizations.

The subjects covered include market analysis, statistics, regulations, transportation, finance, trade terms, and arbitration. There are lists of Department of Commerce publications on foreign trade, directories useful in foreign trade, and private trade journals.

6. *Statistical Services of the United States Government* (Washington, D. C., Bureau of the Budget, Office of Statistical Standards, revised edition, 1959, 40¢).

Included are a listing and explanation of the principal economic and social statistics compiled by the U.S. government.

An appendix lists a bibliography of the principal government statistical publications, classified by issuing agency.

7. *Statistics Sources,* edited by Paul Wasserman, Eleanor Allen, Anthony Kruzas, and Charlotte Georgi (Detroit, Gale Research Company, 1962, 288 pp., $15.00).

This book is a comprehensive up-to-date compilation of sources of government and nongovernment statistics on industries, products, states and foreign countries, and so on, including a plenitude of data compiled by various U.S. government agencies.

The items are listed alphabetically by subjects. An appendix lists addresses of publishers.

II. SELECTED MARKETING BIBLIOGRAPHIES

In the following section are seven different guides to specified marketing areas.

A. TOPICAL

1. *Sources of Published Advertising Research* (New York, Advertising Research Foundation, Inc., 1960, 66 pp., $20.00; free to members).

This booklet is basically a guide to annotated and unannotated bibliographies, abstracting periodicals, directories of individuals and organizations, and a listing of sources of unpublished information in the fields of marketing and advertising.

While each of these categories is heavily weighted with social science sources, this booklet is an excellent guide to general and specialized marketing bibliographies as well.

2. *A Basic Bibliography on Marketing Research,* by Hugh G. Wales and Robert Ferber (Chicago, American Marketing Association, 1956—revision to be published in late 1962—164 pp., $5.00; $3.00 to members).

The focus here is on the main literature published during the period 1939–1955 relating to marketing research.

Organized by subject areas, the bibliography includes sections on background materials (scientific methods, statistics and probability, maps, and so on); techniques (including survey methods, data processing, attitude and opinion measurement, scaling and motivational research, multivariate analysis, and operations research); areas of research (consumer behavior, sales forecasting, media research, industrial research, and so on); research results; research administration; teaching opportunities; and miscellaneous aspects. The bibliography is indexed by author.

3. *A Bibliography on New Product Planning,* by Donald E. Megathlin and Edward J. Hartnett, Jr. (Chicago, American Marketing Association, 1960, 50 pp., $3.00; $1.50 to members).

Here is a selected annotated bibliography of articles from 44 periodicals, plus a listing of association publications, government sources, and selected texts on the topic.

Product planning and research, marketing research, and marketing strategy are the major organizational headings. A list of case histories is also included.

4. *A Basic Bibliography on Industrial Marketing,* by Thomas A. Staudt and William Lazer (Chicago, American Marketing Association, 1958, 233 pp., $5.00; $3.00 to members).

This is an annotated bibliography covering the significant basic periodical literature on industrial marketing.

It is divided into 13 major categories—marketing management, industrial procurement and buying behavior, product policy and strategy, channels of distribution and marketing institutions, physical distribution, management of the sales force, personal selling, sales service, sales promotion, industrial advertising, pricing and credit management, marketing research, export marketing—and 130 subclassifications.

The bibliography is indexed by author, and also includes industrial marketing case problems selected from 19 casebooks.

5. *A Basic Bibliography of Theory and Research Techniques*

in the Field of Human Motivation (New York, Advertising Research Foundation, Inc., 1956, 117 pp., $5.00; free to members).

This is a review of 518 books, articles, and pamphlets published from 1929 to 1956 on social science techniques (such as attitude measurements, depth interviewing, and projective techniques) which are used to study human motives.

There are concise annotations describing and evaluating each item, all of which are in the ARF library. There is an author index, and an introduction to the specialized terminology.

B. CURRENT BIBLIOGRAPHIES

1. *Marketing Information Guide* (Washington, D. C., U.S. Department of Commerce, issued monthly with semiannual subject index supplements, $2.00 per year, formerly *Distribution Data Guide*).

This guide is a comprehensive annotated bibliography of the most current and valuable marketing statistics, surveys, reports, and published materials from commercial, educational, professional, and government sources.

Monthly listings are by source. Semiannual supplements in June and December index and cross-reference the items of the previous six issues by subject. A supplement released with the March issue lists federal government periodicals useful in marketing. This is the most comprehensive guide to current marketing literature.

2. *Marketing Articles in Review,* a regular feature of the *Journal of Marketing* (Chicago, American Marketing Association, issued quarterly, $8.00 per year).

Selected current articles from approximately 175 business, economic, and social science periodicals of interest to marketing practitioners are listed under 23 topical headings.

A brief but comprehensive summary of each article is included. These summaries are a *must* for anyone who wants to keep up to date on the most important current articles in the marketing field.

III. DIRECTORIES

If you are searching for specific information about organizations and people, you will find these directories helpful in getting a good start.

A. BUSINESS ORGANIZATIONS

1. *Guide to American Directories* (prepared by B. Klein and Company, New York, and published by Prentice-Hall, Inc., Englewood Cliffs, N. J., fifth edition, 1962, 448 pp., $25.00)

This guide describes and tells where to obtain approximately 3,000 U.S. directories of retailers, wholesalers, manufacturers, government agencies, and so on, in over 250 categories.

2. *Reference Book of Dun & Bradstreet* (New York, Dun & Bradstreet, Inc., bimonthly; subscription is on an individual contract basis; price depends on number of issues and individual credit reports furnished).

This reference book gives names, lines of business, Standard Industrial Classification code numbers, and credit and financial ratings of over 3 million business establishments in the United States and Canada.

These are manufacturers, wholesalers, retailers, and other businesses that buy on credit. Each listing contains five or more elements of information. The *Reference Book* is revised every two months. Sectional editions are also available.

3. *Thomas Register of American Manufacturers* (New York, Thomas Publishing Company, issued annually, 5 volumes, $20.00)

Here you will find a listing of manufacturers by product classifications. There are over 75,000 different product classifications listed alphabetically in three volumes. Volume IV is a list of manufacturers and their principal products; leading trade names and trademarks; and commercial organizations. Volume V contains an index to product classifications.

B. ASSOCIATIONS

1. *Encyclopedia of Associations* (Detroit, Gale Research Company, 1961, Volume I, 1,010 pp., $25.00; Volume II, 304 pp., $15.00).

National associations and professional societies of the United States are listed in this guide.

Volume I is arranged in broad sections by type of association. Detailed information is provided on 11,482 organizations. Volume II contains a geographical index and an alphabetical list of chief executives.

The sections include business; agriculture; governmental and public administration; scientific, engineering and technical; educational and cultural; social welfare; health and medical; public affairs; fraternal, foreign interest, nationality and ethnic; religious; horticultural; veterans, hereditary, and patriotic; hobby and avocational; athletic and sports; labor unions; chambers of commerce; and Greek letter societies. They are indexed and cross-referenced by name, key word, and subject.

2. *Directory of National Associations of Businessmen: 1960,* by Jay Judkins (Washington, D. C., U.S. Department of Commerce, 1960, 81 pp., 50¢).

This directory contains data on more than 2,000 national trade and professional associations, including number of members, size of staff, chief executives, and mailing address.

Through the use of a key word index, all associations are classified by industrial groups. In addition, the directory lists 100 societies of engineers and scientists.

C. MARKETING AND ADVERTISING ORGANIZATIONS

1. *Bradford's Directory of Marketing Research Agencies,* by Ernest S. Bradford (New Rochelle, New York, but obtainable from A. Bradford Cadman, 1522 Connecticut Ave., N.W., Washington 6, D. C.; biennial, $12.50).

There are some 300 research firms in the United States and abroad listed in this directory, with a description of the research facilities offered by each agency, the date when the firm was established, information on branch offices, scope of operations (local, national, or international), number of staff and field employees, and in many instances information regarding the education and experience of the principals.

In addition, a statement of the types of research in which the firm specializes or has made some notable contribution is usually included. The agencies are arranged geographically with a finding list and personnel index.

2. *Standard Advertising Register* (New York, National Register Publishing Co., annual, 3 volumes, $100.00 with revision service; also sold separately).

Here is a concise record of over 16,000 advertisers, grouped by line of business, with essential facts concerning them: products, executives, advertising agency, advertising appropriations, types of media used, character of distribution, and other points of value. There is a separate index of 19,000 trade names.

An agency volume lists over 3,600 national advertising agencies, including branches, personnel, and so on, with a listing of accounts for 1,900 of these agencies. There is also a geographical index volume of agencies by state, plus 34 foreign countries.

3. *McKittrick's Directory of Advertisers* (New York, McKittrick's Directory of Advertisers, Inc., annual service, $90.00 for either Classified or Geographical service; $120.00 for combination service).

Over 19,000 national and regional advertisers are listed by 66 classifications in this service's Classified volume, with 90,000 key personnel, 24,000 trade names, 12,000 telephone numbers, agencies, advertisers, budgets, and media.

A Geographical volume gives listings by states and cities.

An Agency List volume, published three times a year, gives 29,000 officers and 60,000 accounts of approximately 3,900 U.S. and Canadian agencies (3,300 agencies list accounts). Weekly News Bulletins and regular, cumulative Supplements are also included in the service.

D. MEDIA

1. *Standard Rate and Data Service* (Skokie, Illinois, Standard Rate and Data Service, Inc., issued monthly, except where noted).

A.B.C. Weekly Newspaper Rates and Data (semiannual)	
	$ 3.00 a year
Business Publication Rates and Data	$32.50 a year
Canadian Media Rates and Data	$12.00 a year
Consumer Magazine and Farm Publication Rates and Data	
	$30.00 a year
Films for Television	$10.00 a year
Network Rates and Data	$ 5.00 a year
Newspaper Rates and Data	$30.00 a year
Spot Radio Rates and Data	$37.50 a year
Spot Television Rates and Data	$32.50 a year
Transportation Advertising Rates and Data	$10.00 a year
Medios Publicitarios Mexicanos (quarterly)	$20.00 a year

These publications provide complete information required by advertisers and agencies in preparing and placing advertising in the respective media.

In addition, a wealth of consumer market data is provided monthly as an integral part of the *Newspaper Rates and Data, Spot Radio Rates and Data,* and *Spot Television Rates and Data* volumes. Current statistical market data for states, counties, metropolitan areas, and cities on population, consumer spendable income, total retail sales, retail store sales by seven principal classifications, farm population, gross farm income, and so on are presented. The *Spot Radio* and *Spot Television* volumes also include estimates of radio and TV households by county.

Each series is correlated with available bench marks from federal government agencies and updated regularly.

State maps employ special media symbols for radio, newspaper, and television to designate the types of local media available in each city. Also, Standard Metropolitan Statistical Areas are identified on the media maps.

2. *N. W. Ayer and Son's Directory of Newspapers and Periodicals* (Philadelphia, N. W. Ayer and Son, Inc., annual, $30.00).

Here is a comprehensive listing of approximately 21,700 newspapers and periodicals published in the United States, its territories, Canada, Bermuda, Panama, and the Philippine Islands. The data for a publication include frequency of issue, date established, mechanical sizes, subscription rates, circulation, and editor's name.

Separate cross-indexed lists are furnished for daily newspapers, weeklies, agricultural publications, general magazines, college, foreign language, fraternal, Negro, religious, and trade publications.

Descriptive data, including population, agricultural production, leading manufactured products, rail and airline service, are furnished for approximately 9,100 publication cities and towns.

3. *Ulrich's Periodicals Directory* (New York, R. R. Bowker Co., ninth edition, 1959, 825 pp., $22.50).

This is an international directory of periodicals, classified by subject matter. Each entry includes the periodical's title, subtitle, date of origin, frequency of publication, subscription price, and information about annuals, supplements, indexing services, and so on. The volume covers more than 17,000 worldwide periodicals and lists more than 300 outstanding newspapers of the world, with circulation figures.

IV. GEOGRAPHICAL MARKET AND POPULATION DATA

An abundance of detailed information is available from the following sources. Only the most comprehensive general sources are included.

Supplementing the governmental censuses listed in this section and in Part V are interim reports issued at regular intervals that contain current statistics. Also, individual chapters from the censuses can be purchased separately (see the *Catalog of United States Census Publications,* listed below, for details).

A. U.S. GOVERNMENT PUBLICATIONS

1. *Catalog of United States Census Publications* (Washington, D. C., U.S. Department of Commerce, Bureau of the Census, issued quarterly and cumulated to the annual volume, $1.25 per year).

The catalog indexes all available Census Bureau data. Its main divisions are: Agriculture, Business, Construction, Foreign Trade, Government, Housing, Industry, Population, Miscellaneous.

This is a prime guide to locating U.S. census information.

2. *Census of Population* (Washington, D. C., U.S. Department of Commerce, Bureau of the Census, 1960, published every ten years).

Volume I — *Characteristics of the Population* — describes and cross-classifies number of inhabitants, general population characteristics, and general social and economic characteristics for each state and several possessions, plus a United States summary.

Volume II — *Subject Reports* — consists of approximately 40 reports devoted essentially to detailed cross-relationships on subjects such as national origin and race, fertility, families, marital status, migration, education, employment, unemployment, occupation, industry, and income for the United States as a whole and by region.

Volume III — *Selected Area Reports* — consists of two reports showing selected characteristics of the population for state economic areas, according to size of place where the individual resides.

Census Tract Reports. These reports present detailed information on both population and housing subjects.

3. *Census of Housing* (Washington, D. C., U.S. Department of Commerce, Bureau of the Census, 1960, published every ten years)

Volume I — *General Characteristics* — varies by area in terms of total information supplied, but includes detailed occupancy characteristics, structural characteristics, equipment and facilities, and financial characteristics for each state and several possessions, plus a United States summary.

Volume II — *Standard Metropolitan Statistical Area Analytical Characteristics* — provides considerable data on SMSAs with 100,000 or more inhabitants, with cross-classifications of housing and of household characteristics for analytical use.

Volume III — *City Block Characteristics* — consists of about 500 reports, one for each city with 50,000 inhabitants or more in the 1950 Census or in a subsequent special census, and for about 250 places which have specially requested inclusion in the block statistics program. Includes conditions and plumbing facilities, average rooms, average contract monthly rent, average value, total population, housing units occupied by nonwhites, and persons per room.

Volume IV — *Components of Change* — describes the physical changes that took place since the 1950 Census for each of the 14 Standard Metropolitan Statistical Areas with over one million inhabitants, and three smaller areas.

Volume V — *Residential Financing* — gives ownership and financial information for each of the 17 SMSAs in Volume IV.

Volume VI — *Rural Housing Analytical Characteristics* — contains analytical tables for about 120 subregions in the United States. Statistics are presented separately for nonfarm and for farm units.

4. *County and City Data Book, 1956* (Washington, D. C., U.S. Department of Commerce, Bureau of the Census, 1957, 565 pp., $4.50).

This book is designed to meet the need for summary statistics for small geographic areas.

It is a supplement to the *Statistical Abstract of the United States,* bringing together 133 items of statistical information for each county, state, division, and region; 99 items for each of 172 Standard Metropolitan Statistical Areas; and 130 items for each of 484 cities having 25,000 or more inhabitants.

Statistics from the most recent Censuses of Agriculture, Business, and Manufactures, and from many other sources, include: agriculture; bank deposits; births, deaths, and marriages; business units; city finances and employment; city school systems; climate; dwelling units; electric bills; hospitals; manufacturers; new dwelling units; population characteristics; retail and wholesale trade; services; and telephones. Selected statistics are given for Congressional districts, and population counts are given for smaller urban places.

B. NONGOVERNMENT GUIDES TO MARKET AND POPULATION DATA

1. *Population and Its Distribution: The United States Markets* (prepared by J. Walter Thompson Company, New York, and published by McGraw-Hill Book Company, Inc., New York, eighth edition, 1961, 489 pp., $24.00).

This is a handbook of marketing facts selected from the 1960 U.S. *Census of Population* and the most recent census data on retail trade.

A map of the United States is included, showing over 3,000 urban and rural counties classified by market size.

There are individual marketing maps for each state, and population and retail trade data for each county and each city or town of 2,500 or more population. The major metropolitan markets are classified into three groups of markets, and the information is summarized for each group. In addition, the book shows number of households and number of farms. This collection of Census Bureau facts is arranged in such a way as to be instantly available to the market researcher and is widely used as an aid in establishing the general dimensions of markets and as a source for bench-mark information.

2. *Rand McNally Commercial Atlas and Marketing Guide* (Chicago, Rand McNally and Company, annual, $55.00, with monthly supplements on business conditions).

Here is a complete single-volume atlas of the world, published in a revised and corrected edition each year and leased on a subscription basis.

This volume contains over 500 pages of statistics and maps covering every part of the world, together with indexes of over 100,000 cities and towns. Marketing tables present more than 40 statistical items for each U.S. county. Population figures appear for over 60,000 U.S. localities, the majority of which are available in no other publication.

3. *Sales Management Survey of Buying Power* (New York, Bill Brothers Publishing Corp., annual; published each May or June; 1962 issue, $5.00, and beginning in 1963, $7.00; annual subscription to magazine, $12.00).

This is an annual reference book that is a prime nongovernment authority for population, income, and retail sales data for cities, counties, metropolitan areas, states, and the United States.

It includes *Sales Management* estimates of population and number of households, per capita and per household income, total retail sales and retail sales in nine major categories, plus *Sales Management* indexes of buying power and sales activity for each locale. "Per cent of U.S." figures make this a valuable tool in assigning territories, determining sales quotas, and making sales forecasts.

4. *Editor & Publisher Market Guide* (New York, Editor & Publisher, annual, $10.00).

This guide contains standardized surveys of over 1,500 daily newspaper markets, with data on transportation, population, automobile registrations, housing, banks, utilities, principal industries, number of wage earners, average weekly wages, and principal paydays.

Also given are retail sales data (number of outlets, total and per household sales by commodity group), location of shopping centers, chain stores, shopping days, and nights open. Newspapers and their circulations and names of advertising contacts are included.

5. *Printers' Ink Guide to Marketing* (New York, Vision, Inc., published each fall; this issue, $2.50; annual subscription to magazine, $6.00).

Qualitative portraits are given of over 100 leading U.S. metropolitan markets, including important local trends and developments, population characteristics, industry and employment, financial activity, sales volume, major media, and outlook for the future.

Special sections are also included on farm, leisure, military, Negro, and religious markets; and also business and industrial markets, and international markets. Finally, there is a review of media expenditures by leading advertisers.

6. *Advertising Age Market Data Issue* (Chicago, Advertising Publications, Inc., annual, published in April or May of each year; this issue, $1.00; annual subscription to magazine, $5.00)

Here you will find a comprehensive source guide to hundreds of privately published pieces of data on national markets, regional and local markets, industries, products, and so forth offered by media, trade associations, and other sources.

The 1962 issue contained over 1,900 items. Most of the items are available without charge, and a convenient checkoff order form is provided.

V. ECONOMIC AND BUSINESS STATISTICS

These sources are helpful for business forecasting and market analysis. There are also other volumes of censuses and commodity statistics, including the *Census of Agriculture*, the *Census of Governments*, and the *Census of Mineral Industries*, as well as the *Agricultural Yearbook*, and the *Minerals Yearbook* — all available from the Superintendent of Documents, Washington 25, D. C.

A. COMPENDIUMS OF ECONOMIC STATISTICS

1. *Statistical Abstract of the United States* (Washington, D. C., U.S. Department of Commerce, Bureau of the Census, annual, $3.50).

This volume is a standard summary of statistics on the social, political, and economic organization of the United States, derived from public and private sources.

The book is designed to fulfill two functions: to serve as a convenient volume for statistical reference, and to serve as a guide to other statistical publications and sources. The latter function is served by the introductory text to each section, the source notes appearing below each table, and a bibliography of sources. Emphasis is primarily on national data.

2. *Historical Statistics of the United States: Colonial Times to*

1957 (Washington, D. C., U.S. Department of Commerce, Bureau ·of the Census, 1960, 789 pp., $6.00).

This historical supplement to the *Statistical Abstract of the United States* covers approximately 3,000 statistical time series of various periods from 1789 to 1957.

The material reflects economic, social, and political aspects of U.S. development since the federal government was formally established. Precise source notes indicate where further data can be found.

3. *Survey of Current Business* (Washington, D. C., U.S. Department of Commerce, Office of Business Economics, monthly, $4.00 per year including weekly statistical supplement; single copy, 30¢).

Some 2,600 different statistical series are brought up to date in each issue under the headings of: general business indicators, commodity prices, construction and real estate, domestic trade, employment and population, finance, international transactions of the United States, transportation and communications, plus several headings covering specific raw material industries.

Each issue also includes a review, by the Office of Business Economics, of the current business situation, several feature articles, and brief analyses of significant economic developments.

4. *Business Statistics* (Washington, D. C., U.S. Department of Commerce, Office of Business Economics, biennial — in odd years — $2.00).

This is a comprehensive compilation of historical series, going back 30 years and covering business and market indicators corresponding to those in the *Survey of Current Business.*

5. *Monthly Labor Review* (Washington, D. C., U.S. Department of Labor, Bureau of Labor Statistics, monthly, $6.25 a year; single copy, 55¢).

Information is given on employment, wages, labor turnover, price indexes, and various other current labor statistics.

Recent labor events, book reviews, significant decisions in labor cases, and developments in industrial relations are also discussed.

An annual supplement published in December offers greater detail and historical data.

6. *Federal Reserve Bulletin* (Washington, D. C., Board of

Governors of the Federal Reserve System, monthly, $6.00 per year; single copy, 60¢).

This is a source of statistics on banking, money rates and security markets, finance (government, business, real estate, and consumer), flow of funds, savings, national product and income, production, department store sales, prices, and international trade and finance.

Included is a special national summary of business conditions.

7. *The Economic Almanac* (New York, National Industrial Conference Board, in cooperation with *Newsweek*, biennial, $7.95).

Here is a handbook of useful facts about business, labor, and government in compact and convenient handbook form.

Such items as population, resources, agriculture, prices, banking and finance, public and private debt, communications, transportation, trade, electricity and gas, construction, mining, manufacturing, industry statistics, consumption, savings, and national income are included.

B. INDUSTRY STATISTICS

1. *Census of Business* (Washington, D. C., U.S. Department of Commerce, Bureau of the Census, 1958, 6 parts, compiled every several years).

Volumes I, III, and V provide summary statistics for retail trade, wholesale trade, and selected service trades respectively by geographic areas, plus U.S. summaries. Volumes II, IV, and VI present area statistics by kind of business for counties, cities, and standard metropolitan statistical areas within each state, the District of Columbia, Guam, and the Virgin Islands.

Retail store data are classified by 99 kinds of business groups, number of stores operated, total sales, sales by commodity, employment, legal form of organization.

Wholesalers are classified by 172 kinds of business groups, the functions that they perform, warehouse space, sales volume, and expenses. Data are furnished for each county, and for cities with over 2,500 population.

The service trade census provides data on receipts, employment, number of units operated, and legal form of organization.

Special chapters list data on hotels and motels, laundry and cleaning establishments, and motion picture theaters.

2. *Census of Manufactures* (Washington, D. C., U.S. Department of Commerce, Bureau of the Census, 1958, compiled every several years).

Listed here are geographical and industry data on manufacturers along the following lines: number of establishments, quantities of specific products produced, costs of materials, values added, and wages. Approximately 450 industries and 6,500 commodities are classified.

3. *County Business Patterns* (Washington, D. C., U.S. Department of Commerce, Bureau of the Census and U.S. Department of Health, Education and Welfare, Bureau of Old Age and Survivor's Insurance, issued periodically, $20.00 for complete 1959 set).

This volume shows state and county locations of over 3,000,-000 reporting business units by more than 1,000 kinds of classifications.

Statistics are given on number of business units, employment, and payroll figures. The current edition, published in 1961, covers the first quarter of 1959. Ten parts cover a United States summary and nine geographical divisions.

4. *Media-Market Planning Guide* (Chicago, Advertising Publications, Inc., quarterly; per issue, $5.00, annually, $10.00).

This quarterly supersedes the annual *Market Data and Directory* number published by *Industrial Marketing*. It provides basic sales, media, and trade association facts on 67 industrial markets.

For each industry this guide provides basic sales statistics; tells what and how the market buys; lists sources of available market data; lists trade associations within the industry; and provides advertising rates, mechanical specifications, and circulation figures for trade publications within the industry.

EVALUATION

In many cases the individual using the sources we have mentioned will go on to other sources of data. What standards should he use in appraising the value of information that he finds? We recommend the following standards (all of which we used in making up the lists in this article):

(1) The character of the organization supplying the data should be considered.

(2) The organization's experience, personnel, finances for research, freedom from bias or personal interest, and standards should be considered.

(3) The authority under which the data were gathered and the predetermined standards set for collection of the information are important considerations.

(4) The units in which the data are expressed must be sufficiently defined. Such sample concepts as "house," "consumer," and "automobile" are subject to varying definitions. Composite units are particularly troublesome when comparing different sources.

(5) In every case, a check should be made to determine if more recent data are available from the same or other sources. Figures, sometimes even historical data, are revised as more information is gathered.

Chapter Ten

AUTOMATIC METHODS OF INFORMATION STORAGE AND RETRIEVAL

C. WILLIAM SALM*

JOHN DEARDEN HAS CLASSIFIED information systems into three major types—existing in nearly all companies—and an indefinite number of minor types. The major types—financial, personnel, and logistics information systems—deal mainly with historical *internal* data. Two of the minor systems deal with historical *external* data—the type which we are concerned with in this treatise—about which Mr. Dearden states:

Marketing Information. One of the most important information systems to many businesses is marketing information. The characteristics of this kind of system will differ widely among companies. For example, some systems maintain a great deal of data about such things as competitive actions, customer profiles, and advertising effectiveness; other systems maintain only in-

*The author attended Brooklyn College and Columbia University. As a research chemist, he gained firsthand knowledge of the growing problem of scientific information retrieval, after which he worked on the Air Force's SAGE project—the most complex of on-line information systems. Further computer applications in advertising, marketing and aerospace, plus consulting on the planning and development of computer installations, has given Mr. Salm a keen sense of the ingredients necessary for efficient systems management and operation of data-processing centers. Now located in California's San Fernando Valley, Mr. Salm is currently a consultant on data-processing management and techniques for several private and government organizations.

formation about sales records. A marketing information system tends to be handled completely within the marketing function and usually presents no problem of coordination with the other systems.

Research and Development. Many companies have systems for exchanging information on the results of research findings. Other companies set up systems to examine and store the literature on relevant research.[1]

The telescoping of product cycles, along with narrowing profit margins, keener competition, and the evolution of the orientation of marketing from distribution of what the factory produced to fulfillment of consumer desires, has made the area of marketing information quite critical to the business organization. Information which can help determine, as early as possible, return on investment and various expected costs have become, in turn, critical. In addition to the dollar value of adequate and timely information, the overhead cost of inadequate and redundant information processing cannot be ignored. No introduction is needed to the avalanche of technical literature falling upon research and development (R&D) personnel seeking to make technological advancements. Closing the gap between the originators of such literature and the eventual users is the prime target for information technology.

The magnitude—if not the importance—of the problem of information collection, storage, retrieval, presentation and/or dissemination is in direct proportion to the volume of data involved. Therefore, if the problem has motivated the reader to study this far, a look at some of the automatic methods of *information storage and retrieval* (ISAR) will be worthwhile.

Many organizations have been retrieving information mechanically or automatically for several years, under the name of library services, report searching or miscellaneous

---

[1]Dearden, John, "How to Organize Information Systems," *Harvard Business Review,* Vol. 43, No. 2, March-April, 1965.

processing, using everything from basic card-processing machines to small and even large-scale computers. When considering any kind of general purpose or specialized mechanical, electromechanical or electronic equipment, however, cost and efficiency of operation are usually of major concern. The approach is basically the same as when considering the same aspects of manual systems or methods. A balance or trade-off is sought, evaluating such factors as how soon the system is needed, speed of operation and reliability required, available man-power, facilities and other resources, training required, expansion possibilities, remote collection and/or dissemination required, expected life of equipment and stored data, government specifications and—depending on the aforementioned—cost of developing and operating the system.

ADVANTAGES OF AUTOMATED FILES

The major advantages of a fully automated information file are as follows:

1. *Information.* The facility for automatic indexing allows an infinite flexibility in categorizing to enable a requestor to retrieve all the information he requires, with a minimum of extraneous material included.
2. *Filing.* The actual filing may be accomplished with electronic speeds.
3. *Location.* Whereas a conventional file is usually stationary due to its bulk, an automated file, while also stationary, may be accessed from remote points by electronic methods.
4. *Bulk.* With respect to size, magnetic or micropictorial storage of data results in an appreciable decrease in the amount of space required for a given amount of data.
5. *Retrieval.* The time and effort required for a complete search for all file items relating to an area of interest is reduced from the prohibitive to almost negligible.
6. *Parallel Searches.* More than one automatic file search may proceed simultaneously, while two or more people manually searching through a conventional file may well hinder one another.

7. *Parallel Accessibility.* The same file item is accessible to more than one simultaneous search.

8. *Out-of-File.* Delays due to out-of-file conditions occur when a document has been removed from a conventional file for review or reproduction. As the data never leaves the automated file, these delays are eliminated.

9. *Loss.* Chance of loss when a document is removed from a conventional file is nonexistent in automated files.

10. *Reproduction.* When a copy of a file item is desired, reproduction may be accomplished automatically and immediately.

11. *Reorganization.* The entire file may be automatically reorganized, when necessary, with little or no delay to the users.

12. *Updating.* Additions, deletions, and changes may be accomplished with great facility.

13. *Economy.* In addition to the above economies, many recording mediums, being reusable, are not discarded when a file item is eliminated or replaced. New file items are merely recorded over the old information, eliminating material waste.

14. *Up-to-Date.* The most modern concepts of library science are combined with the current techniques of machine processing.

15. *Expandable.* Operable on current card-processing equipment, with ability for expansion to computer-based systems.

16. *Independent.* In conventional corporate libraries the success of a search often depends on the memory of the technical librarian, when available. If the librarian is not available, the search may be impossible.

Although the increasing size of libraries and data files are a major reason for looking toward automation, the increase in the complexity of the material contained in corporate libraries is presenting an even greater problem. For an automated system, however, increased complexity presents no real problem.

CODING

With respect to costs, the amount of data which the equipment may retain at one time and the rate at which data may be put through the system are major determinants. In this regard, a method of coding the data to reduce the size and speed of the equipment needed must be carefully selected. Encoding, of course, will require eventual decoding or retranslation back to the original information represented by the code. Most often, this may be done automatically within the system, producing directly readable output. As early in the system as possible, the information should be converted into machine-readable form. In many cases, this may be obtained as a by-product of some other operation. For example, the Friden Flexowriter can produce a punched paper tape while typing hard copy. Optical scanning equipment or magnetic ink character recognition (MICR) apparatus can read a number of typed fonts directly. Punched paper tape may be converted automatically to standard punched cards or may be used directly as input to a variety of equipment. The array of direct reading apparatus is advancing far beyond what was thought possible only a few years ago.

Most naturally, encoding establishes the ability for logical classification of data to amplify and augment its basic meaning. The development of a good coding structure is a complicated task which is usually taken too lightly and is assigned too insignificant a position among the many tasks required to implement an automated system. Although those involved are aware that the coding structure has an effect on the efficiency of the operation, the importance of the code is not fully realized. Therefore, before creation of a code, the complete problem should be analyzed and all alternatives examined, to allow the resulting code to be tailored to fit the objectives of the particular organization, rather than just be workable. Some factors to be considered are; the ease of manually assigning and identifying the code, its adequacy for the machine operations anticipated, and its flexibility to allow for increased data volume and/or new categories. All these factors must be balanced against a minimum code size for the highest operational efficiency. Actual coding methods being beyond the scope of this text, the reader is referred to the bibliography following this chapter for a reference on such methods.

INDEXING

Before material may be coded it must be indexed for ease of retrieval. Such indexing is quite different in principle from that used to classify books in the average library,[2] and is designed with an eye toward infinite expansion of the number of categories, as well as increased volume. Thus, the approach to indexing for automatic retrieval departs appreciably from standard concepts, regarding its structure. A popular indexing method, well adapted to automatic equipment, is the use of keywords to identify the salient items of a unit of information, or document, included in the library of stored material.[3] Inquiries to a keyword-indexed file are made by supplying the keyword or group of keywords which specify the subject matter desired. Any documents classified under these keywords will be retrieved, regardless of how many other keywords the same material may be classified under.

The first step in designing an automatic ISAR system is the design of a keyword dictionary, listing all significant

---

[2] The common subject classifications used in libraries limit communication between the author and the user, being dependent on the librarian's ingenuity and the ability of the title to reflect the contents of the document. Keyboard coordinate indexing, on the other hand, allows the information itself to determine the classification to be assigned, depending only on the proper development of a keyword dictionary. An early use of such indexing in a punched card system was by the Linde Company Research Laboratory, for internal progress and technical reports.

[3] The glossary at the end of the chapter defines a number of common words, according to their use in ISAR technology.

words or word groups occurring in the titles, abstracts or texts of documents, significance being defined as giving an indication of the subject matter involved. As can be imagined, preparation of such a list could be an awesome task and yet not include many significant words which could occur in new material received. However, automatic means may be applied here to help develop an automatic system. When information will be indexed by title only, preparation of the dictionary becomes a relatively simple matter of ignoring common title words, such as *a, and, but, for, to,* and certain special words which are common to the functions which the system will serve.[4] When indexing will be based on the contents of the document abstract or the text itself, statistical methods may be performed automatically which can determine significance by frequency of occurrence of words or word groups within the abstract or text, again ignoring common words, regardless of their frequency. Careful analysis and guidance in the creation of such a dictionary will result in easier indexing and more compact, yet more inclusive, queries to the file. The ability to use a variable number of keywords in a query is referred to a multidimensional or multiaspect indexing. Although its use enables much simpler categorizing of material than the choice of a single all-inclusive classification for each document, and increases the chance of retrieving the proper information, the task of training personnel to aid inquirers in the preparation of queries must not be underestimated. The value of any system is only as good as the data entered into it.

A typical file might consist of the titles and location of marketing reference material, such as books and articles, each associated with its corresponding keywords. To inquire about documents on resale price maintenance contracts in the California television industry, one might use in his query the

---

[4]One method of indexing by titles only produces *permuted indexes* and is discussed in a preceding chapter. Such an index is used by Chemical Abstracts Service, publisher of *Chemical Titles.*

keywords; *resale price maintenance, television,* and *Califor-*
nia. In addition, the keywords *fair-trade, appliances,* and
electronics might be included to assure the retrieval of all
desired information. All keywords used in the query would
have to appear in the system dictionary to be carried as keywords in the file. When indexing is done automatically, the
dictionary words are prepared as a by-product. Words of
similar meaning may be equated in either the automatically
or manually prepared dictionaries, to reduce the query words
required for adequate retrieval. In the above example, *resale*
price maintenance and *fair-trade* may have been so equated.

A less flexible file might consist of personnel information
in a particular format, with words describing; color of hair,
age, country of birth, occupation, and sex, along with identification data. These descriptions are not truly keywords in
the sense that has been previously described, since each data
record would have the same set of characteristics described.
Selective retrieval could still be achieved by requesting a list
of all individuals with, for example *brown, male,* and *ma-*
chinist keywords. Notice that the keyword *brown* alone
would be ambiguous if color of eyes was also a keyword. In
this case *brown hair* would be the keyword requested. If desired, the system could be designed to retrieve all records
with at least two of the keywords specified. In almost all cases,
the query must state the keywords exactly as they are described in the index or dictionary, as only the most sophisticated of systems can "recognize" even close appropriations.

A still more precise method is the use of keyword groups,
allowing more detail on the subject matter, yet preventing
extraneous retrievals. For example, if the following were
used to specify document #40;

Keyword Group 40-1: Steel; Carbon; Uncombined; Strength;
Measurement; Research.
Keyword Group 40-2: Steel; Strength; Markets; Sales; Speci-
fications.

An inquiry concerning research on the effect of uncombined
carbon on the strength of steel, or concerning the markets

for steel of different strength specifications, might retrieve the record on document #40 in both instances. However, a query regarding correlations between the amount of carbon in steel and steel sales volumes would not produce this document, as the keywords of the query would not be represented within one keyword group. In all of the above examples the actual documents need not have been stored with the index file, but could have been stored elsewhere, leaving the index file like a library catalog. After determination of the documents desired, they may be fetched elsewhere.

The indexing of keyword groups from the text of documents is a tedious task which must be preceded by careful research into the expected nature of the texts to be encountered. When the variety of information to be incorporated into the same library of data expands, the project can be enormous. However, each of the steps listed below may be eventually handled by fully automatic means. Most manufacturers of automatic data-processing (ADP) equipment are continuously advancing the state of the art in this regard. Even actual language translation by computers is well on its way.

ESSENTIALS OF AN ISAR SYSTEM

1. *Dictionary*. Creation of a dictionary of keyword groups and keywords for the significant elements of each document.
2. *Indexing*. Creation and updating of indexes.
   a) Creation of keyword profiles for new documents entering the system and changing or deleting existing profiles.
   b) Creation and updating of keyword interest profiles for individuals or project groups.
3. *Storage*. Creation and storage of an abstract or storage of the title or entire text of each document.
4. *Dissemination*. Reproduction and/or selective dissemination, or selective notification of document availability, to interested parties, by matching document and interest profiles.

5. *Retrieving.* Preparation of inquiries, as desired, and processing of inquiries for retrieval of document titles, abstracts, or texts.

FILE LOOKUP VS. FILE SEARCH

Although the previous discussion has been with reference to automatic methods, the indexing methods described could be used manually with as much success, high volume or speed required being the only real deterrents to continued manual application.

More important in the design of automatic systems is the determination of the retrieval method to be used. Two major methods are look-up and search. Again, a trade-off must be determined, weighing such factors as volume of material to be indexed and filed, type of material stored, frequency of inquiries, frequency of changes, additions and deletions to the file, and the speed and precision desired. While these factors will differ for each situation, a generalization may be made that a relatively static file may be designed in a way to allow relatively faster access for inquiries. On the other hand, if the volume and/or frequency of changes to the file is high (but not necessarily higher), compared to the number of inquiries to be made, it may be more efficient to design the file to allow for easier updating, even though this usually makes the query procedure less efficient.

FILE LOOKUP

Lookup files are basically composed of a list of keywords. Associated with each keyword are the document numbers indexed under that keyword. For example, a simple system composed of only 10 keywords may be indexed by using Figure 10-1.

With each new addition to the file, a document number is assigned, and that number is added to the list under each

FIGURE 10–1

DOCUMENT NUMBER	KEYWORDS									
	A	B	C	D	E	F	G	H	I	J
1	1		1	1						
2	2				2	2	2			
3			3		3		3			
4					4	4	4			
5	5	5	5	5		5				
6			6					6		6
7			7	7						

appropriate keyword. Queries refer to the selected keywords.[5] For example, a request for a list of document numbers with the following keywords; E, F, and G, would retrieve document numbers 2 and 4. In operation, the document numbers under keyword E (2, 3, and 4) would be compared to the document numbers under keyword F (2, 4, and 5). Only the matching document numbers (2 and 4) would be compared to the document numbers under keyword G. After the document numbers for all selected keywords have been matched, those document numbers common to all are produced in answer to the query. If document numbers under any three out of the four selected keywords are requested, the procedure is somewhat more complicated. Some systems are designed to allow selection of certain keywords as mandatory and others as optional, with respect to the requested keywords. For example, the request statement, "Select all document numbers which correspond to keywords A and B, and to any two of the keywords C, D, and F," would retrieve only document number 5.

The keyword records should be stored in some organized manner for simpler or faster access. For example, they may be arranged sequentially or in order of descending frequency of occurrence. The same principle holds true for the document numbers within each keyword record.

---

[5]This is basically the Uniterm System, developed by Documentation Inc., and generally referred to as coordinate indexing.

FILE SEARCH

As opposed to a file organized for lookup, a search-organized file is grouped by document numbers, with a list of keywords corresponding to each document. The table shown in Figure 10–1 may also be used for indexing such a file. For each addition to the file a single record need be added, containing the document number and associated keywords. This is a simpler means of updating than making an addition to a number of records, as in a lookup file. However, as mentioned in the discussion of file lookup vs. file search, this saving in indexing is offset by a less efficient inquiry procedure.

A query to a search file is processed by examining the entire file. The list of keywords under each document number is compared to the specified keyword combination, and the document numbers corresponding to the successful comparisons are retrieved. The document numbers need not be in any specified order, as all document records are always examined.

Punched Card Methods Using the Lookup Principle

Peek-a-boo

If the number of documents to be indexed is not excessive, this manual method may be quite adequate. The basic recording unit is a card with holes punched to represent document numbers, each document number having an assigned location on the card. For example, if up to 960 or 1,080 documents are to be indexed, the standard 80 or 90-column punched cards used for electronic accounting machines and computers may be utilized. The 12 horizontal rows of 80 or 90 vertical columns each allow 960 or 1,080 locations to be assigned to document numbers. Such cards may be purchased with "push-out" perforations or may be punched mechanically. For each keyword in the dictionary, one card is prepared with a hole punched for each document number indexed under that keyword. When an inquiry is made, the cards for the selected keywords are pulled from the deck and examined for holes common to all selected cards. (Thus, the term peek-a-boo.) From the location of the common holes, the document numbers can be determined. If more documents are to be indexed than there are hole locations on the cards, additional sets of keyword decks may be prepared, for the same set of keywords, but with the additional set(s) of document numbers. Each such deck is examined separately. For up to 10,000 documents per card, Royal McBee's Keydex system is a manual application of the peek-a-boo principle easily adaptable to most files.

Collator

For mechanical retrieval of document numbers, punch cards may be prepared slightly differently. To make use of machines of the collator type, each document number within a keyword group is placed on a separate card. Thus, for each keyword, a deck of cards is prepared. In response to an inquiry, only the decks corresponding to the related keywords are processed. By having each document number on a separate card, the matching document numbers between two of the selected keyword decks may be mechanically separated, or selected, from one of the two decks. The separated cards are then matched to the third keyword deck, thereby eliminating still more cards. The process is repeated, comparing the diminishing set of selected cards with each keyword deck, until all decks have been compared. The remaining selected cards represent document numbers common to all of the keyword decks corresponding to the request. The deck used for separation must, of course, be reconstructed after the selected cards have been listed or otherwise used to answer the query. If the documents thus determined are to be reproduced for the requestor, the selected cards may be used to automatically initiate the reproduction of the proper documents.

IBM Special Index Analyzer

The entire manual/collator process described above may be carried out automatically on the same cards by the IBM Special Index Analyzer. All of the selected keyword decks are placed together in the card feed of this machine. As all decks remain intact, there is no need to reconstruct the one deck which is progressively separated by the collator process. Also, more than one document number may be contained on each card, considerably reducing the size of the card decks required. New entries and changes to the file, and preparation of a list of documents corresponding to the selected document numbers, are also facilitated by this machine. However, as a specialized piece of equipment, it does not have the general purpose usefulness of a collator.

Punched Card Methods Using the Search Principle

Card Sorter

As mentioned in the section on "File Search," all records in the file are examined for each inquiry or batch of inquiries. For use with a general purpose card sorter, the file consists of one card per document, with each punch location on the card representing a keyword. By scanning the entire file, all cards with a particular keyword location punched may be selected. The selected cards are scanned again for the second keyword, etc., until the final selected cards are all those containing a punch for each specified keyword.

Row-by-Row Scanning

Several general purpose card machines, for example, the IBM 101 Electronic Statistical machine and the IBM 108 Card Proving machine, can scan punched cards by horizontal rows. This feature lends itself to unlimited possibilities for file arrangement and retrieval. For example, the first portion of each row may contain the name of a keyword group, such as that mentioned in the section on indexing. The remainder of the row may contain the keywords contained in that group. Abbreviation of keywords and keyword group names enables a sufficient amount of letters to appear in each horizontal row for most purposes. Various types of coding can accomplish this. Using more than one card per document can expand either the number of keyword groups used or the number of keywords per group. The variations depend on the ingenuity of the file designer.

Miscellaneous Equipment

Still other equipment, such as the IBM Universal Card Scanner, enables separation of cards into many categories in a single pass, according to the whim of the user. Although pure punched card methods are limited, when compared to computerized systems, cards still serve as the base of data entry into most computer systems. Therefore, development and operation of a small-scale card system, initially, can supply useful experience with indexing and may give a much clearer idea of what might be desired in a larger system than any other means. The operation of a small-scale system, such as detailed by William F. Williams, should be enlightening to those interested in establishing such a system.[6]

COMPUTERS

Lookup and search techniques with computers may be of infinite variation. Their large memory capacity and assortment of input and output media allow almost any approach to the problem and very high levels of sophistication.

---

[6]Williams, William F., "The First Step to IR," *Business Automation,* January, 1964.

With random access equipment, such as disk file ("juke-box") storage, single queries can be efficiently processed and information retrieved almost instantaneously. With magnetic tapes, an unlimited storage capacity exists. However, the longer the tape files, the more queries should be batched together for efficient processing, since the data on tape must be passed serially to reach the required information. Depending on the internal memory capacity of the computer, as each record of data is passed it can be compared to all the queries of the current batch being processed.

The arrangement of data files for use with computers is an important factor in the efficiency of the system. There are three basic classes of data storage, namely:

1. *Random Access Storage:* typified by the internal magnetic core memory, where all storage locations are equally accessible. This type of storage may be accessed most rapidly, but may be limited, with respect to capacity, as it must contain the instructions for the computer program as well as the data being retrieved.

2. *Cyclic Access Storage:* typified by the internal rotating magnetic drum or external rotating disk, where accessibility is periodic. This is an intermediate classification between random storage and serial storage. The internal rotating drum is not quite as randomly accessible as the internal core storage, since data being accessed must rotate to the pick-up point before it may "read." On the other hand, disk storage is usually referred to as "random storage." However, it is random only with respect to other external storage media.

3. *Serial Access Storage:* typified by magnetic tape or punched cards, where accessibility is dependent on the physical position of the data within the file.
   The card and tape records have no "address" which can be directly referred to. Therefore, each record, from the beginning of the file, must be examined and passed before reaching the desired record. Certain computers, however, have the ability to skip entire groups of tape records.

MICROFILM

An important approach to the intelligence problem is the storage and retrieval of information in pictorial form. The most widely used image recording medium is microfilm, which retains reduced images on photographic film. The common reduction factors of from 10:1 to 40:1 represent an appreciable saving of space. (The reduction factor chosen depends on the resolution required. For example, the fine lines of a drawing may be lost by reducing the drawing to microfilm by a large reduction factor, and then enlarging the image back to the original size.) Space saving, in turn, enables automatic retrieval equipment to pass many more frames per second in search of the desired information, thereby decreasing the access time required, per image, as well as increasing the storage capacity of the system.

The access speed of roll microfilm is hampered by the necessity of passing through the length of a roll of film in searching for a specific image or set of images. To reduce or eliminate this limitation, many methods of "unitized" or discrete record film files have been developed, using individual images or groups of images, physically separated from one another. Single images on unmounted film "chips" and groups of images on strips of film have been successfully employed. A popular method is the use of "microfiche"—a transparent sheet of film on which micro-images are recorded in several rows. An example is the Eastman Minicard system, on which twelve images are recorded per card at a reduction ratio of 60:1.

While most microfilm is of standard silver halide-on-cellulose composition and is exposed and developed in a conventional manner, various other types of emulsions have been developed to enable automatic exposing, developing and filing of photo-images. Some examples are General Electric's thermoplastic recording, photochromic recording, and Kalvar—an emulsion used by IBM's Walnut system, introduced in 1961 and capable of storing 99 million images on film strips. The Kalvar emulsion is exposed by ultraviolet light and developed by heat, eliminating the need for liquid processing and, thereby, facilitating automatic manipulation.

By optically encoding a segment of the film corresponding to each micro-image, the means is established for automatically scanning the various types of films and selectively displaying and/or reproducing the images. With such encoding, indexing methods similar to those described for punched cards may be utilized. The Recordak Corporation's Miracode system uses such indexing to automatically retrieve an image from roll microfilm and display it on a screen for viewing. If a hard (permanent) copy is then desired, the press of a button will produce one. Encoding may also be combined with pictorial data by the use of the popular aperture cards. Aperture cards are standard punched cards with rectangular windows, into which film frames have been sealed, see Figure 10–2.

FIGURE 10–2

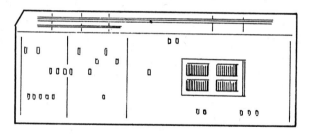

One or several pages of information may be recorded in the photo-image slot, while additional data may be punched, as well as printed, on the remainder of the card. The punched data may be used to automatically sort, store, and selectively retrieve the card, as a discrete unit, from which the image may be displayed and/or reproduced.

A combination processor and reader-printer system by ITEK Business Products can handle roll film, aperture cards, acetate-jacketed single frames or strips, or microfiche. The

Videofile System from Ampex Corporation stores information on magnetic video tape for fully automated high-speed handling and greater flexibility in the compression and updating of stored data. The use of combination search and display systems, such as those described, may limit the flexibility which may be obtained by separating sophisticated search techniques from specialized retrieval apparatus for obtaining the actual documents. On the other hand, a computer may be combined with optical reading apparatus to store and retrieve pages printed in particular fonts. The computer's character-by-character handling of each document page may seem more cumbersome than pictorial representation, but the increased flexibility it allows for manipulation and indexing may prove to be far more efficient and effective for the particular problem at hand.

The National Microfilm Association publishes a book detailing the specifications of hundreds of currently available systems and apparatus, including their prices.[7] It can be seen from this book that small businesses may reap the advantages of the technological breakthroughs already made by the larger organizations—and at costs measuring only in hundreds of dollars. There are usually smaller manual versions of the larger systems, which compete favorably in access time due to the smaller file volumes involved, yet still are capable of storing millions of words.

Don Jenkins, of Magnavox Corp., recently published a rundown of commercially available systems utilizing the roll microfilm concept.[8] Most other current and past issues of *Systems* magazine contain at least one article on microfilm systems. A review of these issues would give any reader an education in the field of ISAR as it pertains to microfilm.[9]

---

[7]Ballou, Hubbard W., *Guide to Microreproduction Equipment* (2d ed.; Annapolis, Maryland: National Microfilm Association, 1962).

[8]Jenkins, Don, "Automated Document Information Storage and Retrieval, Part II," *Systems,* July-August, 1964, and September-October, 1964.

[9]*Systems* is published by United Business Publications, Inc., 200 Madison Ave., New York.

Also, the annual proceedings of the National Microfilm Association are an excellent source for such information.

There are numerous semiautomatic and manual storage and retrieval systems, such as ingeniously organized card catalogues and lists and a variety of copying equipment which may turn out to be the most appropriate means of handling the problem at hand. None of these should be overlooked, even when more sophisticated systems are contemplated, as the smaller items quite often are a useful adjunct.

THE BEST APPROACH

The constantly increasing capacities of equipment and newly developed techniques are continually expanding the horizons of information technology. Almost any current problem in this field may be solved by an efficient solution tailored to the particular situation. Only the effort expended, support received, and imagination of the user can limit the variations developed. To aid in this effort one U.S. firm of approximately 500 employees was conceived for, and is devoted to, research in documentation technology and its application to particular problems.

Development of independent information systems, redundantly using similar input data, has been recognized as an inefficient method of increasing the utilization of ADP equipment. Thus, integrated data processing (IDP) has become the favored direction to follow. Truly total systems, however—a still more advanced concept, leaving little but policy making to human management—is still quite a long way off, in the opinion of this writer, as the state of the art, systems-wise, is not yet equal to the task. More knowledge in the field of management science and the total interrelationships of individuals to organizations and organizations to their various publics (government, employees, community, customers, and others) must first be uncovered.

Yet, if management would isolate and recognize the costs of inadequate handling of information in terms of lost sales, higher operating costs, and other contributing factors to tighter profit margins, its task would be clear. The job of such cost isolation, then, should be undertaken as the first step in deciding the potential gain that may be had from further investigation into intelligence and other information systems.

The extent of the problem should not discourage any potential user. Much information may be obtained from any manufacturer of ADP equipment. The investigator will be surprised at the variety and capacities of current equipment at his disposal. Manufacturer's representatives may aid the user in developing a system tailored to his needs.

The most advisable approach, however, is to employ the services of a competent data-processing consultant or other independent individual to prepare the specifications of the problem at hand and to solicit bids, based on such specifications, to a number of the most likely manufacturers of the type of equipment desired. The proposals may then be discussed with each manufacturer, in order to determine the most appropriate method to be employed. The actual purchase of equipment may not prove necessary, as the population of service centers renting equipment on an hourly or contract basis is increasing rapidly. Such centers are already adequate for the needs of most part-time users.

In addition, professional societies and government agencies may be a source of additional information. In certain cases, perhaps an abstracting service will prove to be the most economical solution to the problem.

The array of methods and equipment, however, is staggering and apt to confuse even one experienced in automated methods for conventional data processing. In addition, the uniqueness of each situation, with respect to its needs, the best methodology to fulfill them, and the resultant choice of equipment or procedures, makes it quite difficult to accept as pat answers the "packaged" solutions offered or even tailored by most manufacturers. This may, in part, be overcome by the development of a table, such as the following:

Name of Equipment	Manu- facturer	Storage Capacity	Cost Per 1,000 documents	Speed of Retrieval	Automatic Reproduction

Many more columns may be added, according to the items of importance for the particular application. Relative values may also be assigned to each feature for each entry made, to assist in arriving at the best conclusion. Collection of such data, however, is not a simple matter, as manufacturers' literature quote specifications developed from a variety of bases, which must be equated. All of these factors point to the need for enlisting the aid of an individual well versed in the application of such equipment to information storage and retrieval. If the volume of information to be collected and stored, and the frequency of information requests, indicates investigation into an ISAR system, there will usually be a device and system which are both adequate and economical for the business volume involved and budget available for such purposes. All that remains is a disciplined and knowledgeable approach to the task of defining and selecting this device.

Aside from providing proper guidance in the choice of a system and the required equipment, an experienced hand can spell the difference between a well-designed system which works well and an equally sophisticated system which is far from successful at solving the real problem. The experienced individual can separate what seems to be the problem from the actual causes to be attacked. In addition, knowledge of the traits of document screeners, library users, and possible pitfalls enables one versed in the subject to establish the proper operating relationships which spell the difference between the ability of a system to satisfy and its failure.

THE HUMAN ELEMENT

Communication is a human problem. So information retrieval, as a solution to a specialized phase of that problem, has to be in human terms. Every system has to be tailored, first, to the people who use it. The results, second, have to be helpful and useful to the people on the receiving end. "We are dealing with knowledge," an IBM executive recently observed of retrieval activities, "and the knowledge is for people. If you don't give them information in a form they can readily use, they won't use it."[10]

GLOSSARY OF ISAR TERMS

ADP. Automatic data processing, using mechanical electromechanical, optical, or electronic equipment.

Dictionary. A list of classifying or keywords, either predetermined for, or derived from, the library of data stored. In the former case, documents are indexed by referring to this dictionary for accepted keywords. In the latter case, the dictionary is prepared as a by-product of the manual or automatic determination of significant words in the data. In either case, the dictionary is referred to in preparing queries to the system.

Document. A full text of information, as an abstract, book, article or report.

IDP. Integrated data processing. A partial combination of ADP systems to effect a greater coordination among systems.

Indexing. Assignment of identifying words and/or assignment to a category to facilitate retrieval.

Inquiry. A query or question put to the system to request the retrieval of all documents or references to documents pertaining to a particular subject, which is specified through the use of keywords.

ISAR. Information storage and retrieval, by manual or automatic means, in systematic fashion.

Keywords. Words indicative of the subject matter of a document, i.e., significant words.

Library. A collection of documents or records specifying the identification and classification of documents, arranged for systematic retrieval.

Permuted index. A list of document titles, in which each title

---

[10]"Mechanizing Information Retrieval," *IBM Data Processor*, Vol. VI, No. 2 (1961), p. 2.

occurs once for each significant word in the title. The entire list is sequenced on these significant words.

Query. See **Inquiry.**

Record. A unit of information. For example, a punched card, a document, or a title with its associated keywords recorded magnetically or on a punched card.

Selected. With respect to punched cards, physically separated from the rest of the cards, based on certain criteria.

Storage. With respect to ADP, the means of recording data, i.e., punched cards, magnetic tape or internal machine memory, microfilm, etc.

Trade-off. Determination of the equilibrium point between two or more important factors, such as: cost vs. time, flexibility vs. reliability, etc.

BIBLIOGRAPHY

Basic Literature

1. BALLOU, HUBBARD W. *Guide to Microreproduction Equipment, 2nd Edition.* Annapolis, Maryland: National Microfilm Association, 1962.
2. VAN NESS, ROBERT G. *Principles of Punched Card Data Processing.* Elmhurst, Illinois: The Business Press, 1964.
3. WILLIAMS, WILLIAM F. "Information Retrieval," *Business Automation* (November, 1963), pp. 20-27; (January, 1964), pp. 24-29, 43; and (March, 1964), pp. 22-29.
4. _____ *Principles of Automated Information Retrieval.* Elmhurst, Illinois: The Business Press, 1964.
5. _____ *Modern Coding Methods.* New York: International Business Machines Corp.

More Advanced Literature

1. CANNING, RICHARD G. "How to Organize Files," *EDP Analyzer,* Vol. 2, No. 10 (October, 1964).
2. _____ "File Management and Data Retrieval," *EDP Analyzer,* Vol. 2, No. 11 (November, 1964).

3. DOYLE, LAUREN. *Library Science in the Computer Age, SP-141,* Santa Monica: System Development Corp., 1959.
4. SHAW, C. J. *The Organization, Retrieval, and Sorting of Information in a Digital Computer, FN-1384, S-1,* Santa Monica: System Development Corporation, 1959.
5. SIEBURG, JACK. "Updating an I.R. System," *Datamation,* Vol. 11, No. 6 (June, 1965).

Chapter Eleven

ELECTRONIC EAVESDROPPING (BUGGING): ITS USE AND COUNTERMEASURES

STEPHEN W. NETOLICKY*

THE RELENTLESS MARCH OF PROGRESS toward the Orwellian society is nowhere better illustrated than in a recent budget request by the U.S. State Department for $1.9 million to finance a "wall-smashing search for hidden spy microphones in U.S. embassies around the world."

Public officials declaim the use of such devices in domestic affairs. The President of the United States is quoted to have sent memos (1965) to his minions saying, "do not use electronic survey equipment unless it is in defense of the nation." At the same time a tax department official describes recent widespread use of these devices in tax cases, as "warped judgment" and "over-enthusiasm" on the part of investigating agents. Still, within the same year, officials have appeared before committees of various types to defend their use of bugging, one recently before the Senate Judiciary Subcom-

---

*The author of this chapter is an industrial consultant who has, for the past three years, specialized in electronics in the communications field. Currently he is president of Dectron Industries, Inc., and prior to this was executive vice-president and general manager of Angeles Electronics in El Monte, California. Dectron manufactures the Secraphone, Delcon Scrambler and Antibug and is headquartered near Los Angeles.

mittee stating that the use of these devices by his agents was proper.

It seems that whether you are for their use or against depends upon whether you are using the equipment, or it's being used on you!

It is into such an atmosphere of confused emotions and morality regarding the propriety of electronic eavesdropping that the Cold War has dropped new technologies of electronics which recently have emphasized the issues. Space-age developments in devices for "bugging," as it is commonly known, are truly amazing, and of a Buck Rogers flavor. Radio microphone-transmitters the size and shape of an olive listen from martini glasses to conversations over a bar. Microphones the size of a small lump of sugar, transmitters no larger, transducers, the use of atomic-powered batteries with great life spans, and transistors, all contribute to the amazing physical change that has taken place. It was but a few years ago that the microphone, transmitter and recorder were of such a size as to require a large vase, a desk-top calendar or a whole telephone base to conceal them, but today the microphone is found in a ring worn on a person's finger, or in a pen, or in the bottom half of a cigarette pack, and briefcases with entire recording units for hours of surveillance are commonly available, being advertised regularly upon the back of the *New York Times* sports section.

Microminiaturization has revolutionized the use of eavesdropping microphones and transmitters.

The concept and art of electronic eavesdropping are not new. It has been available and known to many people for some time, most of them in law enforcement agencies and private investigation. Of course, as with every space-age development, it was drawn and used in Buck Rogers, and for over five years, Chester Gould has referred to these devices in his "Dick Tracy" comic strip.

It is through the advances in technology, permitting cheaper manufacture, more reliability and greater range which have brought John Q. Citizen face-to-face with them.

Another factor, too, has helped the wider use of such devices. This is a changing moral environment and changing attitudes toward personal privacy. It is not unthinkable in today's business world to order a prospective business client or associate to be fully investigated; the methods to be left up to the investigator. In many such cases, the employer knows unusual or extreme methods will have to be used and, in many cases, unobserved surveillance, possibly eavesdropping, will take place in collecting data for the report.

Bugging devices are here. They are being used widely. Only an uninformed, wishful thinker thinks they are rare. Such devices are commonly employed to obtain not only the most closely guarded military secrets, but corporate intelligence as well. With the ability that now exists of implanting a miniature transmitter, the size of your little finger, in such common articles as desk pen sets, cigarette lighters, staplers, as well as on picture frames and other common household articles, some find it hard to feel really safe from being bugged. These are normal people, not paranoid or emotionally upset, but rational folk who know the modern facts of life.

The recent publicity in *TIME* and *LIFE* magazines and elsewhere, given to the olive-sized and -shaped bugging equipment, completely operable while unobserved in a martini glass, must give rise to the speculation that Business Intelligence has come a long way and reaches great depths of effectiveness unless countermeasures are applied.

Laws, state or federal, do not seem to have an effect on the use of bugging equipment as recent court decisions have illustrated. Chief Justice Earl Warren, when he was queried as to the effectiveness of today's regulations, said the fantastic advances in the field of electronic communication constitute a great danger to the privacy of the individual. The Federal Communications Act of 1934 restricts eavesdropping on telephone messages, but says nothing about radio bugs or tape recorders and the Attorney General does not consider divulgence of the information obtained to be improper.

Congressional investigations on the invasion of privacy by certain government agencies, conducted in mid-1965 under the chairmanship of Senator Edward V. Long of Missouri, disclosed that an alarming number of electronic eavesdropping devices, together with peripheral recording and allied equipment, have been sold to the government. Most frequently cited consumers were: the Internal Revenue Service, Food and Drug Administration, Bureau of Customs, General Services Administration, and Bureau of Narcotics. The FBI, surprisingly enough, was notably absent. This, it is felt, is because it purchases its equipment through a blind or its use of budget listings as "consultants." Ostensibly, sales of bugging equipment are limited to those in federal and state law enforcement agencies as well as "licensed" investigators. However, in fact, it is possible for any individual to procure electronic eavesdropping devices and equipment directly under his own, or his firm's name. Naturally, the companies which manufacture this equipment are profit motivated and there is no law against sales of this equipment, even to minors, as there is in firearms regulation. The firms maintain that they are selling to "bona fide" users and who is to prove that someone is not a "bona fide" user.

Technically, in business administration jargon, bugging must be considered as data collection. Perhaps the least emotional way to describe bugging in a marketing operation is to call it "data collection, marketing strategy, competitor, involuntary."

Several companies do a thriving business in the art of locating and removing hidden listening devices. They will for a fee, go to an office, home, or other place, and search by use of electronic detecting devices in an effort to clear out any bugs which have been planted. Their fees start easily at $75 a visit and can run as high as $1,000 just for searching. The average price to check an office and small conference room is $250, nor are these searches as inadvisable as they may seem, considering recent figures developed from inspection of those firms doing business in miniature telephone transmitters. It is reported that in 1965, no less than 250 of such devices were sold in a thirty-day period in the city of Los Angeles. The telephone transmitter is probably one of the hardest to detect. Another high-selling device is the personal transmitter, to be secreted either on one's body or planted within a briefcase or other object.

The possession of this type of equipment, or tape-recording devices, voice actuated, briefcase mounted, which can be left in a competitor's or a customer's office, provides a distinct advantage over competitors. Only three states have made the use (under certain circumstances) of such equipment illegal, California, Illinois, and New York. Aside from federal laws on telephone tapping, few laws cover this topic. The laws which pertain are more oriented toward courtroom procedure and acceptability of evidence (wiretapping and bugging usually being inadmissible).

EAVESDROPPING EQUIPMENT

Electronic eavesdropping equipment comes in a variety of sizes, configurations, and capabilities, usually tailored to meet the specific application intended. The following descriptions are about items currently available and sold by no less than twelve companies openly, with another ten making the items for custom applications. These are U.S. companies. No foreign firms are included.

First let us examine transmitters.

Telephone

Miniature transmitters, the approximate cube and volume of 1.25 inches, are employed by tying directly into the telephone line. This type of listening device is commonly referred to as either a two-line or three-line tap. A common installation consists of direct connection, in series, of the miniature transmitter in the person's telephone line which automatically goes on when the line is activated, with the range, depending upon antenna configuration, of several blocks. As with all these transmitters, they are on a radio frequency, and require that somewhere, within range, there be a receiver which may then feed either into earphones for active monitoring or into a tape recorder also, usually, voice actuated, or both.

When the person is through talking, and the line is disconnected, the transmitter automatically shuts off. In the three-wire tap, after the person has hung up, the receiver acts as a separate microphone and continues to monitor all conversations in priximity of the telephone. This makes it possible to monitor all information received over the phone and continue to monitor after the phone is hung up. A telephone transmitter is probably the most effective bugging device as it is very difficult to detect when not in operation. It draws no current except when in use and even then, it draws from the telephone line itself. There is little, if any, discernible voltage drop which makes its detection difficult by the voltage drop method. Moreover, it can be installed at a junction box some two or three blocks away from the phone line to be tapped. All that is necessary is one time accessibility to the phone line to be tapped. Larger models are available with self-contained batteries as an absolute guarantee against voltage drop in the line and which provide increased transmission range. These devices have varying output, much dependent upon battery life and antenna length. Generally, these are not crystal controlled devices from a power consumption standpoint. Use of the telephone transmitter by private investigators is little discussed because of the necessity to gain access to the telephone line itself, which is illegal under Section 605 of the Federal Communications Act of 1934, thus making it a federal offense to intercept telephone calls.

Personally Carried Transmitters

The next most-favored eavesdropping method is to carry a miniature transmitter in the pocket. The range may be adequate from one to three blocks and dimensions approximate those of a box of matches. This type of transmitter is limited in size only by the battery source being employed as microminiaturization of electronic components has made it possible to reduce the electronics portion to extremely small packages.

This device is frequently used to gather intelligence which is transmitted and recorded by either a briefcase-carried receiver-recorder or by a receiver-recorder unit, attaché case mounted, located within the desired range. As can be seen, this highly mobile unit makes it possible to gather information in the most unlikely places. Microphone's sensitivity is such that it is not necessary to wear the oft publicized flower, jewelry or tie clasp. Transmitters, the size of a package of cigarettes or larger, with self-contained batteries were used until the introduction of these truly miniature units. Prices for the newer units start at $39.95 and go upward to $275 for the transmitter alone. A good receiver for use with telephone taps as well as other diverse applications can approximate $200 and up.

Immobile or "Planted" Miniature Transmitters

Miniature transmitters of all sizes and configurations are manufactured, usually with external power sources, to be employed on the premises where desired intelligence is to be gained. Output ranges on these are from as little as ten microwatts to as much as one-half watt depending upon the size and space available. However, the larger devices and more powerful transmitters have lost favor, in view of the latest units coming onto the market. It is desirable to have as little transmission energy as possible to minimize the probability of detection by the now available radio frequency probes and sounding devices.

Because implanting requires access to the subject's area, it is preferable to have long-life transmitters. Most available transmitters are good from 6 to 20 days with their specified power packs and nonvoice actuation. Since the longer operation requires a larger battery pack, the transmitter itself may be separated from its power supply and microphone to aid in its concealment. Fine wires, tinted to match the surrounding decor, accomplish this. They are impossible to spot unless under active search by a suspicious host. This type is often used on a continuous basis, until batteries are exhausted. Note that the technology of microphone development is now such that one can hear what is being said several rooms away if there is no intervening noise, because the system is designed to automatically load for the decibels being received. This self-compensating microphone is much the same as is used in hearing aids and is far more sensitive than the human ear.

Now that size and configuration have become so flexible, it is almost impossible to name an object or area which cannot be bugged with a stationary transmitter. AC-operated transmitters that fit into light sockets or behind electrical outlets are favored and operate virtually forever, or until detected. Normal procedure is to build the transmitter into a lamp, plant or commonly used item. The transmitter goes on the air whenever the device is turned on. Recent attention has been focused upon testimony about Internal Revenue Service operations and others who bug hotel rooms with voice-actuated or full-time bugs of these types. By alerting the hotel/motel manager that a person under surveillance is going to stay there, it can be arranged to have him shunted to that room which is equipped. In this case, in major cities, microphones and listening devices have been implanted that are connected to a central receiving bank with automatic voice-actuated tape recorders recording each sound. Think of the available and appropriate appliances for such bugs—typewriters, adding machines, clocks, etc.

Transmitters, Carrier Current

Another type of basic transmitter is one which uses the electrical wiring of the office or home itself. The AC-operated transmitter can use existing telephone lines and AC power lines for transmission. This particular method has many drawbacks, as it is necessary to plug the receiver into the same AC line in order to listen because transformers are today often located in offices and right on houses. Moreover, detection is rather simple, in that it is merely necessary to plug into the wall outlet and listen with the appropriate device to see if you can hear your own voice.

MICROPHONES

A common telephone tap, not accomplished by entering the line, is the placement of an induction coil inside or on the line of the subject telephone. Separate power is required. Microphones and simple listening devices (stethescope) can be used with transmitters even when one cannot gain access to a subject area. The commonest use is placement against a pane of glass, door or wall, utilizing the object as a sounding board to listen to the adjoining area.

In the event that the walls are too thick to listen through, a spike mike is employed which consists of a probe which is inserted into a joist and a microphone attached to the end. The joist insures good sound conduction and relays all auditory information from the next room.

The levels of electric current needed in long-term concealed microphones is so small, that it is hard to locate with a flux-flow device, and the microphones and transmitters themselves, usually made of metal, are so small that even metal-hunting and detection devices have difficulty locating them. A person's car can become a sound studio for such devices. Even on the subway, one may be involved with a portable device, not to mention the popular olive-in-the-martini detector.

Not only direct sound pickup, but sound reflection too, can be used. A beam is aimed at a reflector located in the area to be monitored, perhaps on a window or door from a distance. The returned, modulated signal can be translated to speech, although the quality is usually low on these devices. Parabolic microphones increase signal strength.

Little, if any, mention is made in the press of a widespread technique, a type of old-fashioned wire tap which is a direct tie-in with a phone. It is currently used by the government and many firms. By the use of a device, sometimes called a snooper button, a telephone conversation can be monitored without audible click. This is not usually considered true bugging, one of the reasons being that it is done by the head of an agency or by his orders, and is, therefore, more of an internal audit (perhaps in terms of business systems, more related to management information systems than business intelligence). It is easily detected by wire tracing and usually a rather hefty voltage and volume drop is noted when it is in use.

The devices, on the whole, which are deposited in a subject's area, usually limited to a microphone and transmitter and often not even the latter, are now inexpensive enough to be written off and abandoned if located. The gains, however, far outstrip the cost, if no value or moral aspects are involved, for any thinking person can see that just one sale in the missile industry, or a big order in hardware or construction makes eavesdropping attractive indeed. Its use is on the increase. Legislation and enforcement against third party listening is slow, perhaps primarily because the biggest users are the federal and state governments themselves, and who will prosecute them?

Two recent developments, spawned from our space age,

are a microphone-transmitter unit so small that it can be sewn into a person's clothing and, unwittingly, he becomes the agent of the eavesdropper. A second is the laser beam which can be projected against any reflecting object like a window or door or other reflecting object in the area to be interrogated, and reflect a signal back to a unit which translates very small movements into sound.

Although not widely known, a few installations have been made of visual electronic devices. TV cameras, too, have been miniaturized so that the camera can provide inputs directly or through remote wiring, into a transmitter which, in turn, transmits to a remote receiver. Still highly expensive, starting at $700 for battery-powered portable devices, these are bulkier; the smallest camera unit being the size of two 3x5 card files or about an 8-inch cube. As with direct telephone taps, these are more often used for internal security (inside Brinks, banks, and retail stores, etc.) and for shoplifting prevention than for intelligence data gathering. Usually, in investigations, such as insurance claims, a regular camera with film is used, located at a remote point, aimed at the subject area and (because of the high price of film) only run when an operator sees something he believes should be recorded.

Mentioning the use of such TV devices for internal security reminds us that extremely sensitive sound devices, permanently mounted microphones and associated equipment are frequently used as a security measure against intruders. Several large firms in the aerospace industry have "secure rooms" so equipped that the slightest sound sets off a guard alarm.

Half the value of such systems is in the psychological impact upon would-be intruders and, frequently, the devices in stores and secure areas are dummys or mock-ups which provide adequate deterrence.

Parabolic microphone units, in which a sensitive mike is centered in a cone, can be used at remote distances, several hundreds of feet away, to hear what is going on in a subject area.

Some of these devices, tape recorders in briefcases, parabolic mike systems and the like, are advertised publicly, for example, in the *New York Times* Sunday edition. Sales must be sufficient to cause the manufacturers or distributers to expend display advertising rates, which are expensive.

A recent device, an aimed sensor of electrical fields, has been shown to be able to pick up and transmit actual electronic computer contents as the computer is working. Henrik de Kanter of International Marketing Staff, Douglas Aircraft's Missiles and Space Systems Division, has seen this leading to a future occupation within IBM and Remington Rand UNIVAC, namely, the occupation of "Decoy Computer Programmer," who produces counterintelligence programs to confuse eavesdroppers.

FUTURE PREDICTIONS

The growth of the use of all these devices rests upon only a few factors: (1) attitudes of acceptance or indifference to intrusion upon personal privacy, which seem to be increasing, (2) continued availability of inexpensive and ever more powerful devices, (3) sharpened business competition as smaller organizations are eaten up by larger and as technological competence is more homogenous among competitors, so that technological skill is no longer a deciding factor among companies, but instead, slight underbids, skillful marketing and similar tactics take its place.

In 1966, all signs point to a greater use of the devices.

COUNTERMEASURES

The field of countermeasures falls into these topics:

a) Search–Discovery–Removal
b) Override–Interfere
c) Secure Communications–Code

Already mentioned are firms which will attempt to locate "bugs." The general problem is that one never really can be sure that all of them have been found and, secondly, they can be replanted. It is a bit like finding and destroying clover in a large lawn.

Override–interfere is to provide either an audible signal which makes conversations meaningless (unfortunately, usually to the conversants, also) or a radio or wire signal which will eliminate any transmissions. Although, this will not affect bugs which depend upon wire transmission, few do. Thus, "anti-bugging," as it has come to be called, is a powerful defense. The name arises from a device, the "antibug," a product of Dectron Industries, California, which, through special electronic methods, transmits a signal which destroys transmissions from planted or carried bugs.

The last method, secure communications or coding, has as its main problem the fact that people cannot converse well in code. It is recalled that, in both the Far Eastern and European theaters of war in World War II and also in the Korean conflict, American Indians were used on either end of forward telephone lines, in effect, coding the messages. However, no one will deny that transmitting and discussion of things "in the clear" is far superior and tends to prevent errors and misunderstandings.

It is better to nullify the bugging devices by methods (a) or (b), than to use concept (c).

The field of counterintelligence is so complex and so closely guarded for techniques, that we cannot even expose its major areas on these pages, but for the suggestions already made. Consulting with an experienced firm in the area is highly recommended to any organization who has cause to believe they are under surveillance or who want to check before an information leak disaster strikes.

For the interested reader, an article on counterintelligence in electronic eavesdropping from a popular source is recommended (see "When Walls Have Ears, Call a Debugging Man," *Business Week*, October 31, 1964).

The newly developed "antibug" is not mentioned, but has become the major weapon in the war againt undesired intrusion.

Until recently, there has been little done to protect against eavesdropping. This is partially due to general lack of knowledge of what was being done in the eavesdropping area, lack of understanding of possible countermeasures, and lack of motivation to explore these topics.

Knowledge that the "bugging" industry exists, understanding of its basic techniques and realizing the hazards of being exposed to this type of surreptitious listening will together cause a modern careful executive to take appropriate action to prevent difficulties and to assure a satisfactory degree of security.

Preliminary precautions, considered a "must" in any simple self-protection program, include first aperiodic physical searches of a critical area. Areas so chosen would include any corporate conference room used for advanced planning, product development conferences or marketing planning. Usually the top executives offices should be included.

Although the technology of microminiaturization has progressed to permit fantastically small devices, it is most probable that from 1967 to 1970, few of these will be in use and the equipment being utilized during this period will be of a size and configuration that lends itself to being hidden in rather obvious places. Newly changed pictures, wall placards, different office furnishings or equipment or rearranged furniture may be a tip off to newly implanted equipment. In dealing with outsiders, it will be wise to note the person's tie clasp, cuff links, watch and such carried items as a briefcase, these being common microphone locations. If the person is carrying a cigarette case or small battery-operated radio receiver, it is wise to ask to see it, commenting upon how nice it is. Ask for a cigarette or a light, noting both cuff links when exposed, and the cigarette case.

A common technique to minimize eavesdropping may include the use of background music and speaking in soft tones, a common business practice. Turning on a wall speaker in a home, motel, or hotel, to give out music, prevents its use as a gatherer of information as a microphone.

Specialists in the search for hidden equipment, use small metal detecting equipment which can often be rented or borrowed locally from a supply house serving the building industry. A change in the pitch of emitted sound will be noted when the detector is passed near a wired microphone.

It is impossible to assure security on the phone because although you may examine your handpiece and base, it is far too difficult to trace the wire to see that the interloping tap is not on the nearest junction box, it may be downtown, or even at the other end of the connection. The design of the telephone system also has prevented development of any effective jamming signal device. One may guard against leakage of data by induction or tap by use of (*a*) the telephone scrambler at each end of the line, and (*b*) use of an antibug, or (*c*) use of a small neon sign near your telephone when you talk. This foils listening in between ends of the line. Both (*b*) and (*c*) provide defense only from detection within the room in which the call is made. The scrambler is useful only to protect calls between terminals, and is not effective against a planted microphone in the room.

Practical developments such as tightened security laws and controls have led to more use of miniature transmitters and two-line telephone taps, mostly due to the ease of installation. This means the best degree of protection is provided by the joint use of a scrambler and an antibug device. The scrambler, for those not familiar with it, is a small device, portable or stationary, which chops up the transmitted telephone signal making it meaningless noise unless a matching un-scrambler is used at the other end of the line.

The best protection against a wireless microphone is its detection and subsequent removal. These may be readily detected by use of a broad band ultra-sensitive receiver which emits a loud squeal when tuned to the frequency used by the hidden transmitter. The drawbacks to this technique are only the limited availability and high cost of such equipment, commonly used bugging frequencies rarely starting below 30 megacycles and often ranging as high as 520 megacycles. This precludes the use of standard commercial detection equipment. In addition, standard equipment is rarely sensitive enough to detect the small signal emitted by implanted microphone-transmitters unless in close proximity to them. Receivers that cover the 30 to 50 megacycle band, commonly used by eavesdroppers are available for approximately $200. One tuning to 500 megacycles typically costs $500. These can be thwarted by a weak signal and super-sensitive receivers in the hands of an eavesdropping specialist. Many locations defy or deter detection also, because of high ambient RF background radiation. Some "bugging" is using the 85 to 108 megacycle FM band.

Specialists often get a rather high fee for searching offices and conference rooms for hidden devices. The cost of searching a meeting room for 100 persons, in which each chair and person must be "de-bugged" may run as high as $100 for a single meeting.

A new device, the antibug, is available against commonly used transmitters. It is a simple broad band noise generator that emits a strong signal over the same frequencies used in the listening devices, thus overpowering the "bug" no matter what its location, frequency or sensitivity. All the listener hears is white noise, a hissing sound. In the few cases that some speech sounds come through, they are almost always unintelligible or seriously garbled in understanding. The antibug is plugged into a wall socket or carried on the person, and is provided in some of its models with batteries. Producers of antibug, Dectron Industries, claim it to be the only available protection against personally carried "bugging" equipment in common use.

For protection from directional electronic microphones,

cone microphones, parabolic listening devices, spike microphones or acoustical transmitters, the use of which is remote
in distance from the room being monitored, it is suggested
that a sound level be maintained (through music, talk or
taped noise) and the talk which is important and confidential, be carried out in muted tones. Spike microphones and
acoustic transmitters, in a properly loaded room, cannot hear
more than the normal ear.

SUMMARY

We have established in this chapter, that electronic (and
other types) of eavesdropping is being used, and its use is
greater than most businessmen realize. To prevent the reader
discovering, after the fact, that he has been compromised,
that his business secrets are no longer known only to himself
and those he wants to know, and to prevent his unhappy
discovery that his plans, marketing strategy and other matters are known to, and being used by, his competitor, we have
introduced the field of electronic eavesdropping and provided basic guidance on protection. Reasonable vigilance is
wise. We do not encourage paranoid fears which lead to
spending great sums on protection or detection, but we do
recommend that this field receive management's attention
and budget, that aperiodic searches be undertaken, and that
periodic training of top executives include the contents of
this chapter, especially those in positions of trust whose work
is vital to the firm, or nation, and whose offices, conference
rooms, or personal surroundings will contain spoken words
revealing the heart of a firm's intentions.

Electronic eavesdropping is a reality, protection is simple,
action to protect is advisable.

Chapter Twelve

INTELLIGENCE OPERATIONS FOR RETAIL STORES AND CHAINS

BARNETT SUSSMAN*
Consultant on Marketing and Promotion

WHAT ARE THE OPPORTUNITIES for business intelligence (BI) work in retailing?

Most retailers have not taken advantage of new techniques in this field, many are unaware, and some use it but do not realize that they are doing so. In general, retailers are not as advanced as the manufacturers of the products they sell.

With a few exceptions, business intelligence in retail stores is in a most primitive stage. The immediate need is to find questions, not answers. We need to know what retail problems can be solved by the use of BI techniques.

Retailers don't like to admit that there are things they don't know about their customers and about their business. Many are second and third generation members of the trade and they operate as did their parents. But there is a perceptible change coming in this area. This change is caused by the recent growth of huge nationwide retail organizations,

*Barnett Sussman is a member of R. M. Greene and Associates and operates his own retail advertising and sales promotion service in Southern California.

and by the development of a professional management in retail store administration.

As part of a study for a Los Angeles retail supermarket firm, R. M. Greene and Associates questioned retailers on the kinds of business intelligence they felt they needed. A sampling of most of the typical traditional kinds of retail stores was included. Here is an assortment of questions they thought business intelligence should answer for them:

1. Why do I have fluctuations in sales volume?
2. How will an influx of Negroes into my area effect my sales?
3. What changes in zoning can I expect from the new city administration, and will this help or hurt my business?
4. My chief competitor has a new sales promotion. Is this the reason my sales are off?
5. One of my shops has never really "taken off." Is this the fault of the location, the manager, my advertising or what?
6. Should I enlarge my restaurant? Will business continue to grow so I can fill it up?
7. Should I stress quality or price in my advertising?
8. Younger housewives don't seem attracted to my store. What's wrong?
9. One of my competitors just hired a new general manager from the east. What kind of fireworks can I expect from them now?
10. What's the best way to stop my own clerks from pilfering my store?

The retailers wanted data from five areas: (1) his own business, (2) about his customers, (3) about his competition, (4) about his suppliers and trade sources, and (5) about his community as a whole, its laws, its shifting population, and so on.

THE RETAILERS' OWN BUSINESS

The internal affairs of a business are considered management information rather than business intelligence. Business intelligence concerns itself with obtaining facts from outside of the organization. Sometimes the line is hard to draw. For example, how do we classify the behavior of customers once inside the store? However, profit and loss, employee and shelf turnover, gross sales, employee actions, mark-up, percent profit, are management information rather than BI.

INFORMATION ABOUT CUSTOMERS

"When my father started this business," one retailer said, "he knew every one of his customers. Now I'm lucky if I know my own clerks. The other day I tried to wait on one of my own new employees."

Our growing, mobile and restless population makes it hard for a retailer to really know and understand his customers—or those who are not customers. Here are some of the customer-oriented questions the retailers ask:

1. Why do, or why don't, they shop with me?
2. What are my customers' shopping habits?
3. What do they want that I don't stock?
4. What's the best advertising media to get to them?
5. What customers are planning to leave the area (and will they "forget" to settle their accounts)?
6. What determines customer loyalty?

INFORMATION ABOUT COMPETITION

Retailers are always interested in their competition. Most of the successful ones, however, say that too great an interest is an unhealthy state of mind. We hear now and then about the retailer who would peer anxiously out his door down the street where he could see his nearest competitor, so worried about his competition that he didn't take care of the customers he had.

Some of the specific questions about the competition which retailers have are:

1. Who is my competition?

2. How do their stores resemble or differ from mine in price, appearance, atmosphere, etc.?
3. What kind of persons manage my competitive stores?
4. Do they plan to move or remodel?
5. Are any new competitors planning to move into the area? Do any plan to move out?
6. Can my competitors buy cheaper than I can, and if so, how?

SUPPLIERS AND TRADE SOURCES

Progressive retailers are always on the lookout for new items that will sell; sometimes finding new merchandise is harder than selling it. Coming trends in fashion and design are important to clothing retailers. Occasionally, long-range forecasts are made by the business press, like *Woman's Wear Daily*. Usually such media carry short-range forecasts but there seems always to be a need for more business intelligence, especially in clothing, toys, and other fields with fast changing trends.

Unreliable sources, producers of poor quality merchandise, those who have unusually restrictive policies on returns, all of these are of interest to the retailer.

THE COMMUNITY AS A WHOLE

Busy with his own affairs, a retailer often misses changes in his city or business area which may strongly affect his store. Typical of these are political changes, new zoning regulations, gradual changes of dwellings from single to multiple family, new racial or religious groups arriving in the community, new streets or freeways or one-way regulations which can severely change his whole pattern of life. In addition, changes in tax structure, in employee regulations such as hours of work or age limits, changes in parking, or new shopping centers may affect him. All these must be followed (and, in some cases, predicted) by a store owner, and they can slip by easily. Few people bother to go to their community legal meetings and a special interest group can make a motion, have it seconded, hold hearings and have it passed by a local legislative group, all before a merchant even hears of it.

LARGER RETAIL CHAINS

Top management of larger retail chain stores is removed by several levels from customers and sales operations. They tend to depend upon periodic surveys, reports from store owners or managers and newspapers plus trade news sources.

Large-scale operators are more planning conscious than the independents. In order to schedule new stores, they need demographic information, real estate subdividers' plans, industrial developers' concepts, and data from political bodies. A large operator also has more sources of new personnel.

REPORTING FOR RETAIL OPERATIONS

"They gave me raw information," one retailer complained about his business intelligence reports. "They gave me all the facts, and I suppose they're accurate, but their report doesn't help me. I don't expect them to make decisions for me and I don't want their opinions, but their facts must be applicable and clear my way on the decisions I have to make."

Retailers are not trained in statistics, and they must have help if the intelligence reports are to improve their situation.

Retail store managers expect that business intelligence people are well enough trained in retailing to interpret the facts. The retailer who is footing the bill has a right also to expect the BI specialist to teach him how to use the reports. Here are two short paragraphs written to a retailer, one by a BI organization, and the other by a consultant helping the retailer use the report:

The stratified sample means indicated small enough variance

to assure between-item reliability for question 7. Thus the null hypothesis holds that no significant change will take place, this statement at the .01 level of confidence.

Question 7 (about the income of people living in our area) indicated that no drop in average family income is expected. Evidently, as the low-income Caucasians are moving out, the medium-high income Mexican-American population is moving in. Rents have not dropped, and probably will not. The same number of dollars will remain available for food for the family.

Face-to-face reporting is preferable. If possible, the BI specialist should recommend courses of action and discuss on a logical basis, the benefits of each.

SOURCES OF BI FOR RETAILERS

The retail field is characterized by having a newspaper for almost everything. In addition, specialized services have been developed. For example, Willmark Company deals in comparative pricing and protection. They check the behavior of your clerks and they report any unpleasant behavior. They will assist you in training your clerks.

In another field is the Burns Agency. Burns specializes in store protection, investigation of employees and potential employees. Numerous services in the area of customer credit checking includes bureaus, banks, and Dun and Bradstreet. In some large cities the Retail Credit Managers Association has private lists of skips and bad-check passers.

For population shifts and trends, private research will probably be necessary. Census Bureau and local city surveys are usually for other purposes and will not contain the necessary information. Occasionally a school system population shift survey will contain useful information. In general, a search of public studies should precede hiring a private firm. Highway departments, police, traffic, and similar agencies often have recent traffic flow studies which help in site selection. The mere presence of a new competitor—when the competitor is known to use scientific site selection techniques—is a key bit of data.

THE FUTURE OF BI FOR RETAILERS

Since professional BI is expensive, it is not likely that any but the largest independent retail store will now use specialized services other than those like Willmark or Burns. It is, however, probable that in a few years there will be steady BI work for large organizations. The appointment of research directors with demographic statistics and market research as part of their jobs can be expected in a very few years for most major retail chains.

Likewise, BI services of lower cost probably will be merchandisable to the average medium-sized independent in a few years. Centralized computer services for consolidating not only local, but national credit data will develop; such as The Electronic Currency Corporation, of Los Angeles. More and more, the new field of retail business intelligence will improve the profit-making powers of operators who use these services.

Chapter Thirteen

USING BUSINESS INTELLIGENCE TO BUILD THROUGH MERGERS AND ACQUISITIONS

PETER H. STANTON*
President Aerospace Components Corporation
Los Angeles, California

PRESIDENTS AND BOARD CHAIRMEN in American industry are spending a good deal of their time these days taking part in a strange ritual. I call this ritual—which is always performed with stylized gestures, dance steps and incantations—"The Mating Dance of the Merger Bird." One indispensable phase of this ritual is the statement that "2 plus 2 makes 5."

However trite, this business of "2 plus 2 makes 5" is, like all clichés, quite meaningful. It is often possible for two companies, by joining together, to become much more effective and valuable than the sum of their separate parts.

WHY BUY ANOTHER COMPANY?

Let us investigate some of the reasons why managers will look for another company to acquire, whether smaller or the same size as their own.

*Mr. Stanton, a graduate electronics engineer, holds an MBA degree with high distinction from the Harvard Business School. He was formerly president of Astro-Science Corporation, whose sales volume, aided by two major acquisitions, grew from $1 million to $9 million in four years. He is presently president of Aerospace Components Corporation in Los Angeles, California. Mr. Stanton is a member of the Financial Executives Institute and a past member of the Young Presidents' Organization; his biography appears in *Who's Who in the West*.

BASIC FINANCIAL CONSIDERATIONS

Reasons for buying another company, or merging with a similarly sized business include: to add sales volume, profits, or stability to the present picture. Obviously, if a company and the company to be acquired (which I will call "Company X") are both profitable operations, the amalgamation will show higher sales volumes and profits than either company did prior to the merger. This alone, however, should not be the reason for acquisition.

The future return on investment of the combination should be greater than the present return on investment and earnings per share of the stock after merger should be greater than present earnings per share. These are paramount financial considerations to keep in mind when considering a merger or acquisition and many a company has neglected these to its sorrow.

OTHER ATTRACTIONS

There are other things one may want which Company X has. As examples, I might cite: marketing capabilities and access to markets, technical talents, products which are compatible and can be marketed by the same organization and perhaps produced by the same plant facilities, or a publicly held stock if one company's stock is privately held.

INTEGRATION VS. AUTONOMY

Through the merger, one company may wish to broaden its own activities and integrate with Company X if its products, processes, and markets are essentially complementary. On the other hand, one may want to have Company X continue to function as an entirely separate entity with its own self-contained management and in its own plant. Caution should be exercised, however, not to stray too far outside of one's own industry in making an acquisition.

This would become a so-called conglomerate merger with all its well-known pitfalls. It is quite dangerous to purchase a company in an industry so foreign to your own that you have no know-how in it and no understanding of its background and peculiarities, even though many companies have brought this off successfully.

It is of paramount importance that the acquiring management have at least a broad, general knowledge of Company X's problems, markets, products, technology, and the other important parameters which will make the association with Company X a success or failure.

HOW TO ACQUIRE A COMPANY

Without attempting to go into the question of valuation of Company X, which becomes highly technical, let us examine the conventional methods of acquiring other companies, each of which should be gone over with a qualified investment banker, general counsel, tax counsel, management consultant and public accounting firm.

The exchange of stock represents a common situation in which a company issues new common stock to the owners of Company X in exchange for all or part of the Company X's stock. This type of transaction is normally nontaxable, which means that Company X's stockholders will not have to pay any tax until they dispose of the buying company's stock.

Acquisition for Cash or Cash and Notes

Alternately, your company can purchase Company X's stock or its assets for cash, or for cash and a promise to pay additional cash at stated future intervals to the stockholders of Company X. Frequently, a combination of these two methods is used and the purchase is partially financed by an exchange of stock, and partially by the passing of cash, notes, debentures, or other promises to pay.

Contingent Price Method

Another method of purchasing a company is to pay a certain amount at the present time—in stock, cash, or notes—and to leave a portion of the purchase price contingent on future events, generally the earnings of Company X after the merger. This is a particularly attractive method of buying a company if the previous owner-management of Company X is to be retained. It is thereby given a strong incentive for doing a good job of managing after the completed negotiations.

Buying Newly Issued Stock

Another way to acquire a portion of Company X is for a company to buy newly issued X stock from Company X, rather than from Company X's stockholders. This accomplishes only partial ownership, since the old stockholders of Company X retain their stock. It has the great advantage, however, of funneling the cash paid directly into Company X's treasury, where it can be used for expansion capital, and therefore directly benefits the partial owners of Company X.

There are other less-frequently used methods of acquiring companies, and many combinations of those here discussed.

AREAS FOR INVESTIGATION

When you first approach a company with a view to acquiring it or are approached by it, there are, of course, a large number of important areas for you to check out before making a definite commitment to acquire all or part of Company X. Most of these are the same areas that you would check if you were offered the presidency of Company X, or were invited to make a substantial stock purchase in it as an individual investor.

Management and Key Personnel

It is of paramount importance that if the old management is to be retained, you must be satisfied with the quality of its performance in the past plus any other current evaluation of competence. Over and above this, it is vitally important that your management and Company X's management be personally compatible, an often neglected point. A number of mergers go on the rocks because two teams of people, each capable by itself, simply could not get along with each other.

Products and Technical Capabilities

The products of the company to be acquired are an important area for you to investigate in relation to your own, or on their own merits if you are making a diversification move. Take a very close look also at Company X's technical capabilities in terms of personnel, patent position, proprietary strength, and ability to innovate.

Markets and Marketing

The markets for Company X's products must be researched thoroughly with a view to determining whether they are expanding or contracting, and how they can be reached through your own, the original company X's staff, or an autonomous marketing organization. The competitive situation will need to be evaluated. Consideration should also be given to the advertising and public relations picture in relation to the purchasing firm.

Financial Considerations

The new company's statements for at least the past five years must be scrutinized closely. Pay attention to trends, and

take a particularly close look at the most recent developments
so as to guard against the possibility that, even if the general
history of Company X has been good, some disastrous development has not just occurred or is about to happen which
makes the management want to merge or sell out. The commonest danger area subject to manipulation, which should
be investigated thoroughly, is the level of inventories and
any capitalized or deferred research and development expenses in relation to the company's current volume of operations. If these are too high, it is probably a sign that management has not taken its lickings in previous accounting
periods and that profits during those periods have been over-
stated. Accounts receivable should be examined.

Manufacturing Methods

Manufacturing methods and processes, sources of supply,
and other considerations, as related to your own company,
should be reviewed.

Plant Location

Consider whether the location of Company X's plant or
plants is compatible with your own, and how much travel
and communication expense would be involved after a
merger.

Labor and Union Problems

Investigate the union situation of Company X compared
with your own. If you are not unionized, you can probably
expect Company X's union to make a strong effort to organize your operation after the merger. In addition, the whole
area of employee fringe benefits, pension and profit-sharing
plans, of both companies should be examined. Major differences between the two will, in all likelihood, lead to problems after the merger.

The Business Intelligence Problem

The prime problem from an intelligence point of view is that if there is a conspiracy to conceal vital facts, all members of the firm's management are "in the know" and attempts to find out data will be sidetracked, or met with hostility or subterfuge. Great care must be exercised, as the buying company does not want to break relations with this interesting looking acquisition, but still it is vital to gather the data. Investigators are met with threats of withdrawal from negotiations and delicate handling is necessary to pry deeply enough to assure that valid data is acquired. In some cases, in which a tax loss is being purchased or a firm is selling out under pressure, the last few months' operations were under stress and poor records were kept as the owners thrashed about, attempting to save their company.

Aside from these problems, since it may be assumed that a meeting of the minds has taken place, the investigators' problems should be less than in an average business intelligence situation. No secrecy is required and employees are supposed to yield data when asked. Resistance to do so may arouse suspicion by itself.

Special attention should be given to a company whose sales were to one primary customer, for the desire to sell may reflect knowledge that that customer has intentions of halting purchases. Thus some investigation of prime customers may be in order.

Further in at least two cases in the West during 1965, an offer to buy was a blind to gather extensive data on how to eliminate competition and, after data gathering was done, no purchase offer resulted but action did ensue which could only have come of facts learned during negotiations and resulted in severe blows to the two smaller firms, one of which went bankrupt. As part of a counterintelligence operation, it is wise to check that a firm approaching you to buy you out actually has the resources to buy, has shown intent, and can be counted upon to treat your revealed data appropriately.

WHO SHOULD MAKE THE ASSESSMENT?

Since the assessment of a potential purchase or merger should include each major function such as personnel, manufacturing, purchasing, quality control, and so on, some firms who have a full staff assign this as a duty to their own key staff members. A special group is formed in some firms often reflecting all the major areas within the top corporate structure. Many firms attach this group to their planning staff, others to their management methods staff which assess their own regular divisions as well as potential additions to the firm. Many, feeling that their own staff is too busy, possibly not capable, or not too familiar with the proposed new firm's product and methods, hire consultants to do the assessment.

Since the quality of the assessment is vital, a first step in gaining members of a corporate group through acquisition or merger will be to assure that an adequate staff for assessment is ready. If the firm plans to use its own staff, and has doubts about any one staff member, clear arrangements or plans should be made beforehand to fill the gap, through another divisional staff member, through a consultant for that function or through another tactic.

WHAT DATA SHOULD BE COLLECTED?

Many embarking upon the merger route find themselves well stocked with candidates, but understocked with plans to evaluate. The time to plan is well before the opportunity arises.

The guide to what data to collect is implied by the method of evaluation. One method, useful for many different types of choices from among multiple alternatives when there are limited resources, is the decision grid evolved by R. M. Greene and Associates of Los Angeles. In this grid, the alternatives are ranged across the top, and the factors down the side. Each entry cell is given a value or score which can range from 1 to 5, with 1 being the low or undesirable end, 5 being the desirable end. Scoring is done, however, so that over the long range, a normal curve can be fitted over these scores, i.e.:

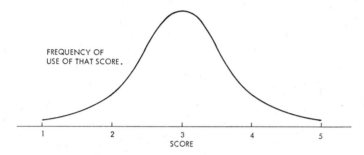

FREQUENCY OF
USE OF THAT SCORE.

1   2   3   4   5

SCORE

Thus, in 100 scorings, the value "1" will be found only about $2\frac{1}{2}$ percent of the time, and likewise the score of "5" would only appear $2\frac{1}{2}$ percent of the time. The scores "2" and "4" would each appear about 16 percent of the time, and the score "3" (average or expected value) would appear approximately 60 percent of the time.

An illustration of such a grid is shown on page 248.

Having developed the factors and written out precisely what the scoring (from 1 to 5) means, the various factors can then be weighted, weights can be multipled by the scores, or added.

The data requirements are clearly indicated by the factors.

SUMMARY

Well thought through, rational decision techniques can provide data requirements for assessment of firms for mergers and purchases. Adequate business intelligence methods can extract that data from the subject firm. Other relevant environmental data is well covered in other chapters of this book. Caution must be used in extracting data from a firm. Unrecognized motivations based upon fear or a desire to conceal essential problems may be important. The quality of the assessors is important, also the design of data collection. Assuming a basically logical system for selection, the only other essential area will be assuring that the system for firm-

assessment is planned, practiced and held in readiness for
the appearance of an interesting opportunity.

ASSESSMENT SYSTEM

FACTOR	Weight	A	B	C	D	E
Expected contribution to sales volume						
Contribution to our profit						
Contribution to our volume						
Expected % return on investment at end of 1st year						
Expected % return on investment at end of 5th year						
Marketing capabilities						
Access to markets we are not in						
Technical talent						
Compatibility of product lines to our existing lines						
Probable success if left with existing management						
Desirability of proposed method of stock exchange						
Total cost of purchase of merger						
Current obligations						
Inventory						
Order backlog						
Reputation (D & B rating, etc.)						
Plant & office condition						
History of stability and growth						
R&D, innovation programs						
Customer spread						
Accounts receivable						
Plant location						
Labor/Union relations						
Personnel program fit						
Other:						

(column header "Firms" spans A B C D E)

Total Score:

Bibliography

BIBLIOGRAPHY

This bibliography covers business intelligence and related topics from 1945 to the present, selecting useful published works available in public sources.

ADELMAN, I. "New Approach to the Construction of Index Numbers," *Review of Economics and Statistics* (August, 1958), pp. 240-49.

ADKINSON, B. W. "United States Scientific and Technical Information Services," *Special Libraries* (November, 1958), pp. 407-14.

ALDEN, BURTON, *et al. Competitive Intelligence: Information, Espionage, and Decision Making.* Boston, Massachusetts.: C. I. Associates, 1959.

ALDERSON, WROE. "Statistical Training for Marketing Research," *The American Statistician* (February, 1953), pp. 9-11.

ALDREDGE, E. S. "Monte Carlo Technique of Operations Research," *Chemical Engineering* (June, 1962), pp. 109-13.

ALEXANDER, RAPHAEL (ed.). *Sources of Information and Unusual Services.* New York, New York: Informational Directory Company, 1958-59.

ALEXANDER, SIDNEY S. "Economics and Business Planning." Reprinted from *Economics and the Policy Maker: The Brookings Lectures.* Washington, D.C.: The Brookings Institution, 1959.

"All the Spies Aren't on the Air," *Television* (January, 1962), pp. 52-55.

ANSOFF, H. IGOR. "Expert Advice on Diversification," *Missiles and Rockets* (July, 1960).

ANTHONY, ROBERT N. "The Trouble with Profit Maximization," *Business Review* (November/December, 1960), pp. 126-34.

"Aries, Others Are Named in Lifting of Trade Secrets," *Oil, Paint and Drug Report* (Aug. 14, 1961), p. 5.

"Available Market Data: Industrial," *Advertising Age* (May, 1958), pp. 143-52.

"Available Market Data: Industrial," *Advertising Age* (April, 1959), pp. 142-52.

BACON, FRANK R., and LEWIS, RICHARD H. "Progress in the Development of Quantitative Market Requirements Models for Use in Long-Range Product Planning," *Seventh International Meeting, Institute of Management Sciences.* (October, 1960).

BARTENSTEIN, F. "Espionage; A Threat," *Oil, Paint, and Drug Report* (Oct. 1, 1962), p. 5.

BARTHOL, R. P. "Learn How to Make Decisions," *Petroleum Engineer* (October, 1960), pp. 10-12.

BATCHELOR, JAMES H. *Operations Research: An Annotated Bibliography.* St. Louis, Missouri: St. Louis University Press, 1959.

BEAUVOIS, J. J. "International Intelligence for the International Enterprise," *California Management Review* (Winter, 1961), pp. 39-46.

BELDA, BERTRAND J. "Income and Expense Planning," *Journal of Accountancy* (November, 1959), pp. 46-50.

BENGE, EUGENE J. "The Expanded Sales Manager and Long-Range Planning," *Sales Management* (November, 1960), pp. 54-56.

BIGELOW, C. G. "Bibliography on Project Planning and Control by Network Analysis; 1959-1961," *Operations Research* (September, 1962), pp. 728-31.

BINGHAM, H. L. "Six Types of Firms and the Management Data They Need," *Business* (1957), pp. 84-91.

BISHOP, J., and RYAN, C. T. "Use Marketing Information for Making Major Management Decisions," *ISA-J* (May, 1962), pp. 41-45.

BOCK, ROBERT H. *An Analysis of the Long-Range Planning Process in a Select Group of Business Firms.* Lafayette, Indiana: Purdue University Press, 1960.

BOLTWOOD, PARKE. "Confessions of an Auto Spy," *SAGA* (November, 1965), p. 20.

BONNER, STANLEY Z. "Reconciling Short-Range Profit Prospects with Long-Range Goals," Section 2, *NAA Bulletin* (July, 1959), pp. 37-46.

"Bug Thy Neighbor," *TIME* (March 6, 1964), pp. 55-56.

BURGESS, R. W. "Meaning of the New Business Census," *Dun's Review and Modern Industry* (June, 1956), pp. 41-42.

BURSK, E. C., and FENN, D. H. *Planning the Future Strategy of Your Business.* New York: McGraw-Hill Book Co., Inc., 1956.

"Business Espionage," *Business Management* (Reprint 1965), 15 pp.

"Business Forecasting: Different Systems the Forecasters Are Using," *Business Week* (September, 1955), pp. 90-92.

"Can Congress Force Steel to Tell All?" *Business Week* (Sept. 15, 1962), p. 30.

CAPON, FRANK S. "Essentials of Corporate Planning," *Controller* (May, 1960), pp. 218, 220, 222.

CASSELS, LOUIS, and RANDALL, R. L. "Six Steps to Better Planning," *Nation's Business* (August, 1961).

CLAPHAM, J. C. "Need for Research in Planning Mechanization," *Engineering Journal* (August, 1961), pp. 47-49.

COE, B. P. "Capacity Stretch," *Industrial and Engineering Chemical* (March, 1962), pp. 47-51.

COHEN, SIDNEY. "How the Retailer Uses Census Tracts," *Journal of the American Statistical Association* (September, 1956), p. 506.

COLEMAN, J. J., and ABRAMS, I. J. "Mathematical Model for Operational Readiness," *Operations Research* (January, 1962), pp. 126-38.

COLEMAN, L. A., and COLE, C. B. "How Much of Your Knowledge Is Yours? Law of Proprietary Rights," *Hydrocarbon Process and Petroleum Refiner* (June, 1961), pp. 208-12.

"Collection of Data from Firms," *Nature* (September, 1962), pp. 500-501.

COLM, GERHARD. "How Good Are Long-Range Projections of GNP for Business Planning," *California Management Review* (Winter, 1959).

COMAN, E. T. *Sources of Business Information.* Englewood Cliffs, New Jersey: Prentice-Hall Inc., 1949.

"Company Organization for Expansion Planning," *Industrial Development* (May, 1959).

"Competitive Gag?" *Newsweek* (July, 1957), p. 67.

COPPOCK, JOSEPH D. *Economics of the Business Firm.* New York: McGraw-Hill Book Co., Inc., 1959.

COVILLE, D. M. "How to Measure the Effectiveness of Manufacturing Planning," *Tool and Manufacturing Engineers* (August, 1962), pp. 62-64.

COX, T. "I've Got a Secret, or Have I?" *Management Methods* (February, 1959), pp. 43-45.

CROXTON, FREDERICK E., and COWDEN, DUDLEY J. *Practical Business Statistics.* Englewood Cliffs, New Jersey: Prentice-Hall Inc., 1948.

"Cyanamid Says Italians Bought Pirated Secrets," *Oil, Paint and Drug Report* (July 2, 1962), p. 3.

DANIEL, P. J. "Application of Operations Research for Site Planning Facilities Support," *Aerospace Engineering* (June, 1961), pp. 26-27.

DAUTEN, CARL A. *Business Fluctuations and Forecasting.* Cincinnati, Ohio: South-Western Publishing Co., Inc., 1954.

DAVIDSON, W. "The Nth Country Problem and Arms Control," *NRA Planning Pamphlet* (January, 1960), p. 41.

DAVIS, R. H. "Business Simulator-Management Game," *Westinghouse Engineer* (November, 1962), pp. 55-60.

"Decade of Military Operations Research in Perspective; Symposium," *Operations Research* (November, 1960), pp. 798-860.

DEUTCH, MORTON. "Bargaining Face—Some Experiments in Bargaining Behavior," *ORSA Nineteenth National Meeting* (May, 1961).

"Developing Product Strategy," *Management Report* (1959), p. 352.

DIEBOLD, JOHN. "Automation: Its Impact on Business and Labor," *NRA Planning Pamphlet* (May, 1959), p. 64.

"Directory of Market Research Organizations," *Advertising Agency Magazine* (May, 1957), pp. 57-58.

"Dishonest Practices: How Management Can Prevent Them," *Textile Industries* (February, 1959), pp. 100-103.

"Do You Know the Law on Trade Secrets?" *Management Methods* (May, 1959), pp. 27-28.

"Drawing a Bead on Drug Pirates," *Chemical Week* (August 4, 1962), pp. 25-26.

"Drug Companies Fear Secrets Might Get out as Result of Proposed Law: Moss Bill," *Oil, Paint and Drug Report* (August, 1957), pp. 172-73.

EFFERSON, C. A. "Organization of the Planning Process." Paper presented to the American Management Association, April, 1960.

ELLIS, J. W., JR., and GREENE, T. E. "The Contextual Study: A Structured Approach to the Study of Political and Military Aspects of Limited War," *Operations Research* (September/October, 1960).

"Engineer Down Firm in Know-How Fight," *Chemical Engineer* (May, 1962), p. 136.

ERNST, M. L. "Operations Research and the Large Strategic Problems," *Operations Research* (July, 1961), pp. 437-45.

ESTES, B. E. "Where to Find Market Research Information," *Industrial Marketing* (June, 1957), p. 156.

EVANS, B. A. "Answer in a Nutshell or Packaged Information for Industry," *ASLIB Proceedings* (August, 1954), pp. 133-39.

EVANS, M. K. "The Accountant's Role in Long-Term Profit Planning," *NAA Bulletin* (July, 1959), pp. 22-36.

"Eyes Everywhere: U.N. Maintains Flow of Valuable Data, Reports, and Surveys," *Chemical Week* (July, 1955), p. 26.

FARRADANE, J. "Information Service in Industry," *Research* (August, 1953), pp. 327-30.

FAYERWEATHER, JOHN. "LRP for International Operations," *California Management Review* (Fall, 1960), pp. 23-35.

"Federal Marketing Services Expand, but Need Encouragement from Business," *Printer's Ink* (October 10, 1958), pp. 37-40.

FEIST, HOWARD N., JR. "Diversification Requires Planning," *Advanced Management* (June, 1959).

"First Southwide Market Research Conference, Miami: With Abstracts and Paper," *Manufacturer's Record* (September, 1957), pp. 43-48; (October, 1957), pp. 32-35; (November, 1957), pp. 32-36.

FISCH, GERALD G., and JACOBY, DEAN L. "Long-Range Planning:

An Approach to Leadership, *Cost and Management* (April, 1959).

FLAGLE, CHARLES D. "Probability: Based Tolerances in Forecasting and Planning," *Journal of Industrial Engineering* (March/April, 1961).

FLEISHMAN, AEROM. "A Survey of Problems, Techniques, Schools of Thought in Market Research," *Industrial Design* (1958), pp. 26-43.

FLOOD, M. M. "New Operations Research Potentials," *Operations Research* (July, 1962), pp. 423-36.

FORRESTER, J. W. *Industrial Dynamics.* Cambridge, Massachusetts: Massachusetts Institute of Technology, 1961.

FUCHS, GERALD J., and THOMPSON, G. CLARK. "Management of New Product Development," *Business Record* (October, 1960), pp. 36-39.

————. "Sources of Economic Intelligence," *Business Record* (September, 1960), pp. 27-33.

FURASH, EDWARD E. "Problems in Review," *Harvard Business Review* (November/December, 1959), pp. 6-8.

GEHMAN, RICHARD. "Executive Spies," *Cosmopolitan* (February, 1958), pp. 70-75.

GERSTEL, STEPHEN. "Drug Spy Collects Interesting Facts," *UPI Release,* Washington, D.C. (April 13, 1966).

GIBIAN, EMIL F. "Long-Range Planning to Offset Increasing Labor Costs," *Management Record* (February, 1959), pp. 66-68.

GOOKIN, R. BURT. "Profit Planning and Control at Heinz," *American Business* (September, 1959).

GORDON, ROBERT AARON. "Business Fluctuations." *Harper's,* pp. 127-52, 449-83. 1952.

GRAY, A. W. "Can Your Cherished Trade Secrets Be Pirated Legally?" *American Machinist/Metalworking Manufacturing* (February, 1960), pp. 105-06.

————. "Don't Lose a Patent by Premature Use," *Chemical Engineer* (January, 1962), pp. 117-18.

————. "Novelty and Patentability," *Machine Design* (August, 1962), pp. 79-80.

————. "Protection of Trade Secrets," *Audio* (April, 1962), p. 23.

————. "Trade Secrets; What the Courts Have to Say," *Product Engineering* (October, 1962), p. 70.

————. "What the Courts Say about Trade Secrets," *Petroleum Refiner* (February, 1957), p. 226.

————. "When a Salesman Switches Jobs," *Purchasing* (August 27, 1962), pp. 77-78.

GREENBURG, L. "New Application of Operations Research," *Operations Research* (March, 1960), pp. 423-24.

GREENE, JAY R., and SISSON, ROGER L. *Dynamic Management Decision Games*. New York: John Wiley & Sons Inc., 1959.

GREENLAW, P. S. *Business Simulation*. Englewood Cliffs, New Jersey: Prentice-Hall Inc., 1962.

"Guarding Detroit's New Cars," *National Petroleum News* (September, 1958), p. 151.

GUYTON, W. J. "Guide to Gathering Marketing Intelligence," *Industrial Marketing* (March, 1962), pp. 84-88.

HARPER, M. "Business Detectives Would Stalk Information; New Profession to Aid Management Proposed." *Petroleum Engineer* (September, 1960), pp. A20d-A20.

Handbook of Commercial, Financial and Information Services, comp. by Walter Hausdorfer. Special Libraries Association. Financial Division. New York, Special Library Assn., 1956.

HAUSER, P. M., and LEONARD, W. R. (eds.). *Government Statistics for Business Use*. New York: John Wiley & Sons Inc., 1956.

HAWTHORNE, R. "Patents and Progress; Editorial," *Space-Aeronautics* (May, 1960), p. 17.

HEENAN, F. E. "Bureau of Ships Work Study Program," *Naval Engineer* (May, 1962), pp. 287-90.

HERRON, LOWELL W. *Executive Action Simulation*. Englewood Cliffs, New Jersey: Prentice-Hall Inc., 1960.

HILSMAN, ROGER. *Strategic Intelligence and National Decisions*. Chicago, Illinois: The Free Press, 1956.

HOGGATT, AUSTIN. "Business Games as Tools for Research," *Proceedings ORSA National Meeting* (1960).

HOLSTEIN, D. "Decision Tables; A Technique for Minimization Routine, Repetitive Design," *Machine Design* (August, 1962), pp. 76-79.

HOOVER, J. EDGAR. "Why Reds Make Friends with Businessmen," *Nation's Business* (May, 1962), pp. 78-80.

―――. "The U.S. Businessman Faces the Soviet Spy," *Harvard Business Review* (January/February, 1964), pp. 140-61.

"How secure can you keep your design secrets?" *Product Engineering* (July 4, 1966), pp. 87-95.

"How a Small Company Plans for Growth," *Dun's Review and Modern Industry* (March, 1959), pp. 63, 120-22.

"How to Be Your Own Economist," *Sales Management* (May 16, 1958), pp. 38-39.

"How to Find out What Your Competitors Are up to," *Management Methods* (July, 1960), pp. 50-52.

"How to Find out What Your Competitor's Doing; Sales Executive Forum," *Industrial Marketing* (August, 1961), pp. 93-96.

"How to Protect Yourself against Business Spies," *Management Methods* (June, 1960), pp. 58-62.

"If You Want to Escalate Know Your Indexes," *Steel* (July 28, 1958), pp. 38-39.

"Industrial Market Data Sources," *Sales Management* (July, 1957), pp. 79-152.

"Industrial Market Data Sources," *Sales Management* (July, 1958), p. 79.

"Industrial Spying Goes Big League," *Business Week* (October 6, 1962), pp. 65-66.

JACKSON, JAMES R. "Learning from Experience in Business Decision Games," *California Management Review* (1959).

JOHNSON, C. F. "Six Types of Firms and the Data Each Needs," *American Business* (May, 1959), pp. 7-9.

JOHNSON, E. A. "Toward Establishment of a Role for Operations Research in Economic Development Programs," *Operations Research* (September, 1961), pp. 743-46.

JOHNSON, ERIK. "On the Formulation and Use of a Multi-Goal

Function for an Industrial Firm," *Proceedings ORSA National Meeting* (May, 1961).

KASHYAP, R. N. "Development of an Integrated Computer System for Long-Range Management Planning and Control," Burbank, Calif. Lockheed Aircraft Corporation (May, 1960).

KAST, FREMONT, and ROSENZEIG, JAMES. "Minimizing the Planning Gap," *Advanced Management* (October, 1960), pp. 20-23.

KAST, R., and ROSENZEIG, JAMES. "Survey of Intra-Company Impact of Weapon System Management," *Engineer's Management* (March, 1962), pp. 37-40.

"Keeping an Eye on the Opposition: Hercules Powder's Information Center," *Chemical Week* (May, 1957), pp. 78-80.

KEMP, L. M., and WHITE, C. M. "Basic Sources of Business Information." *Special Libraries* (April, 1958), pp. 160-63.

KENNEDY, J. D. "Dynamic Business Modeling on the Analog Computer." *Instruments and Control Systems* (September, 1962), pp. 140-46.

KENNEY, THOMAS. "Planning Ahead for Plants Ahead," *Dun's Review and Modern Industry* (March, 1959), pp. 115-19.

KETCHUM, H. W. "Finding New Markets: How the Government Can Help," *Iron Age* (January, 1957), pp. 173-76.

KIBBEE, J. M. *et al. Management Games.* New York: Reinhold Publishing Corp., 1961.

KILBRIDGE, M. D., and WESTER, L. "Review of Analytical Systems of Line Balancing," *Operations Research* (September, 1962), pp. 626-38.

KLEILER, F. M. "Keys to a Rich Uncle's Treasure: Federal Agencies Have Priceless Data," *American Business* (March, 1958), pp. 13-15.

KOCH, EDWARD G. "A Practical Approach to Management Planning and Control," *Advanced Management* (July, 1959).

KOONTZ, HAROLD, and O'DONNELL, C. *Principles of Management.* New York: McGraw-Hill Book Co., Inc., 1959.

KURNOW, ERNEST, and OTTMAN, FREDERICK R., and GLASSER, GERALD. *Statistics for Business Decisions.* Homewood, Illinois: Richard D. Irwin, Inc., 1959.

KUZNETS, SIMON. *Six Lectures on Economic Growth*. Glencoe, Ill: The Free Press of Glencoe, 1960.

LABINE, R. A. "Truth about Industrial Spying," *Chemical Engineering* (February, 1960), pp. 121-26.

LARKE, ALFRED G. "Your Company's Secrets: Are They Safe?" *Dun's Review and Modern Industry* (August, 1958), pp. 44-45.

"Lawsuits Unlimited," *Chemical Week* (Nov. 25, 1961), p. 23.

LEBRETON, PRESTON P., and HENNING, D. A. *Planning Theory*. Englewood Cliffs, New Jersey: Prentice-Hall Inc., 1961.

LEVITT, THEODORE. "Marketing Myopia," *Harvard Business Review* (July/August, 1960), pp. 45-56.

LINDSAY, FRANKLIN A. "The Growth of Soviet Economic Power and Its Consequences for Canada and the United States," *National Planning Association and Private Planning Association of Canada* (October, 1959), p. 27.

LIPP, JAMES E., and STEWART, ROBERT F. "Managing, Planning, and Operations Research," *Proceedings Sixteenth National ORSA Meeting* (1959).

LLEWELLYN, R. W. "Game Information Theoretic Decision Model," *Industrial Engineer* (May/June, 1961), pp. 150-54.

"Long-Range Planning for New Plant Payoff," *Dun's Review and Modern Industry* (March, 1959), pp. 61-62.

LUCAS, ARTHUR W., and LIVINGSTON, WILLIAM G. "Long-Range Planning and the Capital Appropriations Program," *Management Report Number 44: Financial Planning for Greater Profit* (1960).

LUEDER, DONALD R. *Aerial Photographic Interpretation Principles and Applications*. New York: McGraw-Hill Book Co., Inc., 1960.

LUHN, H. P. "A Business Intelligence System," *IBM Journal of Research and Development* (October, 1958), pp. 314-19.

MACCUTCHEON, R. H. "Patent or Secrecy for Shop Tools and Processes," *Tool Engineer* (January, 1957), pp. 94-96.

"Make Your Salesmen Intelligence Agents," *Sales Management* (Oct. 21, 1960), pp. 55-56.

MALCOLM, D. G.; ROSEBOOM, J. H.; CLARK, C. E.; and FAZAR, W.

"Application of a Technique for R & D Program Evaluation," *Operations Research* (September/October, 1959).

MALLAHER, K. A. "Information from the Board of Trade," *ASLIB Proceedings* (May, 1954), pp. 78-85.

"Marketing Intelligence Systems—A Dew Line for Marketing Men," *Business Management* (January, 1966).

"Marketing Planned Five Years Ahead," *Sales Management* (May, 1961), pp. 75-76.

MANLEY, MARIAN C. *Business Information—How to Find and Use It.* New York: Harper Bros., 1955. 265 pp.

MARKHAM, JESSE WILLIAM. *Competition in the Rayon Industry.* Cambridge, Massachusetts: Harvard University Press, 1952.

McCAFFREY, R. L. "Continuing Management Support Is the Key to Healthy Effective Planning Function," *Office Management* (February, 1959), pp. 60-62.

McCORMICK, R. L. "Helping Business Is Big Business: Washington Experts Guide Industry through Capital Maze," *Iron Age* (October, 1958), p. 48.

McCUTCHEON, J. W. "Employee Approximation of Trade Secrets," *Soap and Chemical Specialties* (July, 1955), p. 83.

McDOWELL, IAN. "The Economic Planning Period for Engineering Works," *Operations Research* (July/August, 1960).

McLEAN, JOE. "Long-Range Planning Held Rising Need," *Electronic News* (January, 1961), p. 16.

MEANS, R., and DUFFIN, J. "Minimization Problems Treated by Geometric Means," *Operations Research* (September/October, 1962), pp. 668-75.

MERRILL, H. F. "Guides for Long-Range Planning," *Management News* (November, 1960).

MILLER, B. SPANGLER. *R.C. 254.* Yorktown Heights, New York: IBM Research Center (June, 1960).

MILLER, DAVID W., and STARR, MARTIN. *Executive Decisions and Operations Research.* Englewood Cliffs, New Jersey: Prentice-Hall, Inc., 1960.

MILLER, ERNEST. "Long-Range Planning—An Overview," *Advanced Management* (November, 1960), pp. 8-11.

MORSE, P. M. "International O.R. Activities," *Operations Research* (November, 1961), pp. 910-12.

National Research Bureau, Inc. *Encyclopedia of Business Information Sources*. Chicago, Illinois: The Bureau, 1946.

NEAL, H. R. "How Detroit Guards Auto Secrets," *Iron Age* (November, 1957), p. 98.

"Need Help with Market Research? Your Biggest Answer Man, Uncle Sam," *American Business* (February, 1959), pp. 17-19.

NEMMERS, E. E. *Managerial Economics*. New York: John Wiley & Sons, Inc., 1962.

"New Aries Whodunnit," *Chemical Week* (June, 1962), pp. 20-21.

NEWCOMB, ROBINSON. "Plan Your Part in the Boom," *Nation's Business* (July, 1959), pp. 38-39.

"New Foreign Technical Information Center Offers Service to Business," *Commerce Week* (August, 1958), p. 2.

"New Methods in Mathematical Programming; Texts of Papers from the Second International Conference on Operational Research," *Operations Research* (July, 1962), pp. 437-99.

NICHOLS, W., and HEITMAN, R. E. "Decision Making in Engineering," *ASME Paper Number 59* (1959).

OLSEN, ASKEL G. "How to Plan Research for Profit, Part One: Objectives and Costs," *Food Engineering* (November, 1959), pp. 39-41

———. "How to Plan Research for Profit, Part Two: Managing the Team," *Food Engineering* (December, 1959), pp. 99-100.

"Operational Research, Management's Need," *Engineering* (November, 1961), pp. 652-53.

OSTROW, RONALD J. "Wiretap Cases Bug Nation's Law Officers," *Los Angeles Times* (May 29, 1966), p. 1.

"Overseas Market Research: A Do-It-Yourself Guide: With Data by Subject, by Publication Source," *Dun's Review and Modern Industry* (May, 1957), pp. 105-13.

PACKARD, VANCE. "The Walls Do Have Ears," *New York Times Magazine* (September 20, 1964), pp. 23, 114-16.

PARADISO, L. J. "How Can Business Analyze Its Markets?" *Survey of Current Business* (March, 1945), pp. 6-13.

PATTERSON, MOREHEAD. "How to Prepare for Future Company Growth." *Iron Age* (October, 1959), pp. 75-77.

PAYNE, BRUCE. *Long-Range Planning: Dynamic Discipline for Your Company's Future.* MacKay-Shields Associates Incorporated, 1960.

———. "Long-Range Planning: Special Report," *Chemical Week* (January, 1960), pp. 78-84.

PEARSON, ANDRALL E. "An Approach to Successful Marketing Planning," *Business Horizons* (Winter, 1959).

PENROSE, EDITH TILTON. *The Theory of the Growth of the Firm.* New York: John Wiley & Sons, Inc., 1959.

"Planning in Today's Management; Panel Discussion," *Aerospace Engineering* (April, 1962), pp. 56-57.

PRESTON, LEE E. "A Longer Look at the Sixties," *California Management Review* (Fall, 1960).

QUINN, JAMES B. "The Challenge of Effective Planning for Research: Part One," *Chemical and Engineering News* (January, 1961), pp. 78-84.

———. "The Challenge of Effective Planning for Research: Part Two," *Chemical and Engineering News* (January, 1961), pp. 106-12.

———. "Long-Range Planning for Industrial Research," *Harvard Business Review* (July/August, 1961).

RAPHAEL, M. "Guides to Business Information Sources," *Business Literature* (May, 1957), pp. 142-43.

RATES, R. D. "CICRIS: Cooperatives, Industrial and Commercial Reference and Information Service," *ASLIB Proceedings* (March, 1957), pp. 83-84.

REAM, N. J. "Planning and Control in Engineering Management," *ASME Paper Number 59* (September, 1959).

REES, T. H., and KENT, A., and PERRY, J. W. *Automatic Correlation of Information for Purposes of Commercial Intelligence.* New York: Interscience Publishers, Inc., 1958.

RICHARDSON, WILLIAM W. "The Accountant's Opportunities as a Profit Planner," *NAA Bulletin* (July, 1960), pp. 3-10.

———. "Significance of Company Forward Planning," *NAA Bulletin* (January, 1960).

RIGGLEMAN, J. R., and FRISBEE, I. N. *Business Statistics*. New York: McGraw-Hill Book Co., Inc., 1951.

RODGERS, O. E. "Competitive Position as Measure of Engineering Progress." *ASME Paper Number 58* (March, 1958).

"Rooting out Data That Distort Business Forecasting," *Business Week* (March 19, 1960), pp. 190-92.

SCHER, V. A. "Protecting Your New Ideas," *Textile World* (June, 1960), pp. 38-39.

SCHLAIFER, ROBERT. *Probability and Statistics for Business Decisions*. New York: McGraw-Hill Book Co., Inc., 1959.

SCHRAMM, ROBERT W. "Where Is Your Company Headed?" *Petroleum Refiner* (November, 1959), pp. 361-65.

SCHWEYER, H. E., and MAY, F. P. "Criteria for Capital Expenditure," *Industrial and Engineering Chemical* (August, 1962), pp. 46-50.

SCOTT, DON H. "A Brief Look at Management in 1970," *Sales Management* (November, 1960).

―――. "Failure to Make Long-Range Plans," *Sales Management* (1960), pp. 38-40.

SENEY, WILSON. "Financing for the Long-Range," *Dun's Review and Modern Industry* (July, 1960), pp. 43-45.

SHELLEY, TULLY, JR., and PEARSON, ANDRALL W. "A Blueprint for Long-Range Planning," *Business Horizons* (Winter, 1958), pp. 77-84.

SIMON, HERBERT A. "Management by Machine: How Much and How Soon," *Management Review* (November, 1960).

SIMS, E. RALPH, JR. "Industrial Technical Intelligence: Tool for Long-Term Planning and Prevention of Technological Surprise," *Advanced Management* (July, 1959), pp. 18-20.

"Simulation and Gaming: a Symposium," *American Management Association* (1961).

SMITH, JACK. "Ex-Army Man Tracks Down Industrial Spies," *Los Angeles Times* (February 11, 1962), pp. 1-2.

SMITH, PHILIP A. (ed.). "The Impact of Computers on Psychological Research," *SDC, SP-119* (October, 1959).

SMITH, RICHARD AUSTIN. "Business Espionage: Long-Range Planning for Management," *Harper's* (1958), pp. 358-72.

"Snooping Electronic Invasion of Privacy," *Life* (May 20, 1966), pp. 38-47.

SNYDER, RICHARD M. *Measuring Business Changes.* New York: John Wiley & Sons, Inc., 1955.

SOMMER, ARTHUR V. "Considerations in Evolving a Long-Range Plan: a Case Study." *Master's Thesis MIT, School of Industrial Management* (1959).

SOMMERS, A. T. "Forecasting and the Diffusion Indexes," *Analyst's Journal* (February, 1958), pp. 23-27.

SPECIAL LIBRARIES ASSOCIATION. FINANCIAL DIVISION. *Handbook of Commercial, Financial and Information Services.* (comp. by WALTER HAUSDORFER). New York: Special Library Association, 1956.

SPENCER, M. H., and SIEGELMAN, LOUIS. *Managerial Economics: Decision Making and Forward Planning.* Homewood, Illinois: Richard D. Irwin, Inc., 1959.

"Spying for Profit," *Time* (July, 1959), pp. 59-60.

STEINER, GEORGE A. "How to Forecast Defense Expenditures," *California Management Review* (Summer, 1960).

STEINER, GEORGE A. (ed.). *Managerial Long-Range Planning.* New York: McGraw-Hill Book Company, Inc., 1963.

STESSIN, LAWRENCE, " 'I Spy' Becomes Big Business," *New York Times Magazine* (November 28, 1965), pp. 105-8.

STEWART, N. "When to Tell Your Secrets; Managers' Need to Know Must Be Weighed against Risks of Carelessness," *Nation's Business* (June, 1962), pp. 62-64.

STOLZE, W. J. "Decision Making as it Affects Long-Range Planning," *Engineering Management* (March, 1962), pp. 33-36.

———. "Long-Range Planning in the Electronics Industry," *Master's Thesis MIT, School of Industrial Management* (1960).

———. "Measuring Effectiveness of Technical Proposals and Marketing Effort in Military Electronics, *IRE Transactions on Engineering Management* (June, 1960), pp. 62-66.

"Taking Dead Aim at Industrial Mata Haris," *Factory* (March, 1961), pp. 164-65.

"Talking Too Much Can Hurt You; Three-Year Story of a Patent Fight," *Business Week* (January 28, 1956), p. 116.

THOMPSON, KENNETH L. "Long-Range Planning for a Growing Firm," *Journal of Accounting* (March, 1960), pp. 39-43.

THOMPSON, STEWART. "New Dimensions in Creative Planning," *The Business Quarterly* (Summer, 1959).

TOMBACH, HAROLD. "Business Intelligence," System Development Corporation, *SP-59*. April, 1959.

TONGE, FRED M. "The Use of Heuristic Programming in Management Science." Rand Corporation, *P-2127*, November, 1960.

"Trail That Led to Spy Charges," *Business Week* (November 25, 1961), pp. 28-29.

"Twenty-Four Newspapers Market Studies Available to Agencies," *Cities Advertising Agency* (October, 1957), pp. 75-76.

VANCE, STANLEY. *Management Decision Simulation.* New York: McGraw-Hill Book Co., Inc., 1960.

VANDENBERG, JACK. "Auto Makers, Too, Conduct Espionage," *Los Angeles Examiner* (June, 1960), p. 40.

"Vast Conspiracy, Asserts Aries," *Chemical Week* (December 16, 1961), p. 21.

VAZSONYI, ANDREW. "Optimum Mix of Offensive and Defensive Advertising," *Ramo-Wooldridge Corp.* (July, 1960).

VICKER, R. "How Industry Is Using Overseas Science Scouts: Abstract," *Management Review* (August, 1960), pp. 37-39.

WALLICH, HENRY C. "The Cost of Freedom: A New Look at Capitalism," *Harper's* (1960).

———. "Here's a Way to Real Growth," *Nation's Business* (September, 1960).

WASSERMAN, PAUL. *Information for Administrators: A Guide to Publications and Services for Management in Business and Government.* Ithaca, New York: Cornell University Press, 1956.

WATKINS, H. W. R. "Operational Research," *Chemical and Industrial* (March, 1962), pp. 447-50.

WEEKS, S. "Uses of World Trade Information Service," *Foreign Commerce Weekly* (September, 1957), p. 21.

WEILAND, PAUL E. "Long-Range Planning for Public Utilities," *Public Utilities Fortnightly* (December, 1959), pp. 969-76.

WESSEL, ROBERT H., and WILLETT, EDWARD R. *Statistics as Applied to Economics and Business.* New York: Henry Holt and Company, 1959.

"What Is a Trade Secret?" *Machine Design* (March, 1960), pp. 105-107.

WIKSTROM, WALTER S. "Factors in Manpower Planning," *Management Record* (September, 1960), pp. 2-5.

WORTHAM, DR. A. W. "Planning Is Essential to Corporate Success," *News Front* (April, 1961).

WRIS, ANREN. "Are You Tomorrow Minded?" *Management Review* (February, 1961).

YALE, JORDEN P. "Elements in Long-Range Planning," *Advanced Management* (May, 1961).

YASPAN, ARTHUR J., and HALBERT, MICHAEL. Information-Collection Procedures," *Operations Research* (August, 1957), p. 582.

YEAGER, P. B. "Company Secrets Have Reasonable Protection," *Nation's Business* (October, 1959), p. 14.

YOCUM, JAMES C. *Information Sources for Small Business.* Small Business Handbook Series. Columbus, Ohio: Ohio State University, B-3, 1949.

Appendixes

Appendix A

INDUSTRIAL ESPIONAGE*

EDWARD E. FURASH

Much publicity has been given lately to the practice of "industrial espionage" by American business. Articles and news items have implied that, more than ever before, executives are out to steal secrets from their competitors. To find out how often such activity occurs in business, who does it, and what top management thinks about it, HBR *made this study. By detailed questionnaire and depth interview we examined both the unlikely and the likely places for spying, and gathered data on the prosaic as well as the romantic aspects of securing information about competitive activities. Edward E. Furash, Assistant Editor of* HBR, *is the reporter.*

—THE EDITORS

"If your company has a secret—and what company hasn't?—hold on to it tight, tighter than you have in the past. According to at least one large detective agency, attempts to steal corporate secrets are growing. . . ."—*Dun's Review and Modern Industry,* August 1958.[1]

"Ironically, our high-minded and idealistic society has made industrial espionage one of the important vertebrae, if not the very backbone, of its economy. . . . Spying is as common as the

---

*Reprinted from *Harvard Business Review,* Nov.-Dec., 1959.
[1]Alfred G. Larke, "Your Company Secrets: Are They Safe?" p. 44.

forty-hour week. 'In business,' one executive stated . . . 'it's not only ethical to steal secrets, it's obligatory. If you're planning to stay in business, that is.' "—*Cosmopolitan,* February 1958.[2]
    "Ever meet an industrial spy? Quite possibly you did, without knowing it. For according to those whose business it is to steal your secrets, there's more industrial espionage going on today than ever before."—*Fortune,* May 1956.[3]

    Every executive has some things he wants to know about his competitors in order to predict their reactions to new strategies by his company. He needs such information in order to give his salesmen "talking points," to beat the quality of a product of his competitor, and so on. At the same time, there is some particular information about his own company that he does not want anyone else to know. These secrets, for the most part, relate to highly prized processes and know-how that give him some marketing advantage over competitors.
    How far will competitors go to get such information? Recent articles and news releases claim that some executives will do just about anything to get these secrets. According to some self-professed industrial spies interviewed in this study, more factory keyhole peeping is going on today than ever before in the history of American business. But executives, when queried, deny that it is prevalent in business. Those who make the charge counter with cries of "hypocrite" and claim that those who do it most will deny it the loudest.
    It is true that most businesses today probably face tougher competition than ever before. At the same time, a high premium has been placed on all kinds of information that will give a business some competitive advantage. Whether these factors have placed such great pressure on today's executive that he is willing to attempt to steal key information from his competitor is something that has yet to be proved.
    That is why we wanted to try to pin down some facts and figures. Our quantitative findings are based upon 1,558 completed questionnaires—1,250 machine tabulated, the balance inspected

---

[2]Richard Gehman, "Executive Spies," p. 71.
[3]Richard Austin Smith, "Business Espionage," p. 118.

and found to have no significant differences—which represents a 21% return from our mailing to a cross section of *HBR* readers.

The vast majority of the business executives who read HBR *say that, although they would like to know many things about their competitors, they would gather this information only through methods that they considered open and aboveboard— no matter how tough the situation!* Indeed, few executives consider the activities publicized in such articles as those quoted above to be either prevalent or laudatory. In fact, many say they are doing something about *improving* the atmosphere in their industry to establish better competitor relations.

In essence, much of the smoke may be without fire and may result from the confusion of routine and quite ethical procedures for competitor intelligence with the definitely questionable activities of espionage. To put these questions in perspective, let us examine the questionnaire responses and then consider them in the light of the more qualitative interviews and voluntary comments.

FORMAL METHOD

Executives were asked to describe the system used in their companies to gather information about competitors. Their answers can be found in Exhibit I. Though there are differences by size of company, only a minority use any formal system, even among large companies.

However, the fact that a company does not have a "formal" method for gathering and evaluating competitor information does not mean, necessarily, that such information is of no importance. Nor does it mean that the company does not do a good job of using what information it does obtain. In order to discern the importance of information about competitor activities, as well as the satisfaction that the executive feels with his company's system for gathering it, we asked:

"Do you think your company should have a more organized and more systematic method for gathering, processing, analyzing, and reporting information about competitors?" The answers:

Yes 56.6%   *No* 43.4%

EXHIBIT I

KIND OF ORGANIZATION DEVELOPED FOR GATHERING INFORMATION
ABOUT COMPETITORS, BY SIZE OF COMPANY

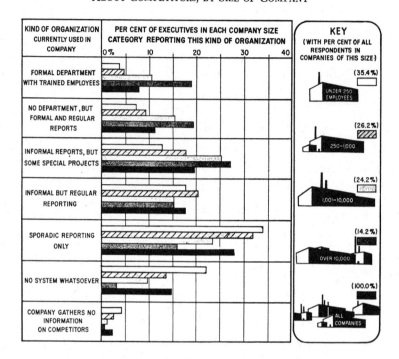

As shown in Exhibit II, executives in firms with more formal systems are less likely to want an improved procedure for handling competitor information than are those in companies with few or no methods for gathering and evaluating this material. But almost all say that information on competitor activities is quite important in the daily conduct of their businesses, and the majority would like to improve the system currently used in their companies, at least to the degree that they could be certain that important information would be recognized and circulated among the executives who need such knowledge for planning or strategy purposes. Industry differences are negligible.

One sharp exception to this trend is those executives whose companies gather *no* information about competitors. Informal comments written on the questionnaires indicate that most of

EXHIBIT II

EXTENT TO WHICH EXECUTIVES WANT A MORE FORMAL, SYSTEMATIC
METHOD FOR GATHERING INFORMATION ABOUT COMPETITORS
(*as percent of executives in companies using each method*)

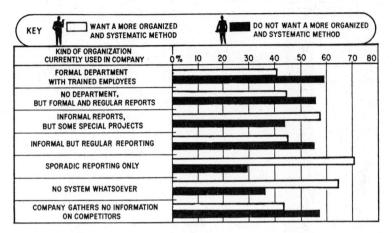

these executives (bankers, for instance) feel that this information is not important in their businesses, or that the few facts they do need are readily available.

WHAT AND HOW?

If having information about competitor activities is important, then what specific facts do executives want most? The executives were asked to indicate on a long list of possible items —with room for additional ones—the *three* kinds of information about competitors they considered to be most important to a firm in their industry. Their responses can be found in Exhibit III.

The informal comments show that the most important information desired by the majority—facts about competitor pricing activities and strategy—is especially significant in a period of rising costs, and in situations where personal selling is an important component of the marketing mix.

How do companies obtain information? Most executives feel that company salesmen are the most fruitful source of informa-

EXHIBIT III

KIND OF INFORMATION ABOUT COMPETITORS THAT EXECUTIVES
FEEL IS IMPORTANT TO COMPANIES IN THEIR INDUSTRY

PER CENT OF ALL RESPONDENTS CONSIDERING THIS INFORMATION IMPORTANT		WHO WANTS THIS INFORMATION THE MOST ?			
KIND OF INFORMATION ↓	↓	INDUSTRIES MOST INTERESTED	PER CENT OF INDUSTRY EXECUTIVES ↓	COMPANIES MOST INTERESTED	PER CENT OF COMPANY-SIZE EXECUTIVES ↓
PRICING	66.8%	RETAIL & WHOLESALE TRADE CONSTRUCTION MANUFACTURING CONSUMER PRODUCTS	87.4 % 76.9 % 66.9 %	250-1,000 EMPLOYEES	69.6%
PROMOTIONAL STRATEGY	40.9%	RETAIL & WHOLESALE TRADE BANKING COMMUNICATIONS	70.9% 69.4 % 46.2%	UNDER 250 EMPLOYEES	47.8%
RESEARCH & DEVELOPMENT	35.6%	ENGINEERING MANUFACTURING INDUSTRIAL PRODUCTS	62.1 % 49.0%	OVER 10,000 EMPLOYEES 1,001-10,000 EMPLOYEES	54.4% 31.7%
SALES STATISTICS	27.4%	TRANSPORTATION RETAIL & WHOLESALE TRADE COMMUNICATIONS	46.3% 41.0% 38.5%	1,001-10,000 EMPLOYEES	27.2%
MANUFACTURING PROCESSES	24.8%	MANUFACTURING INDUSTRIAL PRODUCTS ENGINEERING	36.2% 32.0%	OVER 10,000 EMPLOYEES	31.1%
COST DATA	24.2%	CONSTRUCTION ENGINEERING	41.0% 27.6 %	1,001-10,000 EMPLOYEES	25.5%
EXPANSION PLANS	19.6%	BANKING TRANPORTATION	32.4% 31.7 %	OVER 10,000 EMPLOYEES	24.3%
COMPETITIVE BIDS	18.3%	CONSTRUCTION ENGINEERING	46.2% 41.4%	UNDER 250 EMPLOYEES	21.0%
PRODUCT STYLING	17.5%	MANUFACTURING CONSUMER PRODUCTS	35.5%	1,001-10,000 EMPLOYEES	18.1%
FINANCING	5.7 %	BANKING TRANSPORTATION	16.2% 9.8%	UNDER 250 EMPLOYEES	8.6%
PATENTS & INFRINGEMENTS	4.7%	MANUFACTURING INDUSTRIAL PRODUCTS	8.2%	OVER 10,000 EMPLOYEES	6.3%
EXECUTIVE COMPENSATION	2.3%	BANKING CONSULTING COMMUNICATIONS	8.9% 7.7% 7.1 %	UNDER 250 EMPLOYEES	4.3%

tion about the activities of competitors. The second most valuable source is published information, followed by personal or professional contacts with executive counterparts. A summary table
of these findings can be found in Exhibit IV. Analyzing these ap-
praisals for industry differences, we find that:

- 52% of executives in the manufacturing of industrial
products and 44% of those in the manufacturing of consumer products state that their salesmen furnish "much"
or "extensive" information about competitors.

- 69% of executives in the retail and wholesale trades
and 66% of executives in transportation indicate that their
salesmen furnish "some," "much," or "extensive" information about competitors.

- 47% of executives in consulting and business services
and 39% of those in banking feel that their salesmen furnish "little" information or "none."

- 52% of executives in banking, 47% of those in transportation, and 40% of those in communications and en-

EXHIBIT IV

AMOUNT OF INFORMATION ABOUT COMPETITORS OBTAINED BY COMPANY FROM VARIOUS SOURCES

(as percent of all respondents)

Source of information	Amount of information obtained					
	None	*Little*	*Some*	*Much*	*Extensive*	*Total*
Company salesmen	10.1%	12.6%	36.6%	25.6%	15.1%	100.0%
Published sources	5.6	17.8	40.6	20.6	15.4	100.0
Personal or professional contacts with competitors	4.1	14.9	50.2	22.8	8.0	100.0
Company suppliers	14.2	26.7	45.0	12.2	1.9	100.0
Advertising agencies, consultants (excluding formal marketing research)	37.5	35.1	21.6	3.9	1.9	100.0
Hiring employees of competitors	52.7	33.7	10.9	1.9	0.8	100.0
Undercover activities by company employees	84.2	12.9	2.2	0.3	0.4	100.0
Undercover activities for company by outside agency	87.7	9.2	2.4	0.3	0.4	100.0

gineering obtain "much" or "extensive" information from published sources.

- 25% of those in wholesale and retail trade state that they receive "much" or "extensive" information from company suppliers or customers.
- 40% of executives in banking indicate that they receive "much" or "extensive" information from personal contacts with executives of other firms.
- Over 60% in *every* industry feel that their companies receive "some," "much," or "extensive" information from such personal contacts by executives.

There are sharp differences in the degree to which companies of various sizes use these several sources of information:

- 52% of executives with companies having more than 10,000 employees indicate that their companies receive "much" or "extensive" information from company salesmen, compared with only 25% of executives in companies of less than 250 employees.
- 44% of executives with companies of more than 10,000 employees report that their companies obtain "much" or "extensive" information from published sources, compared with only 26% of executives in companies with under 250 employees.

Such statistics may only reflect the fact that a large company has more salesmen and, therefore, more opportunities to gather information. On the other hand, they may reflect a difference in the ability of the company to afford the "luxury" of organizing to obtain and report competitive information.

The importance put on salesmen as sources of information about competitors is underscored by the chief executive of a consumer products company who writes that "a good system of salesman reporting about competitor activity is the best way we know for getting the information that is most important to us— the information necessary to meet competition and sell effectively." This statement is also a good indicator of the nature of the competitive intelligence conducted by American business: *most business firms gather information about the immediate activities of competitors in order to meet competition more effectively at the consumer or customer level.*

SPYING ACTIVITIES

But what about the type of activity that, in all justice, must be called espionage or, more strongly, spying? Better suited to popular journalism, by virtue of its sensational, not to mention romantic, aspects, the frequency of such spying has been the subject of all too few serious studies.

A group of students at the Harvard Graduate School of Business Administration found that, in a survey of 200 companies, some 27 percent reported that spying or other types of undercover information collecting had recently been discovered in their industry. Of these, 20 percent thought that this activity was increasing, 70 percent indicated no change, and 10 percent thought it was decreasing. The report did not list the kind or number of industry groups involved or the possible duplication of instances to which these companies referred.[4] This evidence would suggest, at least, that some executives *think* that spying is being done in their industry. To estimate the extent of such activities, we asked executives whether in their companies they had observed or heard of various kinds of activities. It can be seen from their replies, summarized in Exhibit V, that when all industries are surveyed, the active incidence of spying turns out to be surprisingly low.

EXHIBIT V

EXECUTIVE OPINIONS OF THE AMOUNT OF SPYING AND
SECURITY ACTIVITIES IN THEIR INDUSTRY
(as percent of all respondents)

Activity	Have heard of	Have observed	Have not heard of or observed	Total
Authorized spying on the part of your company?	5.7%	4.4%	89.9%	100%
Spying *against* your company?	17.5	7.2	75.3	100
Employee fired for revealing secrets?	8.9	4.9	86.2	100
Tightening of company security?	12.1	34.7	53.2	100
Unauthorized spying by company employees?	11.4	7.1	81.5	100

[4] *Competitive Intelligence* (Watertown, Massachusetts, C. I. Associates, 1959), p. 61.

In every case, the frequency of occurrence of industrial espionage is higher for those who report indirect as opposed to direct knowledge of the event. An evaluation of these responses by company size reveals that only in the case of tightening company security is there a serious difference between large and small companies. Executives in large companies report more instances of tightening company security (39.7 percent observed, 14.9 percent heard of) than those in smaller companies (24.9 per cent observed, 9.0 percent heard of). Again, this difference may merely reflect the fact that larger companies have more money available for such services, rather than a difference in the need for security.

On the basis of industry, only those in retail and wholesale trade observe a greater than ordinary amount of *unauthorized* spying by company employees (12.6 percent observed, 12.6 percent heard of). Similarly, those in banking report less spying *against* their companies (9.9 percent heard of, 3.6 percent observed), while those in construction report considerably more (24.4 percent heard of, 12.6 percent observed). Two striking industry differences in firing employees were reported; more instances are cited by executives in engineering (17.3 percent heard of, 6.9 percent observed), and in consulting and business services (12.9 percent heard of, 10.0 percent observed). Finally, executives in the several industries report dissimilar frequencies of instances of tightening company security:

	Heard of	*Observed*
Engineering	3.5%	65.5%
Manufacture of consumer products	12.0	40.0
Retail & wholesale trade	14.2	32.3
Banking	4.5	13.5
Transportation	7.1	11.9

If only key executives had real knowledge of, or participated in, company spying activities, then the low incidence of certain activities reported would have quite a different meaning. With this possibility in mind, we analyzed the responses for differences in reporting by executives in various management positions; the results are shown in Exhibit VI. We also analyzed the responses

EXHIBIT VI

EXECUTIVE OPINIONS OF THE AMOUNT OF SPYING AND SECURITY
ACTIVITIES IN THEIR INDUSTRY, BY POSITION LEVEL
(as percent of respondents in each position category)

Activity	Position level*	Have observed	Have heard of
Authorized spying on the part of your company	Top	3.8%	5.4%
	Upper middle	4.2	5.7
	Lower middle	7.2	7.2
Spying *against* your company	Top	7.2	18.7
	Upper middle	7.2	15.3
	Lower middle	7.2	16.1
Employee fired for revealing secrets	Top	5.7	9.1
	Upper middle	3.7	8.4
	Lower middle	3.6	7.2
Tightening company security	Top	32.4	11.5
	Upper middle	39.0	12.1
	Lower middle	28.6	8.9
Unauthorized spying by company employees	Top	7.8	10.7
	Upper middle	4.9	12.8
	Lower middle	17.9	7.2

*Top management (54.2% of all respondents): chairman of board; board member; owner; partner; president; vice president; treasurer and secretary-treasurer; secretary to corporation; general manager; general superintendent; administrative director and controller; and assistants thereto. *Upper middle management* (32.3% of all respondents): plant or factory manager or superintendent; functional department heads (e.g., advertising, sales, production, procurement, industrial relations, and so on); division, branch, or section manager or chain store manager; and assistants thereto. *Lower middle management* (4.5% of all respondents): supervisor; office manager; traffic manager; chief accountant; foreman; coordinator; finance manager; and so on.

according to the age of the executive; see Exhibit VII. Note that for nearly all the specified activities more of the younger executives have heard of or observed the activity in question than have older executives.

A general question such as the one asked does not provide a good indicator of the incidence of specific activities, or the kinds of situations in which these activities are taking place. For example, in those instances where the executive has only heard of the activity, the number of different events involved cannot be discovered, nor can the degree to which reports are influenced by industry jitters or word-of-mouth magnification.

EXHIBIT VII

EXECUTIVE OPINIONS OF THE EXISTENCE OF SPECIFIED
ACTIVITIES IN THEIR INDUSTRY, BY AGE
(*as percent of respondents in each age category*)

Activity	Age	Have observed	Have heard of
Authorized spying	Under 35	7.2%	9.0%
on the part of	45–49	3.6	5.1
your company	Over 60	3.0	3.0
Spying *against*	Under 35	8.3	17.3
your company	45–49	5.1	16.4
	Over 60	4.6	15.2
Employee fired	Under 35	5.4	4.4
for revealing	45–49	5.7	10.1
secrets	Over 60	9.2	6.2
Tightening com-	Under 35	37.7	10.6
pany security	45–49	36.4	14.3
	Over 60	20.2	7.7
Unauthorized spy-	Under 35	5.9	16.5
ing by company	45–49	10.8	12.9
employees	Over 60	4.6	4.6

Moreover, spying against the company can include patent infringement investigations and lawsuits by competitors, as well as cases of secret-stealing; and security may have been tightened for a number of reasons other than to prevent competitors from learning company secrets.[5]

WHAT FREQUENCY?

To indicate the frequency with which various *specific* espionage activities occur in business, executives were asked to estimate the degree to which companies in their industry use various devices to gather competitive information.

Their responses to this question (see Exhibit VIII) support the evidence cited earlier, for example, that only 0.5% of the executives feel that their companies obtain much or extensive information from undercover activities by company employees or hired agents. Similarly, the data in the exhibit show that the activities that can be labeled as spying (bribery, wire tapping,

---

[5]See Harvey Burstein, "Not So Petty Larceny," *HBR* May–June 1959, p. 72.

EXHIBIT VIII

EXTENT TO WHICH EXECUTIVES THINK COMPANIES IN THEIR INDUSTRY USE SPECIFIED PRACTICES TO GATHER INFORMATION ABOUT COMPETITORS

(as percent of all respondents)

Practice	Extent of use						
	Never	Rarely	Occasionally	Frequently	Regularly	Do not know	Total
Comparison shopping	24.8%	13.4%	19.4%	13.8%	15.6%	13.0%	100.0%
Indirectly pumping competitors	7.3	14.6	39.3	21.7	7.2	9.9	100.0
Surveillance of competitor's activities	11.8	13.7	22.5	20.1	20.4	11.5	100.0
Hiring employee of competitor	16.6	32.7	27.3	8.8	1.7	12.9	100.0
Rewarding competitor's employee for information	67.4	14.3	1.1	0.3	0.1	16.8	100.0
Wire tapping or other electronic eavesdropping	78.8	3.7	0.7	0.0	0.2	16.6	100.0
Misrepresentation so as to enter plants	65.0	15.0	3.7	0.2	0.1	16.0	100.0
Posing as buyer or supplier	54.7	17.0	10.6	2.0	0.2	15.5	100.0
Planting confederate in competitor's company	66.1	12.4	1.8	0.2	0.2	19.3	100.0

misrepresentation, confederates, and posing) have a low order of use by competitors.

The main divergence in opinion is on the topic of employee hiring. Here executives generally feel that little or no information about competitors is obtained from such sources. Surprisingly, however, the same executives also feel that competitors practice this activity to a considerable degree—37.8%! Part of this radical divergence may be due to the nature of employee hiring, a topic covered later in this article.

If these espionage activities occur in industry, are they increasing or decreasing? To obtain a measure of the change in frequency of these activities over time, the executives surveyed were asked whether in the past two years espionage or spying activities in their industry had increased or decreased. Here is what they feel has happened to these activities:

Increased	11.7%
Remained the same	49.3
Decreased	2.3
Never existed	36.7

Exhibit IX contains the responses to this question analyzed according to industry.

ASKING THE "SPIES"

Another way to find out if spying activity is increasing is to ask those employed in business security services, as business investigators, or those holding themselves forth as "industrial spies." Their experiences have been recently published in a number of popular articles and used as evidence of the prevalence and increase in espionage activities.

A number of these individuals were interviewed for this survey. Many of them feel that the number of cases involving personal perpetration or investigation of industrial espionage is increasing. However, they are *not* able to indicate whether this increase in investigations is due to an increase in espionage activities per se or to an increase in companies' sensitivity to espionage.

They were asked to describe the nature of the cases, other than purely protective, referred to them by business. By their testimony, the majority of these cases consists of situations in

EXHIBIT IX

EXTENT TO WHICH EXECUTIVES THINK SPECIFIED ACTIVITIES HAVE
VARIED OVER PAST TWO YEARS IN THEIR INDUSTRY

PER CENT OF ALL RESPONDENTS	INDUSTRY	AS PER CENT OF EXECUTIVES IN EACH INDUSTRY			
		"INCREASED"	"REMAINED SAME"	"DECREASED"	"NEVER EXISTED"
23.8%	MANUFACTURING CONSUMER PRODUCTS	13.1%	52.9%	3.4%	30.6%
34.4%	MANUFACTURING INDUSTRIAL PRODUCTS	11.9%	55.4%	2.1%	30.6%
3.1%	CONSTRUCTION	16.2%	56.8%	0.0%	27.0%
2.3%	ENGINEERING	17.2%	61.6%	0.0%	21.2%
5.6%	CONSULTING AND BUSINESS SERVICES	10.6%	46.4%	4.7%	38.3%
8.8%	BANKING, INSURANCE, INVESTMENT	5.4%	30.3%	0.0%	64.3%
3.3%	TRANSPORTATION	12.2%	36.6%	0.0%	51.2%
10.1%	RETAIL AND WHOLESALE TRADE	5.6%	57.2%	1.6%	36.6%
4.1%	COMMUNICATIONS	5.6%	44.4%	7.4%	42.6%
4.5%	OTHER INDUSTRIES	7.1%	28.4%	1.8%	62.7%

which management feels that an employee is stealing material
or embezzling funds. Many of the remaining cases are requests for
"management audits" which consist of supplying the client with
undercover operatives to be employed for the purpose of reporting on employee activities. Again, most of these audit cases involve
thefts; others are the investigation of foreman bias, slowdown
on a production line, or simply a check on the general efficiency
of company operations.

Many of the investigators interviewed feel that management is
becoming more "intelligence conscious"—implying that management is using investigation more and more to check on the internal health of the organization. As one investigator put it,
"Management often wants the peace of mind we can give them
through an internal audit. We often uncover stealing by employees and misconduct that management never would have
thought existed."

Another major category of cases which are referred to by the
investigators concerns investigations for lawsuits or patent in-
fringements. In these cases, the company counsel or attorney
usually hires the investigator. Typically, the investigator has to
find out about the activities of a competitor in order to get

evidence on a patent infringement. Another type of assignment is to get evidence or affidavits for a lawsuit against a buyer or supplier.

When asked about cases of outright spying to gain advantageous information for its own sake, most of the investigators were reluctant to answer, and could cite fewer cases than one would expect from earlier published statements. Only after lengthy inquiry would they indicate the frequency with which such cases are offered to them. Apparently, with few exceptions even for those who call themselves "industrial spies," the majority of their contacts are for infringement or lawsuit cases in which the hiring management has some legal grounds for the investigation. When asked for specifics, they most often would repeat published cases or cite cases of industry "jitters." In the words of one investigator:

"One company in the industry might pull a dirty deal. The others get so scared that soon everyone has a private investigator following everyone else. The only one who gets anything out of it is the investigator. The people in the industry don't even learn as much as they could find out in the course of regular competitor contacts!"

Another investigator when interviewed stated that he "had not had a case of outright spying in almost three years." Few others could recall more than one case in the previous six months.

Whether one case in six months is too many or too few is a question for the business community to decide. More to the point is the fact that, whether the demand for "corporate spying" is increasing or not, the bulk of such activity is in the realm of legal investigations for patent infringement, lawsuits, and theft. Whether spying is proper conduct even in such "legal" situations is the more immediate question for the business community to decide.

ASKING THE DETECTIVES

A final source of information on the magnitude of industrial spying activity comes from those firms employed in industrial security. Many executives in these companies report that more cases of information leaks are being discovered because of the increasing use of management audits. But they also are not sure whether this means that spying is on the increase, or that companies are getting better at spotting it.

Others feel that many of the cases of wire tapping are internal company matters, and that the rare cases of outright spying activity have been blown up by the press, or used by industries as a vehicle for publicity.

When asked whether his company was receiving more cases of information leaks than in the past, John O. Camden, Vice President and General Manager of Pinkerton's National Detective Agency, Inc., emphatically replied:

"On the contrary. I believe we are called in less frequently than in the past for cases of information leaks, in spite of the fact that we are now serving ten times as many clients as we were ten years ago. Of course, there are exceptions, but they are so much in the minority that they do not present a problem. Most companies gather sufficient information in the course of daily contact with their competitors and through their salesmen and suppliers to have a very good idea of their competitors' abilities. Spying is unnecessary and unwanted.

"Let me cite an illustration. Several months ago one of our clients advised us that a competitor had come to him and told him that he had been offered the secret formula for preparing certain materials that our client's company was manufacturing. Our client had spent millions of dollars in research for this process. The competitor told him that he had been approached by a man who said that for $50,000 or $100,000 he could get complete information concerning the formula and process of manufacturing itself. The man who came to him was not an employee of the competitor or our client, but merely a go-between engaged in selling information as a business. We, through investigating and certain other phases of our work, were able to determine the identity of the employee who was going to provide the information, and he was apprehended.

"I mention this particular situation as an illustration of the fact that a good deal has changed in the attitude of businessmen. The competitor would have profited considerably by having the information, for only one or two companies are able to produce the material. I think that you'll find that this is the attitude of the vast majority of businessmen."

THE CAUSES

Whatever the incidence of espionage activity, there must be some reason for it. Perhaps it is due to the moral character of the particular businessman engaged in it; on the other hand, it might be caused purely by conditions or pressures in the business world. To estimate causation, we asked executives what they felt would lead to an increase in industrial espionage. Here is their vote:

Decline in ethical standards	77.0%
Tougher competition	53.3
Self-defense	37.5
Executive stake due to stock options	6.6
Miscellaneous	3.3

But there are notable industry exceptions to the above averages —viz., engineering, where 87 percent feel that a decline in ethical standards would be the cause, and 63 percent feel, in addition, that tougher competition would be a contributing factor; and consulting, where 88 percent feel that a decline in ethical standards would be the precipitating factor.

BOUNDARIES OF MORALITY

What, then, do executives consider to be "ethical" and "unethical"? To discover this, we asked them to express their approval or disapproval of various situations that have occurred in business. Exhibit X shows what executives consider the moral and ethical boundaries, with a breakdown by age.

Of twelve situations presented, four are approved by a majority of all executives, and one leaves them nearly evenly divided. Some interpretation may be helpful:

Comparison shopping—practiced for quite some time by retailers and manufacturers of consumer goods—is the most emphatically approved. The similar, but more recent, practice of "scouting" is approved by a somewhat smaller majority of executives. In certain respects, both these activities can be considered above board, since they occur in full public view.

The third most approved practice—moving into a test

EXHIBIT X

EXECUTIVE OPINIONS OF VARIOUS SITUATIONS
THAT HAVE OCCURRED IN INDUSTRY
(*as percent of executives in each age category*)

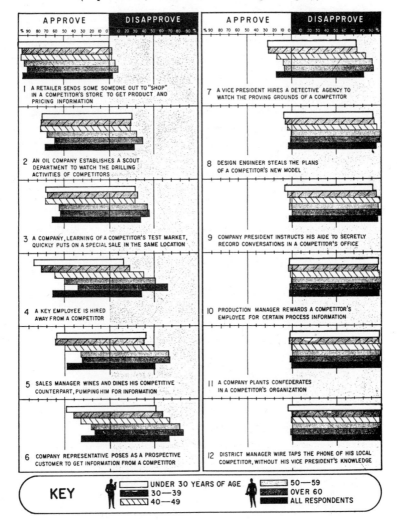

KEY — UNDER 30 YEARS OF AGE / 30—39 / 40—49 / 50—59 / OVER 60 / ALL RESPONDENTS

market—raises an interesting problem. A company can readily learn of a competitor's test, through trade commentary, press releases, and salesmen. The question is whether or not to engage in *counter*intelligence.

The fourth situation the executives approve of—by a scant majority, in this case—is that of hiring employees from a competitor. This issue contains both the possibility that the man is hired for his abilities and the possibility that he is hired for the information he has.

As for the one topic where the executives are almost evenly divided, further analysis by industry indicates a majority of executives in manufacturing industrial and consumer products, engineering, and transportation approve of "wining, dining, and pumping" competitor counterparts, while the majority in all other industries are against it.

In general, for the other situations discussed, there are few variances in aggregate opinions among executives in different industries. Small as these variances may be, however, they may be great by comparison, and can cause the atmosphere of one industry to be quite the opposite of that of another. Here are some differences:

● *Consulting,* where more executives (75%) favor hiring away employees; 25% approve of watching a competitor's proving grounds; and 8% approve of planting a confederate.

● *Engineering,* where executives are split evenly on the issue of employee hiring, but where 73% of executives approve of breaking into a test market.

● *Retail and wholesale trade,* where 48% approve of posing as a buyer or supplier.

● *Banking,* where 51% of executives disapprove of breaking into a test market.

● *Transportation,* where 10% of executives approve design stealing.

Despite these instances of variation in industry ethics, there are many more situations on which agreement is widespread. It is a matter of more or less, not one of black and white.

AGE DIFFERENCES

Strong similarities do not exist in the opinions of executives of different ages. *In nearly every case the younger executive is more likely to approve of a situation than an older executive.* In some instances, their opinions are so different as to be completely opposite. Here are two revealing, even startling, examples:

Executives over 50 disapprove of hiring away employees, whereas executives under 50 approve; and the younger the executive is, the more likely he is to approve! Of course, this might be a reflection of the position he holds in the company. However, the opinions of executives in different management positions (see Exhibit XI) do not differ nearly as markedly as do those opinions of executives in different age groups.

More probable is the possibility that younger men prefer to consider themselves "available" for hire and are eager to reach out for new opportunities. Older executives, perhaps, see less opportunity to make a change, have stronger feelings of being "set" in their current position, or find themselves in situations where they recognize the problems of maintaining a staff of effective personnel, and consequently prefer not to hire away employees, lest someone start hiring away from them. More light will be thrown on this point later.

Younger executives are more in favor of "wining, dining, and pumping" competitor counterparts than are older executives. (The exact reversal in opinion seems to come at about age 45, with those below 45 in favor, and those above 45 against.) Again, remembering that young men are more likely to be in lower management positions, top-management opinions are not as markedly different from other management positions as are the opinions of younger versus older executives. *In fact, the differences in opinion on all situations presented might very well represent quite separate ethical standards on the part of younger and older executives.*

In order to evaluate this hypothesis, we analyzed the opinions on the two revealing situations on the double basis of the executives' age *and* position in the company. Exhibit XII shows how dominant the age pattern is.

EXHIBIT XI

Executive Opinions of Various Situations that Have Occurred in Industry, by Position Level

(as percent of executives in each position category)

Situation	Top management		Upper middle management		Lower middle management	
	Approve	Disapprove	Approve	Disapprove	Approve	Disapprove
A retailer sends someone out to "shop" in a competitor's store to get product and pricing information	95.7%	4.3%	96.3%	3.7%	96.4%	3.6%
An oil company establishes a scout department to watch the drilling activities of competitors	71.2	28.8	76.6	23.4	75.0	25.0
A company, learning of a competitor's test market, quickly puts on a special sale in the same location	64.1	35.9	68.7	31.3	58.9	41.1
A key employee is hired away from a competitor	59.0	41.0	68.1	31.9	69.6	30.4
Sales manager wines and dines his competitive counterpart, pumping him for information	47.5	52.5	52.0	48.0	44.6	55.4
Company representative poses as a prospective customer to get information from a competitor	32.5	67.5	32.6	67.4	39.3	60.7
A vice president hires a detective agency to watch the proving grounds of a competitor	16.3	83.7	18.8	81.2	32.1	67.9
Design engineer steals the plans of a competitor's new model	4.2	95.8	6.9	93.1	9.9	90.1
Company president instructs his aide to secretly record conversations in a competitor's office	4.1	95.9	2.9	97.1	7.1	92.9
Production manager rewards a competitor's employee for certain process information	2.9	97.1	1.5	98.5	1.8	98.2
District manager wire taps the phone of his local competitor, without his vice president's knowledge	1.2	98.8	0.9	99.1	0.0	100.0
A company plants confederates in a competitor's organization	1.6	98.4	2.5	97.5	7.1	92.9

EXHIBIT XII

EXECUTIVE OPINIONS OF TWO SITUATIONS THAT HAVE OCCURRED IN
INDUSTRY, BY AGE AND POSITION LEVEL
(as percent of executives in each category)

		Situation		
		"A key employee is hired away from a competitor."		"Sales manager wines and dines his competitive counterpart, pumping him for information."
Age group (as percent of all respondents)	*Approve*	*Disapprove*	*Approve*	*Disapprove*
Under 30 years of age (7.2%):				
Top management*	79%	21%	59%	41%
Upper middle management	92	8	53	47
Lower middle management	100	0	50	50
30–39 years of age (29.2%):				
Top management	78	22	62	38
Upper middle management	75	25	60	40
Lower middle management	77	23	50	50
40–49 years of age (32.9%):				
Top management	58	42	49	51
Upper middle management	68	32	52	48
Lower middle management	42	58	20	80
50–59 years of age (22.8%):				
Top management	50	50	35	65
Upper middle management	45	55	33	67
Lower middle management	50	50	25	75
Over 60 years of age (7.9%):				
Top management	35	65	30	70
Upper middle management	20	80	46	54
Lower middle management*	75	25	66	34

*Number of respondents in this age-position category is very small.

TEST CASES

It is one thing, however, to ask an executive to approve and disapprove of another's actions and to try to infer from this what he would do, and entirely another to *know* what he would do. To get some indication of how the executives in the survey would react in certain situations, we asked executives to indicate the methods for gathering information that they would use. Their replies are presented in Exhibit XIII.

EXHIBIT XIII

**EXTENT TO WHICH EXECUTIVES WOULD USE SPECIFIED METHODS FOR GATHERING
INFORMATION IN HYPOTHETICAL BUSINESS SITUATIONS**

(as percent of all respondents)

Situation		Method for gathering information					
	Forth-rightly ask the competitor	Hire a competitor's key employee	Indirectly pump the competitor	Bribe a competitor's employee for information	Plant a con-federate	Use wire tapping
1. "Your company wishes to enter a new field in which a competitor is strong, your company lacks know-how."	68.9%	42.3%	40.8%	1.1%	0.5%	0.3%
2. "Your company is considered leader in the industry, but another company has done some valuable research you don't have."	61.6	41.5	25.9	1.2	0.6	0.4
3. "Your company's sales have declined rapidly due to activities of a competitor that you don't know how to match or beat."	45.7	40.2	39.6	3.4	2.6	0.7
4. "You seriously suspect your competitor of patent infringement."	72.4	26.6	10.4	10.4	5.7	1.5

Each of the cases presented represents an increasingly difficult competitive situation. Though the differences in percentage points are not great, there is some indication that certain, albeit few, executives would be willing to use the more undesirable activities as competition stiffened. Further analysis in detail shows:

● In every situation except the first, young executives are less willing to speak forthrightly to competitors than are older executives.

● In all four situations, younger executives are consistently more willing to use the questionable activities than are older executives, though in the last two the magnitude of the difference is small.

● In each situation, those in engineering are more willing to use employee hiring than are those in other industries.

● In each situation, executives in banking, investments, and insurance are more willing to speak forthrightly to competitors than are those in other industries.

Finally, we asked the executives whether they thought most companies in their industry would have answered the same as they did, or have reported more or fewer practices. Here is their verdict:

The same	77.5%
Fewer	3.1
More	19.4

In other words, most executives feel themselves to be typical of others in their industry; there is no suggestion that they see themselves as exceptionally "pure." Manufacturing has the largest proportion of those who do feel their competitors would do more.

But note that even in manufacturing, the individuals willing to practice spying activities represent a distinct and very small minority. Thus, even in situations in which the company has been wronged legally, only a small proportion of the executives surveyed would use any of these activities. As one manufacturer put it: "If an executive has let his company decay so far that he has to resort to these activities rather than honest research efforts, then he deserves to be a loser."

The attitude of younger executives raises thornier questions:

Are younger executives more honest and realistic in their appraisal of business ethics and activities than their older counterparts? Are the older executives reporting what they think they "ought" to say?

Does an executive temper his opinions and activities as he grows older? Does he become more "ethical" in his opinions, less willing to do the "unacceptable" in competitor relations? Do his experiences force him to conclude that higher standards are the most fruitful means for company success in the long run?

Are younger men governed by a different set of ethical rules than their elders? Does this difference represent the opinion of two different generations of management? As time goes on, and today's young men attain higher positions, will the ethics of business practice condone more and more such activities?

Each of these hypotheses describes a different business world for today and the future. Which hypothesis will be the more accurate in time is an interesting topic for more intensive research. Traditionally, the second hypothesis has been the more accurate. But the Editors wonder how executives reading this analysis feel, and will be very interested to see their comments.

EMPLOYEE HIRING

One of the consistently controversial issues coming to light in this survey is the practice of hiring away employees from other companies as a possible means of getting information about competitors. In focusing on this issue we asked the executives:

"To your knowledge, has your company hired a key employee from a competitor . . . in the past year?" The replies:

Yes 21.1%   *No* 78.9%

The very largest and the very smallest companies report the lowest incidence of this practice (16.8% *Yes*). The industries in which the frequency is greatest are engineering (41.4% *Yes*) and communications (30.8% *Yes*); the one with least frequency is banking (12.0% *Yes*).

However, the successful hiring of an employee takes more than just an offer of a new job; it also takes an employee who is willing to leave his company. Many more offers were made than were accepted in order to achieve the 20 percent rate of successful hirings given above. In order to discover how executives would act on a new job offer, and therefore gain a measure of their loyalty to their current employers, we asked them what they would do if they were offered a better job by a competitor of their present company.

Here is a summary of the various courses that executives say they would take:

Reject the offer immediately	23.2%
Inform superior, consider a counteroffer if made, then make a decision	55.0
Inform superior, resign, accept new position	11.6
Accept new position, then inform superior	10.2

On the surface, then, up to 22 percent of the executives are willing to leave their current employer immediately, and 55 percent are willing to consider the new offer seriously. This is quite a problem in view of the fact that most executives cite employee loyalty as their primary defense against industrial spying. Employee hiring is a form of such spying, though not usually recognized as such.

There are some interesting variations in opinion in this area:

• Top executives are least likely to consider the new job offer seriously, but one should hardly feel comforted by this, since most of the seven percentage points above the average for all executives represent the opinions of owners or partners. But the lower down the management ladder one goes, the more likely it is that a man will be willing to consider a new offer seriously, or leave his current employer outright.

• As might be guessed, younger executives—especially under 40—are more willing to consider or accept a new job outright than are their older counterparts.

• Executives in engineering and transportation are least loyal to their employers, with only 3 percent willing to reject an offer outright, and over 35 percent willing to accept another job very readily, without considering offers from their current employer.

A far better measure of loyalty, however, is the amount of information that an executive is willing to give a new employer about his previous company. To measure this, we asked executives what they would do if they were not obligated (by contract) to their previous employer not to reveal his secrets. They say they would:

Withhold key information from new employer	16.5%
Feel the new company entitled to all abilities and key knowledge one possesses, if required	78.4
Volunteer key information about previous employer	5.1

Few executives, then, would be actively disloyal to their present company and use such secrets to enhance their position in the new company. But these differences in opinion show up:

● Only 2.8 percent of those executives in top management would volunteer information about their previous employer; 19.3 percent would withhold it voluntarily.

● Younger executives are more willing to volunteer information about a previous employer (7.5 percent under 40 years of age would, but only 2.6 percent over 40 years of age). In addition, three times as many older executives are willing to withhold information voluntarily.

● Executives in engineering are far less likely to withhold information voluntarily (only 3.4 percent would), and slightly more likely to volunteer it (7.5 percent would). But by far the majority of executives in engineering (89.5 percent) would have to be asked for it before the new company would get it.

In effect, companies that rely on employee loyalty as a method of keeping secrets safe have to recognize that, on an average of 8 times in 10, the employee will give the information to a new employer, *if he is asked for it.*

How does the new employer feel? We asked:

"What knowledge would you expect a new employee to contribute to a new job in your company?" The answers:

All knowledge and abilities   75%
Would exclude competitor's secrets   25

But expecting an employee to give all of his loyalty to his new company after he has been hired is quite different from going out to hire the employee *for the sole purpose* of obtaining the competitor's secrets. In the hypothetical situations discussed above, a *maximum* of 45 percent of the executives surveyed would hire an employee for that purpose alone.

Again, for the situations posed, young executives are the most willing to hire away an employee as the solution. In fact, the majority of all executives less than 40 years old (52.5 percent) would use this practice to obtain the information necessary to enter a new field, or to find out how a competitor was beating them in the market place. In all situations, far fewer of the older executives would hire away an employee for this purpose, and the proportion of executives over 40 years of age approving the practice in these two situations never exceeds 35 percent, and indeed, for executives 50 or over, never is greater than 20 percent. There are no appreciable industry differences.

It is clear, then, that hiring away employees to get information would be attempted by a substantial portion of this sample of executives, especially the younger ones, and that the majority would approve of this practice for various other reasons. The industry in which the practice is most approved and would be most attempted is engineering, comprising mostly companies in the electronics, design, and advanced research and defense industries.

Interviews with executives in the electronics industry reveal that on occasion information has been stolen by hiring away an employee. However, most of them feel that there have been few instances in which *considerable* information was lost in this way. These executives say that a far more important cause for employee switching is the shortage of highly trained electronics engineers which forces companies to bid against each other for capable men. Naturally, some loss of minor information occurs in the process. According to William M. Tetrick, President of Farrington Manufacturing Company:

"Fortunately, we have had little difficulty in keeping our employees. In the industry as a whole, however, engineers are switching as rapidly as salaries can be raised to attract them. It's a matter of having to find the personnel who are competent and can supply the skills necessary to do the job, not one of trying to steal secrets by hiring employees away.

"Suppose, for example, we needed a top-flight mechanical engineer. I would inquire as to where the best men in this field are currently employed, and endeavor to discover who might be unhappy with his present position. Naturally, I'd want to get the best man available. But if he were working for one of our competitors and there was the slightest suspicion that in hiring him we would be stealing some of their information, I would take the second-best man. If this second man were unhappy in his present job, and the work we were doing was more to his liking, then I would offer him the job. We want the man for his abilities, not for his information about our competitors."

This same attitude was reflected by many of the executives surveyed, through informal comments. "We hire a man because of his ability and general knowledge," wrote the president of a retail clothing firm. "If he's with a competitor and he isn't happy, then maybe our organization is the place for him."

On this issue, Thorndike Deland, Sr., Senior Partner in Thorndike Deland Associates (management consultants specializing in executive placement), said:

"In fact, for the clients we serve, I don't know of a single case in which a firm has hired a man for the purpose of getting any secrets or information about his previous employer, for the simple reason that they already had them. They gathered the information in the course of normal trade contacts and competition. The man was hired for his ability, not for the competitor's secrets. *Many companies fail to recognize that a man has to be unhappy or discontented with something in order to leave.*"

CONCLUSION

Though the results of this survey indicate that the frequency of industrial spying and secret-stealing in American business is quite low, a number of sore spots were brought out.

(1) There is strong evidence of a sincere difference in opinion and in ethical standards between younger and older men in industry. The younger executives are far more willing to condone activities that older executives will in no way countenance. Whether this portends a change in business and management ethics for tomorrow and hence an increase in industry spying is for more foolhardy prophets to try to answer.

(2) The practice of hiring away executives and employees is condoned by the majority of executives in this survey, and a large number of executives say they would practice it in order to gain information about competitors. Furthermore, executives are quite willing to consider seriously or accept readily a new job. For the individual firm, this indicates a greater stake in keeping its executives happy in order to keep information at home, as well as to ensure an effective job in running the company. Careful screening to get good executives is a partial solution, but keeping an executive motivated after selection is just as important and certainly is no easy task. When asked about this, Willard E. Henges, President of Graybar Electric Company, Inc., whose policy of executive selection and promotion is from within, replied:

"We feel the best motivator of all is good income. It's the best lubricant in the world for an organization. We use, in addition to direct compensation and stock ownership, merchandise and various executive benefit plans. But equally important in an organization is to create an opportunity to achieve these rewards by providing the executive with opportunity to develop and to use his abilities, and by creating an atmosphere which encourages him to do this."

(3) One way to keep secrets at home, in the event that an executive does decide to leave, is a contract restraining him from giving information for a period after he vacates his present job. Along these lines, we asked:

"Would your present company require by *formal* contract or understanding that you *not* disclose certain information to a new employer?" The response:

Would require	14.3%
Would not require	27.6
No company policy	58.1

As might be expected, more top executives are bound by such a contract than middle-management people. As for industry differences, even where this practice is most prevalent—manufacturing of industrial and consumer products and engineering —the figure is only about 18 percent of executives. Over half of all companies have *no* policy on this matter.

(4) Although competitors may not be out in great numbers stealing secrets, the survey did not reveal, by any means, that competitor relations are perfect. In fact, from informal comments and interviews we gathered many indications of concern about competitor relations. Many executives are worried because they feel that their competitors do not compete fairly in the open market place. But far more frequent are the indications of industry distrust, or hypersensitivity to competitor reactions and competitor activities. We received a number of opinions from executives as to what should be done to improve competitor relations. For example:

"In selling goods to American industry, success depends more on the contribution made in the way of new products, new processes, new methods, and better ways of doing things, than it does on worrying about what the competition is doing—or *planning* to do. Suppliers to industry are mostly honest, ethical, intelligent, have a sense of 'service' and make better contributions to industry when there is good, fair competition to serve as a stimulant." [Vice President of an industrial products company]

"The key to success is to create such a dynamic, aggressive organization that you don't need to worry about what your competitor is doing. The executive who is depending on spying to keep his company on top is bound to fail, for he will not be prepared for the day when the information doesn't come in. The best defense against spying is solid research and marketing on your own part." [President of shoe manufacturing company]

Mr. Henges summed up these sentiments nicely when he said:

"We would much rather see our competitors selling electrical products according to what we consider to be the real needs of the user. However, our competitor is entitled to his own opinion as to what and how to sell. It's up to him to handle the situation as he sees fit, and we have no right to challenge his opinion. We believe our competitors have the same problems we do—and we try to solve them in the best way we know of: in a sound, businesslike, and honest manner. In this way, we help to lead industry practices in what we consider to be the right direction. Experience has shown that competitors will follow if we set a good example and show that our way is best in the long run. To do this, you have to play the course, and *not* the competitor."

Many groups across the country are trying to create an atmosphere in business wherein competitor relations can be eased. We asked the executives in the survey what device within the business community would most ease a difficult competitive situation to the benefit of nearly all. Some 65 percent of all executives feel that sharing information more freely would be the best first step though they agree that not all companies would benefit equally.

Outside the business community, at least one service organization, the Rotary Club, is trying to do something about improving competitor relations. Its program, according to Mr. Deland, who serves as Chairman of the New York Rotary Club's Vocational Service Committee, "is to encourage fair play and communications within an industry, through providing opportunities for members to make personal contact with their competitors and thereby fostering mutual understanding and improved service." The symbol of this program is the "Four-Way Test," which the Rotary encourages trade and professional associations to adopt and distribute: Is it the truth? Is it fair to all concerned? Will it build good will and better friendships? Will it be beneficial to all concerned?

Just as there are individuals participating in spying activities, there are many more who condemn them and work actively through industry leadership to create an atmosphere of good competitor relations. True, no article can claim to be completely authoritative in reporting the incidence of spying activities in business. After all, the objective of good espionage is to get the secret without ever getting caught or telling that you have it. Perhaps those who practice it the most also do disclaim it the most. The executives reporting in this survey, however, indicate that for the business community as a whole industrial espionage is an insignificant and frowned-on practice. Many of them also feel that it has received publicity out of all proportion to the frequency that such activity actually occurs in business, and hope that such publicity will help control rather than encourage it.

Appendix B

HOW THEY SELL

Ex-CIA Man Gathers Market Intelligence for Westinghouse Air Brake

'Agents' Pick Top Prospects For an Off-Highway Truck, Check on Rivals' Activities

Former Ike Aide Shuns Spies

FREDERICK C. KLEIN
Staff Reporter of *The Wall Street Journal*

PITTSBURGH—When Edward J. Green came to Westinghouse Air Brake Co. in 1953, fresh from a top job in the Central Intelligence Agency, he was dismayed by something a budding sales boss with a more conventional background might never have thought of. "I was shocked at how little was understood about getting and processing information," he says. "We got reports from salesmen and read the trade journals and that sort of thing, but what we learned wasn't being put together in an organized way in time to aid decisions."

So Ed Green began organizing a sort of business CIA at "Wabco," and intensified his efforts when he became marketing vice president in 1959. Using market researchers, salesmen and engineers as "agents," the company today spends about $1 million a year collecting information on customers and competitors. And its approach, though far removed from anything the layman might think of as "salesmanship," has paid off in results any sales

boss of the glad-hander school might envy. Reversing a previous
slump, Wabco's sales of air brakes, signaling devices, road graders,
off-highway trucks and other railroad, construction and industrial
equipment have spurted almost 42 percent in the last two years,
to a 1963 record of $241 million.

No cloak-and-dagger work has gone into producing these results. Ed Green firmly declares he is "opposed to industrial spying
in any form." Indeed, he thinks actual espionage is overrated
even in gathering political intelligence. He had little contact with
it himself; his jobs with the CIA and its predecessor, the wartime
Office of Strategic Services, were all administrative. Even so, he
says, he discovered that 80 percent of the information collected
by the CIA came from "overtly obtainable sources."

ATTUNED TO THE FIELD

But tapping those "overtly obtainable sources," Ed thinks,
is as important in sales as in diplomatic planning—and especially
in Wabco's capital-goods field. The company, he says, averages
about five years to think up a new product, design it, produce it
and begin selling it—and "that's too long to waste on a piece of
equipment" that won't sell. Moreover, many of Wabco's customers, which include railroad, construction, mining and oil
firms, have been caught in a cost-price squeeze in recent years and
are tending to base their purchases on cost analyses, rather than
friendship with suppliers or the showmanship of sales presentations.

As a result, says Ed, now a big-framed 55, "the days of the
back-slapping salesman are a thing of the past with us. The only
way to make a sale today is to convince the customer that the
equipment you will make will do a job cheaper and better than
what the competition has to offer"—and for this, he's convinced,
complete, accurate information is the major "must."

To get that information, Ed has organized a system whose
thoroughness reflects not only his intelligence training but his
personality. "Ed Green is the most organized person I've known,"
says a Wabco colleague. "When he was a baby, I'll bet he told
his mother where to stack the diapers."

RESEARCHING THE REDS

Applying this talent to Wabco, Ed Green today has employees reading and analyzing dozens of technical and trade journals, poring over U.S. Census Bureau equipment shipment reports, and scrutinizing research reports such as those prepared by the Stanford University Research Institute. To get ideas for product designers and engineers, Wabco even keeps tabs on Communist research, by looking through the CIA's Consolidated Translation Survey reports on technological developments in Red countries.

And that's only the beginning. To guide salesmen, the company compiles exhaustive dossiers on customers and prospective customers. Currently it's highly interested in selling automated transit gear to subway and elevated train operators. So a shelf at Wabco's Switch & Signal division headquarters in Swissvale, Pa., near Pittsburgh, bulges with blue-covered, loose-leaf volumes detailing the plans of every major city in the U.S. that's considering new facilities or major service expansions. They include even the nickname of every member of every major transit authority in the country.

In the field, the salesmen themselves constantly roam through customers' plants and offices, quizzing production men and purchasers on company activities, plans and needs, and filing regular reports, many on forms Wabco supplies, on any data they pick up.

"I see Wabco people frequently, and they're in constant touch with our operating people," reports John W. Barriger, president of the Pittsburgh & Lake Erie Railroad, a long-time Wabco customer. "They ride our trains and talk to our foremen. They know our brake needs as well as we do."

Competitors get an equally thorough check. Wabco engineers, on orders from headquarters, regularly attend technical talks given by engineers of competing firms. "Knowing what theories the competition is interested in can give you a clue to what kind of (product) applications they have in mind," says Mr. Green. Wabco also keeps files on all executives of competing companies. When a rival firm names a new sales boss, it can tell its salesmen immediately what he did in his previous job, and thus how tough a competitor he can be expected to be.

The system is still being refined, too. Early this year, Ed began requiring salesmen to fill out "lost business reports" whenever a competitor beats out Wabco on a contract worth $10,000 or more. The salesman must compare Wabco's bid with competitors' bids on such things as price and delivery time, interviewing the buyer for details if the bidding wasn't public. Then he must summarize why he thinks Wabco lost—and he's encouraged not to spare himself if the fault was his own.

Ed Green's experts—one to three full-time intelligence analysts at each of the seven Wabco divisions, plus a central staff of three market researchers—analyze such reports for clues as to how selling tactics can be made more effective. Recently a salesman reported that he hadn't called on a railroad often enough to discover that it was about to let an equipment contract earlier than scheduled, and a rival got the award before Wabco could submit a bid. Instead of chewing him out, Wabco took this as a clue to how that railroad is likely to operate on contracts of the type involved, and now schedules regular sales calls to guard against future surprises.

AN EMBARRASSING EARFUL

This was neither the first nor the most striking case in which the information turned up by Wabco's elaborate intelligence network proved to be embarrassingly simple—though vital. In 1961, Wabco sent researchers to ask road builders and municipal highway departments why they weren't buying its road graders. They got an earful of things that might seem obvious, but yet had been overlooked. Among other things, the customers complained that Wabco's three-model line included neither the high-performance machines that contractors need to shape roadbeds, nor the low-cost, low-horsepower models cities use to maintain road shoulders. And they objected that the placement of controls was too different from the road graders their drivers were accustomed to operating.

So Wabco expanded its line to include both high performance graders and a low-cost stripped-down model for municipalities, and adjusted the placement of controls. Sales rose 14% in 1962,

13% in 1963, and so far this year are up 20%. And Wabco claims to have boosted its share of the grader market 21% between 1960 and 1963, running a stronger third to Caterpillar Tractor Co. and Jeffrey-Gallion Manufacturing Co.

At other times, the payoff from Wabco's intelligence work has come in accurate selection of sales targets for a new product. Between 1957 and 1960 the company was field-testing prototypes of an off-highway truck, called the Haulpak, featuring a new suspension system that allowed the lumbering vehicle to haul a bigger load on a lighter body, increasing speed and reducing its turning radius. While doing so, it set its researchers to surveying potential markets.

TRACKING DOWN THE QUARRIES

Using sources such as *Pit & Quarry Magazine,* Wabco drew up a list of all 2,200-odd stone quarrying operations in the U.S. It then sent men to interview many of these operators, analyze their jobs to see if they were large enough to use a high-priced Haulpak (they cost as much as $130,000 each), and seek information on their equipment buying plans. It thus selected the 350 best immediate prospects, and armed salesmen with brochures, flip-charts and job analysis figures tailored specifically to each quarry on which the salesmen would call.

Similar investigations targeted coal and ore mining and road building prospects, and Wabco hit them all with immense success. Sales of the Haulpak in 1961 leaped 183% over the introductory year of 1960, and have doubled since, Wabco says. Industry sources say the company, on the strength of the Haulpak's success, is challenging the long-standing leadership of General Motors Corp.'s Euclid division in the $60 million a year off-highway truck market.

"Wabco stole a march on the industry with the Haulpak," says R. G. Rhett, purchasing director of Kennecott Copper Corp. "When they showed us we could move more ore at less cost on our particular jobs, we bought them." Kennecott since early 1962 has bought 66 of the 65-ton-load Haulpaks, for an average of about $100,000 each.

A TRANSIT COUP?

Advanced intelligence on customers' needs further has enabled Wabco to design new products, or product adaptations, for specific markets, and to pick out the best features of its products to emphasize in sales presentations. Late last year Wabco salesmen and engineers assigned to prepare bids for equipment to be used on a test track on which the San Francisco Bay Area Rapid Transit District will try out various kinds of transit gear picked up a tidbit of news from District engineers. They learned, and reported to Wabco headquarters, that the District was seeking an alternative to the cast-iron truck suspension gear long used in transit vehicles, such as subway and elevated-railway cars.

Wabco immediately went to work adapting its Hydrair off-highway truck suspension system—the one that made the Haulpak possible—to transit cars, a totally new use. Already, it has won a $284,000 contract to test the system on the Bay Area's 4.4-mile track. If successful, the system could win a $2 million contract from the Bay Area Transit District, and possibly still more lucrative contracts in other areas of the country. The Bay Area test track has been planned as something of an industry showcase for advanced new equipment, and transit officials all over the U.S. will be watching its operations with intense interest.

In a different field, Wabco's Air Brake division in 1959 was awaiting the outcome of railroad tests of a combination of a new type of brake rigging and brake shoe it had developed largely to make railroad-car brakes work more efficiently. But it knew the new gear also would enable a manufacturer to make railroad cars bigger without making them heavier—and its salesmen reported that car makers just then were putting on their drafting boards designs for railroad cars bigger than any that had been seen. So "we switched our sales approach to emphasize the weight reduction angle," says William Ayres, Air Brake Division product sales manager.

ENTER THE "PREGNANT WHALE"

This rapidly proved to be the right pitch. "The fact that Wabco had such a rigging available," and made its virtues known, "was one reason we decided to go ahead with our big 'pregnant whale' tank cars," says Stuart Moyes, chief engineer at General American Transportation Co.'s tank car division at Sharon, Pa. The "pregnant whale," completed in 1961, is 65 feet long, and carries a 32,800-gallon load. Before it appeared, General American's largest tank car was 55 feet long and carried 20,000 gallons.

Still, customers say Wabco some years ago wasn't doing a very good job of anticipating customers' needs even on the railroads, let alone in the other industries it sells to. "Wabco until recently was a pretty stuffy outfit," says one veteran railroad man. "For a long time they got by on their reputation for reliability. It's only lately that they've realized the railroads are getting more progressive—more receptive to new ways to cut costs and improve service. Wabco perked up just in time."

INSURANCE, POLITICS AND INTELLIGENCE

That "perking up," most observers agree, can in large part be traced to Ed Green and the fresh viewpoint he brought to the company.

"I HUMOR THE FACTORY"

Though Ed Green and the intelligence approach he brought to Wabco are widely credited with a major role in this turnaround, they haven't been universally popular; some people feel the focus on planning has been overdone. Since he took office, Ed has urged dealers for the company's LeTourneau-Westinghouse earth-moving equipment division, who are independent businessmen, to make up formal, five-year projections of the buying plans of their customers. "That would be great if we had a half-dozen men to work on it," says one L-W dealer. "I kind of humor the factory along that I do it."

In other respects, too, Ed runs a tight ship. Salesmen are limited on entertaining of customers. They do take customers out frequently, but for lunches and occasional dinners rather than nights on the town. "We prefer that our men stick to business," says Ed.

The salesmen, incidentally, no longer get commissions either;

they work for a salary plus incentive bonuses. Wabco wants holders of advanced college degrees as salesmen, and feels such men won't want to gamble on commission selling—especially in a field where sales efforts may take a long time to pay off. Humphrey O'Dell, a successful salesman says he once had to feed a railroad technical reports on certain Wabco equipment for three years before the line would buy any.

SPARE-TIME WORK

Ed is "available" to others besides Wabco salesmen. He holds offices in several trade associations, writes frequently for trade magazines, and is a much-sought speaker at trade association meetings and management seminars. He says he carries on most of this spare-time activity "because marketing is my hobby," but indicates some of it helps Wabco's intelligence effort, too: "Getting together with other executives keeps me posted on new developments."